DRIVING
FORCES

DRIVING FORCES

The Automobile, Its Enemies, and the Politics of Mobility

JAMES A. DUNN JR.

BROOKINGS INSTITUTION PRESS
Washington, D.C.

About Brookings

The Brookings Institution is a private nonprofit organization devoted to research, education, and publication on important issues of domestic and foreign policy. Its principal purpose is to bring knowledge to bear on current and emerging policy problems. The Institution maintains a position of neutrality on issues of public policy. Interpretations or conclusions in publications of the Brookings Institution Press should be understood to be solely those of the authors.

Copyright © 1998 by
THE BROOKINGS INSTITUTION
1775 Massachusetts Avenue, N.W.
Washington, D.C. 20036

Library of Congress Cataloging-in-Publication data:

Dunn, James A., 1943–
   Driving forces: the automobile, its enemies, and the politics of mobility /
by James A. Dunn, Jr.
      p.   cm.
   Includes bibliographical references and index.
   ISBN 0-8157-1964-7 (cloth : alk. paper)
   ISBN 0-8157-1963-9 (pbk. : alk. paper)
   1. Transportation, Automotive—Government policy—United States.
   2. Local transit—Government policy—United States.
   3. Transportation and state—United States. I. Title
   HE5623.D86 1998   98-25420
   388.3'21'0973—ddc21   CIP

9 8 7 6 5 4 3 2 1

The paper used in this publication meets the minimum requirements of the American Standard for Informational Science—Permanence of Paper for Printed Library Materials, ANSI Z39.48-1984

Typeset in Times Roman

Composition by AlphaWebTech
Mechanicsville, Maryland

Printed by R. R. Donnelley and Sons
Harrisonburg, Virginia

Acknowledgments

I would like to express my gratitude to the following individuals for their assistance. Anthony Perl made helpful comments on drafts of several chapters. His insights on rail policy were particularly valuable in chapter 5. Richard Harris's comments contributed to improving chapters 1, 2, and 3. Robert Fishman's help on chapter 6 was also useful. None of these colleagues, however, is responsible for my interpretations and conclusions.

William Felix and George Morris helped get prompt access to state and federal documents. William Threlkeld provided research assistance for chapters 2 and 3. James Nettleman, Judy Odom, Elaine Navarra, and the staff of Rutgers' Paul Robeson Library provided excellent reference, circulation, and interlibrary loan service. Nancy Davidson was professional and supportive as acquisitions editor for Brookings. Barbara de Boinville edited the manuscript promptly and efficiently. Carlotta Ribar proofread the pages, and Julia Petrakis prepared the index. Rutgers University's Faculty Academic Study Program provided a semester-long sabbatical leave during which the first half of the manuscript was written.

For Bernadette

Contents

       Washington versus Detroit   51

       Policy Entrepreneurs and the Politics
          of Adversarialism   53
       The New Social Regulatory Regime   57
       The Road Not Taken: Positive Public Leadership   58
       Ronald Reagan and the Politics of Restoration   63
       Between Regulation and Partnership: The Politics of
          Propulsion Systems   70
       The Results of Regulation: The Politics
          of Evaluation   76
       Toward a Postpetroleum Benefits Regime?   79
       Vehicles of the Future   81
       Conclusion   83

4   Restoring Urban Transit:
       Between Protection and Rejuvenation   85

       A Policy Window for Public Transit: Building a
          New Benefits Regime   87
       Closing the Window: Fiscal Retrenchment and
          the Privatization Challenge   92
       Evaluating the Results of the Transit
          Benefits Regime   98
       Transit as Policy Monopoly and as Symbol   107

5   Intercity Passenger Rail:
       Subsidies, Speed, and Suspense   112

       The Disappearing Railroad Blues   113
       The Amtrak Regime: Design Deficit   116
       Reinventing Amtrak: Partnership, Privatization,
          or Liquidation?   121
       Beyond Amtrak: The Allure of High-Speed Rail   128
       Potential High-Speed Rail Corridors in America   129
       State Attempts to Promote High-Speed Rail   132
       The Prospects for Fast Trains: Stakeholders in a
          New Promotion Regime   137

Tables

1

THE AUTOMOBILE AND ITS ENEMIES

The Making of a Policy Vanguard

In the ways that matter directly to individuals, the automobile transportation system's performance is superlative. It produces more trips each day, each week, each year than any other mode of transportation. No other mode of transportation attracts as many consumer dollars, employs as many workers, consumes as much steel, glass, and rubber, and has a greater impact on the country's economy and society. There were 200 million motor vehicles registered in the United States in 1993, some three-quarters of which were cars. This amounted to approximately one car for every 1.8 people.[1] The automobile is the *solution* to most Americans' transportation problems and has been for at least two generations.

In addition to the automobile's success as a means of transport, it has succeeded in becoming a powerful social symbol, a cultural icon, and an emotional outlet for millions of people in our society. Journalists and pundits are always writing about the American "love affair with the automobile." Academic psychologists have written about the "deeper" significance that modern drivers attach to their cars. These subconscious meanings range from the sexual to the religious, from a fashion statement to a tool of aggression.[2] As a political scientist writing about transportation policy, I am reluctant to psychoanalyze, deconstruct, or otherwise plunge into a search for the "hidden meanings" of the car. I prefer to stick to observable facts in the political and transportation realms. But before discussing the prospects for changes in public policy toward the automobile, I want to point out three important political-psychological aspects of the auto's success as a means of transportation.

The first aspect can be expressed by a term that is much in vogue: "empowerment." Ownership of an automobile empowers an individual to make a vastly wider range of choices relating to personal mobility than he or she would have without a car. Auto drivers are freed from the constraints of the fixed routes and rigid schedules of train or bus riders. They can choose many more destinations; select the companions, if any, traveling in their vehicle; carry much more luggage than they could on a bus; never have to stand because all the seats are taken; stop for refreshment when they want to; listen to their favorite music or news; and not worry (too much) about being mugged while waiting at the bus stop or subway station. That this sense of empowerment really exists is revealed by the fact that the owners of 160 million American autos pay thousands of dollars every year to empower themselves and ensure that they have these choices.

The second politically relevant aspect of the auto's appeal is "equality." The auto provides a kind of individualist equality that is particularly well suited to American values. It is true that auto manufacturers and advertising firms devote immense ingenuity to stratifying and segmenting the car-buying market. And it is also true that there is a very large economic gap between the driver of a battered 1980 Chevette and one who owns a brand new Mercedes. But when they both are on the open road, or stuck in a traffic jam, or circling the block searching for a parking spot, there is a fundamental equality in their condition as automobilists that unites them across class, racial, ethnic, and religious lines as few other aspects of our society can. The opportunity, indeed the right, to own an automobile is one of the most important "down payments" on the practical material equality of living that is the most attractive promise of American democratic capitalism.

The third point about the automobile's success is its very comfortable fit with U.S. political traditions and administrative capabilities. Of course, the automobile could not have flourished as it has without a great deal of public investment and support. The kind of support the automobile needed from the public sector was exactly the kind of support that American public authorities and agencies were best suited to give. Public support for the auto was incremental—that is, it started small and grew over the years. It was based on highway programs that stressed partnership between federal, state, and local authorities and that provided greater mobility choices for individuals and plenty of opportunities for private businesses to profit. Auto-supportive policies were, for the most part, not very controversial or heavy-handed. They did not try to restrict other modes such as trains or transit. Those few policies that involved direct government regulation of individuals' behavior (such as driver licenses and speed limits) were commonsense requirements aimed at establishing the minimal amount of order needed for the system to function effectively.

The Automobile as a Problem

Given the tremendous success of the automobile, one might expect a virtual consensus that such an achievement should be preserved and enhanced. One might expect the experts to recognize the automobile's virtues as much as the people and concentrate their efforts on making it even better. But no! In discussions of transportation policy, a growing number of very vocal critics and analysts see the automobile not as a solution but as a problem, and auto policy not as a success but as a failure. If they have their way, future policy toward the auto will reduce its convenience and utility, not preserve it.[3] These "enemies" of the automobile choose not see it as the most successful mode of transportation and the most popular means of personal mobility ever created. Instead they view it as a voracious consumer of irreplaceable energy resources, a major source of greenhouse gases, a killer of tens of thousands of accident victims, and a destroyer of calm and cohesive communities. They urge enactment of policies to discourage people from using their cars. They want Americans to take public transit, ride share, pedal bikes, or walk—in other words, to abandon the very same cars that provide such mobility and a sense of empowerment and equality.

The chasm between the critics' view of the auto and the way the average motorist (which is almost the same as saying the average citizen) sees her car is puzzling and troubling to both sides. The situation has been labeled by one auto critic "the enigma of automobility."[4] The adversaries point to the actual and potential negative consequences of mass automobility, which are felt overwhelmingly as long-term collective problems. "Don't those short-sighted motorists see that they are driving the planet toward its doom?" they exclaim. The motorists fire back: "Increase gas taxes by a dollar a gallon to discourage driving—over my Congress-man's (politically) dead body!" It would be foolish to deny that the auto-mobile has had negative effects, along with its positive ones. Yet many of the critics' policy recommendations are worse than useless because they are politically unpalatable to the majority of Americans. By making it ap-pear that solutions to auto-related problems will require millions of Ameri-cans to give up their cars and their suburban lifestyles, they make it seem that nothing at all can be done to deal with the auto's negative side effects.

This gulf in perceptions and prescriptions between the auto's enemies and the motoring masses is disturbing. There are real problems created by mass automobility that need to be addressed. But the shrill rhetoric and doomsday predictions of the auto's critics are surely exaggerated. Their policy proposals ask millions of individuals to make major tangible sacri-fices in personal mobility in order to achieve nebulous planetary benefits at some time in the future. These proposals must be held to very strict stan-dards of scrutiny for their impact on mobility and for their political sustainability. Poorly thought out and ideologically driven policies are not what is needed. In World War II the gas rationing program asked American motorists, "Is this trip really necessary?" In the 1990s the federal govern-ment's employer trip reduction program came perilously close to telling employers they had to develop a plan to discourage their employees from driving to work alone or face stiff fines.[5] This ride-sharing boondoggle proved politically unacceptable, but only after wasting millions of dollars and uncounted thousands of hours of planning time in private businesses and public institutions. It is folly to expect millions of Americans to give up their cars without a wrenching social and political backlash. Yet, as we will see, that is the ultimate goal of the anti-auto forces that are taking on an increasingly prominent role in the discussions about future transportation policy.

This book explores the political process by which the auto's adversar-ies have risen to prominence in the transportation debate. It attempts to as-sess how far they have moved the debate over the past thirty years and how much farther they are likely to move it in the next thirty. The auto's ene-mies have done a necessary and valuable job by calling attention to a range of collective problems related to the automobile. But in their zeal to spread the word about the automobile's problems, they end up downplaying the real advantages of the automobile and ignoring its importance for tens of millions of American citizens. Their most prominent anti-auto policies all too often take the form of elitist social engineering schemes that minimize the practical and political difficulties of replacing the auto as the center-piece of our surface transportation system.

Thus this book takes a skeptical look at the major policy initiatives undertaken to tax, to regulate, and to provide alternatives to the automobile. What were the rationale and the specific goals of these policies? How much were they influenced by the adversarial sensibility? How well have they achieved their goals? What kinds of policies could address the negative aspects of the automobile while preserving its benefits?

The remainder of this chapter fleshes out the story of the enemies of the automobile—their origins, values, hopes, and strategies. What makes them think that they can successfully push adoption of anti-auto policies in the most auto-dependent nation in the world? Chapter 2 examines the political and institutional factors that made promotion of highways such a successful program in America. It also looks at efforts to modify the rules that have linked highway taxes to highway spending, and the responses of highway supporters to preserve this regime. Chapter 3 describes the political dynamics between Washington and Detroit over regulating the automobile's safety, emissions, and energy characteristics, and it explores the directions this important relationship might take in the future. Chapter 4 explains efforts to revive public transit as an alternative means of mobility and shows how limited the possibilities for transit really are. Chapter 5 does the same thing for intercity passenger trains. It analyzes the political weaknesses of Amtrak and the serious administrative-financial hurdles to revival of the rail mode by means of high-speed rail technology. Chapter 6 describes how the auto's enemies have rethought the meaning of mobility and developed a holistic approach to transportation as an alternative to automobility. It also assesses the substantial problems that will face attempts to fit their new vision of holistic transportation into America's institutional and intergovernmental structures. The last chapter presents a politically realistic politics of mobility—one that preserves the real benefits of the automobile while building public support for policies that can improve its social utility and reduce its negative effects on the environment.

The Rise of the Adversarial Temperament

The decade of the 1960s transformed values, changed social relations, challenged established authority in institutions and politics, and fostered experimentation in public policy.[6] The civil rights crusade, the opposition to the war in Vietnam, women's liberation, environmentalism, and other social movements proclaimed the need to bring down old hierarchies and established ideas.[7] This period of extreme cultural ferment provided fertile soil for the growth of an anti-automobile sensibility that has been surprisingly influential in shaping transportation policy. The revisionist view of the automobile springs from what has been called the "green tradition" in American thought and literature.[8] This line of thought, exemplified by Ralph Waldo Emerson, Henry David Thoreau, and Walt Whitman in the nineteenth century, seeks an alternative to the prevalent antisocial individualism of American culture and finds its inspiration in a reconnection with the natural world.

In the twentieth century social critics and urbanists like Lewis Mumford and Jane Jacobs drew on the values of this tradition and focused them on the problem of what modern technology, especially the automobile, was doing to America's cities.[9] The 1960s began with a few irascible anti-auto voices crying in the wilderness and ended with an outpouring of books, articles, and reports that were extremely critical in their assessment of the automobile's impact on America. Within a few years the private car and the whole industrial and social apparatus that supported it were redefined by the critics in very negative terms. In this "consciousness-raising" exercise the automobile suddenly went from being a proud achievement of American industry to being a relentless oppressor and a menace to civilization.

The adversaries of the auto seemed to feel toward it a kind of Old Testament moral and esthetic aversion. To them the car represented something crass, materialistic, and arrogant. The drive-in society, the high-rolling Big Three automakers, and the disintegration of urban communities in the 1960s seemed to drag the American dream down from its lofty pedestal into a pit of grasping individualism and sleazy commercialism. Their vision was of a fall from grace of a people led astray by their own *Insolent Chariots*, tempted down *The Road to Ruin* by the *Superhighway-Superhoax*. The final battle was approaching. It would be *Autokind v. Mankind*. Only through repentance could America move *Beyond the Automobile*.[10]

These early adversaries did not want to solve specific problems caused by the automobile. They defined the automobile as a problem in and of itself. They were not interested in the details of highway congestion, traffic accidents, air pollution, or urban sprawl as such. It was the whole gestalt of the auto as the central sociocultural icon of our society that they wanted to eliminate. One of the most thoughtful of them, historian James J. Flink, wrote that the country had passed through three stages of automobile consciousness. Stage one was from the pioneering years of motoring until Henry Ford's tremendous success with mass production of his Model T. In this period attitudes and institutions favorable to the motor car developed rapidly and laid the groundwork for its success. Stage two, from 1911 until the end of the 1950s, saw the "mass idolization of the motor car" and the transformation of America into "the car culture." The third stage began in the 1960s. It would lead to a popular revulsion against the excesses of the car culture and to an attempt to put the auto back in its proper, much diminished, place in our society.[11]

In his 1975 book entitled *The Car Culture*, Flink asserted that the energy and environmental troubles of the 1970s had sounded the "death knells of the automobile culture." That culture and its values were "no longer tenable." We were living through the "ending of the age of automobility." He could foresee the emergence of "an alternative future characterized by true community and expanded democracy, free from the privatism, materialism, escapism, and exploitation that the automobile culture encouraged." That future was within our grasp. "Achieving it requires only our will, intelligence, and collective effort."[12]

A similar optimistic view of the possibilities for change was developed by Emma Rothschild in her 1973 book *Paradise Lost: The Decline of the Auto-Industrial Age*. Her argument reflected the belief of virtually all the auto's enemies of the period: the auto's overwhelming success came about because the system had been rigged in its favor. In her words "the sustenance of social and institutional partiality . . . provided roads, a favorable tax structure, a dispersal of cities and jobs . . . encouraged the decay of alternative modes of transportation, and suspended rational calculations of the costs of auto development and auto waste." Despite this the tide of history was moving away from Detroit and the automobile. "[I]t is exactly this structure of social support that seems most unreliable in present auto troubles . . . auto power is comprehensible, contingent, reversible." In the next ten or twenty years the real costs of the auto would become ever more evident. Coalitions that had supported the auto in the past would "disintegrate." Struggles over government regulation of the industry "are certain to intensify."[13]

At about the same time another anti-auto analysis appeared that went beyond Flink's broad "stages of consciousness" and Rothschild's "social and institutional partiality" as causal factors in the auto's dominance. Bradford Snell pointed the finger at specific culprits: giant corporations that had conspired to undercut alternatives to the auto. Snell prepared a report for the U.S. Senate Subcommittee on Anti-Trust and Monopoly, which resurrected the obscure 1949 case of *U.S.* v. *National City Lines.* In that case the government charged General Motors, Standard Oil of California, and Firestone Tire and Rubber with forming a holding company, National City Lines, which acquired transit firms in some forty-five cities.[14] The holding company then proceeded to dismantle the streetcar lines, replacing them with GM buses on Firestone tires. All three giants—GM, Firestone, and Standard Oil—were found guilty in federal court in Chicago of antitrust violations. GM was fined $5,000, and its treasurer was personally fined $1.

Snell's report went on to recommend that the government use the antitrust laws to break up GM (as well as Ford, Chrysler, and American Motors) into separately owned constituent units to enhance competition in the auto industry. GM's bus and rail divisions would, of course, also be spun off into independent corporations. After the breakup "auto makers' current power to raise substantial sums for lobbying . . . to fight rail transit by charging higher-than-competitive prices for their motor vehicles" would be eliminated. Snell also recommended that the government encourage entry of new competitors into the bus and rail equipment manufacturing sector by means of "guaranteed Government loans, tax incentives, and other benefits."[15]

So many anti-auto and pro-transit writers took up Snell's theme (without subjecting it to much critical scrutiny) that it stands to this day as the conventional wisdom for the decline of transit. Among transit advocates, rail buffs, and auto adversaries, it is virtually an article of faith that giant corporations subverted democracy and the market in conspiring to foist cars and highways on a nation that really did not want them.[16] The theme that the auto's triumph had been the result of natural human shortsightedness and selfishness was supplemented, even replaced, by the charge of organized collusion by powerful economic forces. The people did not simply make the wrong choice; they were not really given a choice. Both democracy and economic freedom were subverted by manipulative, exploitative, and conspiratorial measures.

How should we evaluate the prophecies, predictions, and accusations of these adversaries of the auto from twenty-five years ago? We can deal with their specific predictions rather summarily. Clearly, their hopes for an immediate revolution in transportation and community planning were not realized. Developments in the 1970s and 1980s showed that Detroit can take quite a beating in both the market and in Congress without the automobile losing any ground to other modes of transportation. Americans will as readily drive a Toyota as a Taurus. They will burn reformulated gasoline or gasohol if they have to. They might even take to electric or hybrid vehicles when the price and performance characteristics are right. But they will not flock to a lifestyle that includes strong metropolitan land-use controls, high-rise living, and greatly increased dependence on public transit. A retrospective observer might reasonably accuse Flink, Rothschild, and the other early critics of wishful thinking. They confused the fact that the auto was no longer at the pinnacle of its prestige with the prospects for replacing it with public transit and planned communities. They conflated cyclical declines in profits of U.S. auto manufacturers with a presumed decline in the attractiveness and importance of the auto in the transportation system. And they vastly overestimated the American public's eagerness to give up the personal mobility and the convenience of the car.

What about the accusation that the downfall of transit and the rise of auto dominance were the product of a vast conspiracy? It is still being given respectful attention in anti-auto circles. In 1996, for example, PBS showed a television documentary, "Taken for a Ride," based on Snell's charges. But many economists and historians regard as ludicrous the charge that a conspiracy of auto interests produced the dramatic modal shift away from intercity and urban rail against the will of the American people. In the 1974 Senate hearings UCLA economics professor George W. Hilton called Snell's thesis "so completely oversimplified that it is difficult to take seriously." Hilton presented the Senate subcommittee with a detailed analytical and factual rebuttal of the antitrolley conspiracy theory.[17]

In the 1980s Scott Bottles's research on how Los Angeles adopted the automobile led him to conclude that "Snell's presentation was riddled with factual errors and faulty logic. . . . The historical record . . . simply does not support his interpretation." The Los Angeles Railway Company, for example, had already decided to replace its obsolete trolleys four years before National City Lines acquired the company, but World War II intervened. Bottles notes that "it was GM's attempt to monopolize the sale of buses that bothered the government," not a conspiracy against streetcars. He goes on to point out that "the real irony of the conspiracy theory" is its portrayal of the traction companies as "virtuous, responsible public utilities trying to fight off the evil designs of the automobile manufacturers." The reality was just the reverse. "Angelenos adopted the automobile in protest against the inefficient and seemingly corrupt railway companies."[18]

Sy Adler, an associate professor of urban studies at Portland State University, notes that the streetcar conspiracy story even surfaced in the popular animated film *Who Shot Roger Rabbit?* and is just as fictional. Adler writes that "everything Bradford Snell wrote . . . about transit in Los Angeles was wrong."[19] Cliff Slater studied the economics of streetcars versus buses. He concluded that "GM did not cause the destruction of the streetcar systems. Streetcars were being replaced all over the world by buses on about the same time line as in the United States. GM simply took advantage of an economic trend . . . that was going to continue with or without GM's help."[20] Historian Mark Foster says current critics of the automobile are "guilty of presentism, the cheap wisdom of perfect historical hindsight." They reinterpreted the record to discover "evidence of a conspiracy of realtors, automobile producers, and government officials to fleece the general public."[21]

The revisionists' goal is to delegitimize the modal shift from rail to road. If it was prompted by sinister and selfish interests to exploit the public, it was not a true democratic choice, they argue. Delegitimizing the past makes it more plausible to assert that their hoped for policy measures to restore railroads and transit systems—and to restrain automobile use—are the true democratic policies because they embody real long-term community needs.

It is certainly true that the commercial success of the automobile and highways was reinforced by the political success of highway supporters. But what the critics decry as a deformation of democracy is, from a less partisan and more analytical point of view, nothing more than politics as usual in our wide-open, rough-and-tumble republic. What could be more natural for growth coalitions than to use every advantage at their disposal to get and keep the kind of public policy support they need? Isn't that exactly what the railroad "robber barons" and the urban "traction magnates" did when their modes were in their early stages of growth?

The critics are historically anachronistic and politically unrealistic in thinking that the struggle between the modes could have had a different ending. A strong and far-sighted central government would have had to intervene steadily and skillfully in support of unpopular privately owned rail and public transit companies and against the growth of individual automobile ownership, free highway travel, and decentralized suburban land development. In the years when autos were becoming the dominant mode of transportation, the political support for such a massive public intervention was virtually nonexistent. The highway growth coalition helped enhance the capability of the federal and state governments to plan and build highways. It promoted policies that kept the focus of these new capabilities on highways, but it did not set out to destroy other modes that the majority of the American people wanted to protect.

Revisionist "presentism" does a disservice to the critics' own agenda by underestimating the extent to which autos and highways fit the values of American political culture and the administrative capabilities of American governments. It creates unrealistic expectations that remedying the situation will be a relatively straightforward matter. Simply reverse the bad decisions of the past, launch programs to rebuild the rail and transit lines, raise the costs of owning and operating cars, and in a few years the problems of the auto will be solved. The experience of the past several decades shows this to be wishful thinking.

Have auto critics today recognized these mistakes? Have they changed their analyses or their views? In a 1988 book *The Automobile Age*, Flink frankly admitted that "mass personal automobility appears to have a new lease on life. . . . [A]utomotive technology is making cars safer, less polluting, and more energy efficient with every model year." Despite this progress, he is still opposed to the car culture. He writes that "mass transit remains safer and cleaner still, as well as considerably cheaper when all costs are considered." His moral and historical judgment on the car culture is unshaken. The car has not been "a historically progressive force for change in American civilization since at least the 1960s." The automobile age may be over. "It remains to be seen," he writes, "whether the renaissance of automotive technology can make mass personal automobility viable even in the most affluent nations long past the turn of the twenty-first century."[22]

Although the specific predictions of the prophetic auto critics turned out to be wrong, and their historical charges of conspiracy overblown and erroneous, their consciousness-raising won "disciples." The visceral hostility to the auto and its culture are clearly still present in the next generation. But what does this generation of adversaries make of the automobile's continued dominance as a mode of transportation? Do they acknowledge progress in making cars safer and cleaner? Do they still expect the end of automobility in the near future?

The well-known environmentalist author Bill McKibben writes, "The progress we've made in solving environmental problems is deceptive: we're making no progress at all on the deeper problems, *because they do not spring from the same sources.* One set stems from a defect in the car; the other set comes from the very existence of the car."[23] Cleaning hydrocarbons and nitrogen oxides from auto exhaust can reduce smog and reduce health risks to asthmatics. But the carbon dioxide in even the cleanest auto emissions contributes to the greenhouse effect and endangers our planet. McKibben cites the U.N. Intergovernmental Panel on Climate Change in support of his belief that the world cannot support its population if everyone lives like middle-class Americans. "It's terrifying to imagine Asians owning cars in the same numbers as we do." It is immoral and impractical for us to ask the underdeveloped nations to remain underdeveloped while we continue to enjoy our luxuries, first and foremost our automobiles. The only way out of the dilemma is for Americans to "rethink what we mean by 'development'"—that is, to substantially reduce our auto ownership and usage. "We need bicycles and we need buses, and we need to make them seem as marvelous as Miatas."[24]

James Howard Kunstler wrote two books, *The Geography of Nowhere* and *Home from Nowhere*, that focus on the by now familiar litany of damages that the automobile has wrought on the physical and esthetic environment of our communities. For him the automobile suburb "combined the worst elements of city and country with none of the best parts." He describes it as "noplace"—"a trashy and preposterous human habitat with no future."[25]

Like the earlier enemies of the car, Kunstler believes "the Auto Age, as we have known it, will shortly come to an end." In his view "the great suburban build-out" is "bankrupting us both personally and at every level of government." He dismisses suburban development in the 1990s as "the mindless twitchings of a brain-dead culture, artificially sustained by the intravenous feeding of cheap oil." Soon he expects a "paradigm shift" in American society, the adoption of a new "comprehensive world view shared by a critical mass of citizens" that may result in "convulsive social change," like the abandonment of Leninist communism in the Soviet Union. Americans will not abandon capitalism, but they will have to abandon their present "exhaustive" economy for a "sustainable" one.[26]

Sustainability, Kunstler argues, precludes "mass automobility," Americans' reliance on cars for all the functions of daily living like shopping, commuting, and recreation. The end of mass automobility means that "every adult need not be compelled to bear the absurd expense of car ownership . . . as a requisite of citizenship." To achieve this we will have to "reacquire the lost art of town planning and radically revise . . . the zoning codes" to rebuild our towns and cities. Even blighted urban neighborhoods and cities that have been written off as hopeless can be rescued. "There is no reason why Cleveland, Detroit, and Harlem could not become as finely functional and spiritually gratifying as Paris."[27]

Putting "the Motor City" on a par with Paris will take some mighty powerful changes in urban planning and zoning codes. But Kunstler is undaunted. "The adjustment may be painful for a nation that views car ownership as the essence of individual liberty. . . . But the future will require us to make this adjustment."[28] The car culture "reflects much confusion over the ideas of freedom and democracy." Its view of democracy is that "all opinions, like votes, have equal value." Its definition of freedom is "whatever makes you happy. This is the freedom of a fourteen-year-old child."[29] But more than juvenile truculence perpetuates the car culture. Kunstler sees in it a moral and spiritual dimension: "We have the knowledge to do the right thing; we lack only the will. . . . [T]he inescapable conclusion is that our behavior is wicked, and that we are liable to pay a heavy price for our wickedness."[30] Here is the prophetic temperament breaking out again with a vengeance.

Jane Holtz Kay is the architecture and planning critic for *The Nation* and author of the 1997 book *Asphalt Nation: How the Automobile Took over America, and How We Can Take It Back.* She too believes that the "old consciousness is waning and with it confidence in our car-bound destiny." We are at the beginning of "a millennium that will either . . . stop the asphalting of America—or propel us down a ruinous path." She too feels that the remedy lies in better land-use planning: "the cultivation of a landscape that values place more than passage, that restrains auto mobility in the name of human mobility, that re-thinks the way we live." Like Kunstler, she is enamored of the "New Urbanism" planning movement, but she has a more activist temperament and agenda. She calls for personal opposition to the auto at all levels: "fight a Wal-Mart or install a speed bump . . . attend a meeting or follow a state planning process . . . picket a congressman or call and write a legislator." She is heartened because she sees anti-auto sentiments spreading from the Birkenstock and sneaker-wearing crowd who attend Greenwich Village conferences on auto-free cities and clamor for "devehicularization" to the suit-and-tie-clad engineers and traffic planners meeting in suburban Howard Johnsons' executive suites to discuss "Implementing Regional Mobility Solutions."[31]

From Prophecy to Organization: The Vanguard Strategy

For the most committed enemies of the auto, then, the fact that cars are less polluting, safer, and more energy efficient now than they were twenty-five ago is no consolation. Such minor progress just lulls us into a false sense of security, dulls our outrage, demobilizes the ranks of protesters. In fact, the auto's hard-core opponents regard their most important goal as maintaining a sense of urgency and an awareness among opinion leaders of the downside, even the "dark side," of automobility. They link the auto to as many of society's ills as they can—from the need to spill "blood for oil" in the 1991 Gulf War to the assumed causal connection between automobility and the potential disasters of global warming. Their constantly repeated views now form a position on the spectrum of policy options that cannot be ignored in the debate over the auto's role in the transportation system.

A growing number of environmental and resource conservation institutes, think tanks, and policy organizations, using somewhat more temperate language, reiterate the enemies' case that things cannot go on this way much longer. The Worldwatch Institute, the World Resources Institute, and the Union of Concerned Scientists build their policy recommendations on the basic proposition that the role of the automobile is unsustainable (as well as undesirable) in the long run. "The lifestyle Americans have grown accustomed to cannot be supported indefinitely," write the authors of the World Resources Institute study *Car Trouble*. "It is tempting to put off long-term remedies . . . but we are running out of time. . . . [W]e must recognize that we are part of the natural world, not its owners or rulers."[32]

The long-term goal of auto adversaries today and yesterday remains very much the same: the end of automobility as we know it. The means of attaining it are sketched out in a recent report of a blue ribbon panel on urban transportation policy for the twenty-first century.[33] The report's author, Elmer W. Johnson, was formerly a vice president of General Motors. But he has turned on automobile civilization with the zeal of a convert. Like Flink and the early prophets, he sees "America's individualist and consumerist culture" as the chief obstacle to the end of automobility. To change the culture requires a "more enduring concept of leadership." Contemporary politics, he laments, is dominated by "a rather dismal concept of leadership" that limits itself to market research and polling, that is afraid to offend voters, that goes for quick fixes and avoids deep-rooted problems. Therefore, the anti-auto program must be one of "social learning and consensus building [that] will take years." The reformers "must build a small, but powerfully persuasive, community of concerned citizens . . . to develop a visionary and hopeful program that spells out the seriousness of the nation's social ills and . . . tough but equitable solutions . . . to address these ills."[34]

This is a blueprint for a "vanguard" strategy—an elite group of anti-auto activists whose progressive ideas and individual agendas complement and reinforce one another. The anti-auto vanguard will operate in the policy process like an "advocacy coalition." Unlike ordinary interest groups, an advocacy coalition is made up of "actors from a variety of public and private institutions at all levels of government who share a set of basic beliefs . . . and who seek to manipulate the rules, budgets, and personnel of governmental institutions in order to achieve [their] goals over time."[35] Political scientists Paul Sabatier and Hank C. Jenkins-Smith note that advocacy coalitions are patient; they promote policy changes that will take a decade or longer.[36]

Ideas, not interests, are the glue that holds advocacy coalitions together. They "resist information suggesting that their basic beliefs may be invalid or unattainable and they will use formal policy analyses primarily to buttress . . . those beliefs."[37] They may show flexibility in secondary matters, such as which policy instruments or political tactics are most likely to achieve their overarching goals. For example, the anti-auto vanguard will remain committed to its core belief that auto use must be drastically reduced, but it might shift tactically away from promoting public transit to car pool mandates as circumstances warrant.

There are three key elements of the vanguard's long-term strategy. First, it must continue consciousness-raising among policymakers and the general public. There is no doubt that the auto's enemies are working very hard on this. The World Resources Institute's booklet entitled *The Going Rate: What It Really Costs to Drive* has become one of the most widely circulated pieces of anti-auto propaganda since the Snell report. This booklet argues that the automobile enjoys huge "hidden" subsidies (up to $300 billion). It cites $85 billion worth of free parking at shopping malls, factories, and office complexes, as well as $25 billion of defense expenditures to protect access to Persian Gulf oil supplies. Its policy recommendation, of course, is reduction of these subsidies. The auto must be made to pay its "true social costs." Once people are confronted with paying the full costs of the car-dominated transportation system, they will be much more willing to consider adopting alternatives to the automobile.[38]

Arguments that the auto is being unfairly subsidized are not new, but *The Going Rate* got more visibility than most. And, like most such arguments, one can challenge many of the assumptions on which its calculations and its conclusions are based. For example, ascribing $25 billion of annual military expenditure to the automobile is extremely dubious. It assumes that the world's only remaining superpower would have no reason to maintain its existing level of carrier groups and air wings if the United States were self-sufficient in oil. And counting $85 billion in free parking as a subsidy is odd accounting, to say the least. The private owners of these parking lots paid to acquire, pave, light, and (increasingly) police them. No taxpayer dollars are involved. Indeed, the property owners pay real estate taxes on all their property, including parking lots. On the side of the balance sheet reflecting public revenues generated by the auto, *The Going Rate* counts only gasoline taxes, registration fees, and tolls levied directly on the auto. It ignores auto-related revenues that flow into public coffers from traffic violations fines; state and local sales taxes on automobiles, auto parts, and auto repairs; and the many kinds of taxes and fees levied on the tens of thousands of service stations, new and used car dealerships, car washes, and commercial parking garages that dot the American landscape.

The second element of the vanguard's strategy, after raising the public's consciousness, is effective lobbying of the legislature. The most notable success in this regard is the Surface Transportation Policy Project (STPP), formed in the fall of 1990 to lobby the Congress and to raise public awareness. Its self-described mission is "to help craft a new transportation program that focuses on moving people and goods, rather than vehicles . . . to better serve the environmental, social, and economic interests of the nation." Some of the groups that make up the STPP's network include the Environmental Defense Fund, the American Planning Association, the Rails to Trails Conservancy, the National Resources Defense Council, the Bicycle Federation of America, America's Coalition for Transit Now!, and the Friends of the Earth.[39] The first fruits of lobbying by the STPP were provisions of the 1991 Intermodal Surface Transportation Efficiency Act that authorized more flexible funding for nonhighway projects.

Third, the vanguard's strategy is to build bureaucratic momentum and convey a sense of inevitability regarding the adoption of its program. To this end the vanguard has become a vocal part of the "policy community" that is consulted and represented on interdepartmental panels, task forces, and advisory committees. In September 1994 President Bill Clinton appointed a Policy Dialog Advisory Committee to consider ways of reducing greenhouse gas emissions from cars to 1990 levels by the year 2005. Of the thirty members, eleven represented auto and oil interests; thirteen were from vanguard groups like the STPP or from state and local transit authorities and energy offices. At its first meeting the group agreed to make decisions by consensus.

Given its vision, commitment, and sense of purpose, the vanguard always receives a respectful hearing and sometimes its views can be made to appear in the majority. After eleven meetings of the policy dialog committee over the course of a year, no consensus could be reached on what to recommend. However, this did not stop seventeen members (representing all but one of the vanguard groups and none of the auto and oil groups) from issuing a "Majority Report" that recommended the adoption of virtually the entire vanguard policy agenda as the way to reach the greenhouse gas reduction goals.[40] This agenda is extremely ambitious (see table 1-1).

Problems with the Vanguard's Agenda

The intent of the policies in table 1-1 is to shift a large number of daily trips from the automobile-highway system to other modes (public transit, ride-sharing, walking, and bicycling), and to restrain or reverse the pattern of suburban sprawl development. In other words, they seek to bring about a massive modal shift from one dominant pattern of transportation and land use to another. In the past such modal shifts have always involved replacing an older transportation technology with a newer one that offered greater output in terms of mobility. For example, railroads moved passengers and freight farther and faster than did canals and soon relegated barge traffic to a much less profitable market niche. But the newer mode also required greater inputs in terms of land, labor, and capital. Achieving the vanguard's goal would be the first modal shift in transportation history to reverse the process by restricting physical mobility and restraining land development.

This perspective enables us to see more clearly the basic political flaw in the vanguard's vision and agenda. It is not just that the vanguard overstates the seriousness of *the problems* being caused by the automobile. If estimates of premature deaths caused by auto emissions over several decades run from 70,000 to 700,000, it will come down strongly behind the higher number.[41] This is understandable, given the vanguard's role as consciousness-raisers. In principle, these exaggerations are correctable by fur-

Table 1-1. *The Vanguard's Policy Proposals for the Automobile*

Policies to increase cost
  Increase motor fuel taxes
  Impose or increase taxes on employer-provided parking
  Increase annual registration fees
  Institute a vehicle miles traveled (VMT) fee
  Raise annual fees on trucks

Regulations modifying vehicle design
  Increase fuel efficiency standards
  Require use of modified gasoline and diesel fuels
  Require use of alternative fuels (natural gas)
  Institute enhanced inspection and maintenance requirements for vehicle emissions systems
  Require marketing of zero emission vehicle (electric cars)
  Provide incentives and "feebates" for purchase of fuel efficient vehicles

Travel behavior modifications
  Institute congestion pricing of peak-hour road use
  Require employee ride-sharing
  Institute transportation demand management measures (high occupancy vehicle lanes)
  Improve public transportation, especially rail modes
  Improve intermodal planning
  Regulate land-use planning to discourage auto use

Source: Policy Dialog Advisory Committee, *Majority Report to the President to Recommend Options for Reducing Greenhouse Gas Emissions from Personal Motor Vehicles* (http://essential.org/orgs/public/citizen/COMEP/transportation/cartalk.html); James J. MacKenzie, Roger C. Dowet, and Donald D. T. Chen, *The Going Rate: What It Really Costs to Drive* (Washington, D.C.: World Resources Institute, 1992); and Deborah Gordon, *Steering a New Course: Transportation, Energy, and the Environment* (Washington, D.C.: Island Press, 1991).

ther studies and by refinement of methodology and assumptions. The most fundamental flaw in the vanguard's approach is that it systematically underestimates *the benefits* of automobility. Most of the auto's benefits are enjoyed first and foremost by individuals, and the auto's adversaries simply ignore or denigrate this type of benefit. This enables them to convince themselves, for example, that a policy of inducing people to get out of their cars and into mass transit is just as beneficial as one that permits continued car use. After all, transit still enables people to move from point A to point B. If one responds that people would rather go from point A to points C, D, E, and Z on their own schedule while listening to a new CD on their car stereo, the vanguard tends to respond with condescending comments about advertising hype, false consciousness, the costs of sprawl, global warming, and shifting paradigms.

The vanguard is deeply averse to acknowledging the material and psychological value of the auto to millions of individuals. As a result, it is attracted to policy solutions that often appear, and sometimes are, both ineffective and undemocratic. In the process of raising the public's consciousness to the collective costs of the car culture, the vanguard has raised its own consciousness to stratospheric heights. Thus the cures they prescribe for auto ills are either so unpalatable as to be ineffective in the small doses that the public is willing to swallow, or so drastic that they might do more harm than good if they were ever adopted.

In most American communities there is no system of transport technology and land-use planning that offers citizens more convenience, comfort, and security than the automobile. Enacting and implementing enough of the vanguard's policy agenda to "level the playing field" and make other modes sufficiently attractive to induce auto owners to give up their automobility is an unprecedented social engineering challenge. It would seem to require regulations so intrusive, taxes so high, and central planning so comprehensive as to be beyond the pale of American experience. Even if major portions of the agenda were enacted into law, it is far from clear that they would produce the desired outcomes in terms of decreased auto use and a return to transit-friendly land-use patterns. For instance, peak-hour road pricing on the main arteries in and around the heart of the metropolitan area might prompt businesses and individuals to move farther out beyond the range of such measures. Furthermore, it is virtually certain that the laws and taxes necessary to discourage driving would not be accepted by voters. The vanguard threatens to take away the tangible embodiment of their personal freedom, their car, without offering a superior substitute, thus provoking a backlash against the whole program.

Issue-Attention Cycles and Types of Transportation Policies

If the vanguard's policy proposals are fraught with administrative difficulties and seem to be beyond the bounds of political acceptability, why bother to analyze them? Why should we be concerned with policy proposals that do not have a chance of adoption? The answer is that times change. Old problems come to seem more serious and new ones surge to the forefront of public concern in what Anthony Downs has labeled the "issue-attention cycle."[42]

Downs sees five stages in this cycle. In the "pre-problem stage" the condition exists but has not been brought to public attention. In the second stage, what Downs calls "alarmed discovery and euphoric enthusiasm," the issue receives massive coverage by the media and politicians as they real-ize its political potential and tout their preferred solutions. But by the third phase, many are "realizing the cost of significant progress." After a while stage four, the "gradual decline of intense public interest," sets in as the public and the media get bored, discouraged, or distracted by another prob-lem. Finally, the issue moves to the "post-problem stage" of lesser atten-tion and spasmodic recurrences of interest. The programs and institutions that were created at the peak of interest still have to be funded and adminis-tered, however, and they often appear not to have truly solved the problem.

Because the automobile is so deeply woven into the fabric of Ameri-can society, it is connected in one way or another to most of society's prob-lems. When policymakers believe they are facing a crisis that is related to the automobile, they are most likely to turn to the ideas and proposals that have been around for years. John Kingdon has studied how policy propos-als get put on the agenda for action. He notes that "solutions float around in and near government, searching for problems to which to become at-tached." The same solution, such as federal aid to mass transit, was at-tached successively to the problems of congestion, air pollution, and en-ergy as each rose and fell in prominence without making a major dent in any of them. Kingdon quotes one of the policy advocates doing the repack-aging of solutions as saying: "There is nothing new. We are resurrecting old dead dogs, sprucing them up, and floating them to the top."[43]

Federal policy toward the automobile has gone through the is-sue-attention cycle numerous times over the years (see table 1-2). Each time public attention and policymaking focused on different aspects of the problem that needed to be solved. Each time different types of policies and policy solutions were chosen to address the problem. Programs, laws, and regulations created as the solution to one set of difficulties (for example, freeways as a response to congestion) become part of the problem in other areas (for example, the decline of transit). The result has been a disjointed and decentralized approach to overall transportation policy.

The policy types shown in table 1-2 distribute costs and benefits in characteristic patterns that affect how groups will organize to support or oppose a policy. *Promotion* entails offering public incentives (land grants, tax incentives, federal matching funds) to private entrepreneurs or to gov-ernments to induce them to build transportation facilities (railroads, high-ways, transit systems). Promotion can lead to a scramble to get a goodly share of what is being offered for one's own business or constituency. It also can spur complaints that too much promotion is being done for a rival

Table 1-2. *Issue-Attention Cycles in Federal Automobile Policy*

Problem	Policy solution	Type of policy
Basic road construction (1916–32)	Federal-aid partnership	Promotion
Congestion (1956–65)	Interstate highways; highway trust fund	Promotion
Decline of other modes (1964–80)	Transit and train subsidies	Protection/rejuvenation
Safety (1966–69)	Safety standards	Regulation
Pollution (1970, 1990)	Clean air standards	Regulation
Energy (1975–79)	Fuel economy standards	Regulation
Industrial competition (1980–84)	Import quotas; regulatory rollback	Protection
Suburban sprawl (1991–)	Flexible funding (Intermodal Surface Transportation Efficiency Act); holistic transportation	Rationalization
Global warming (1993–)	Technical standards; Partnership for a New Generation of Vehicles; zero emission vehicle mandates; vehicle miles traveled reductions	Regulation and rationalization

mode. (For example, public transit advocates charge that too much federal aid goes to highways.) *Regulation*, on the other hand, involves government rules and mandates that increase costs for a relatively small number of businesses or individuals (for example, auto manufacturers) in order to provide benefits for others (for example, less air pollution for the public).

Protection/rejuvenation policy aims to halt the decline of a transport mode and perhaps even to restore its competitive attractiveness. Public subsidies are offered for new capital and for operating expenses (for example, federal urban mass transit assistance). The principal direct beneficiaries of such subsidies are the employees (unionized workers and management), companies that build transit equipment and infrastructure, regular commuters, and cities that can bring in federal subsidies. Conflict arises over whether the investments of public money are producing the benefits they are intended to achieve. (In other words, are more people actually riding transit?) Finally, *rationalization* policy involves efforts by planners to shift the competitive balance between different transport modes in order to maximize the social benefits and minimize the social or external costs. Attempts to reduce peak-period highway congestion and lower automotive air pollution by shifting trips from individual cars to shared-ride vehicles are examples of the urge to rationalize transport policy. Such efforts require strong institutional and legal tools and are likely to provoke acrimony among drivers and confusion among local officials, especially if the policy instruments are selected by the anti-auto vanguard.

But the vanguard's ideas are not the only possible policy solutions. Floating around in the policy debate are positive, solution-oriented proposals that have a chance of being adopted and could alleviate real auto-related problems. The aim of these proposals is to help people go where they want to go faster, or cheaper, or more conveniently. Policies that drastically increase automobile taxes or severely restrict auto use do not meet this standard. Policies that encourage the development of less polluting, more fuel efficient vehicles do. What is needed is practical criteria to separate the positive policies from the negative ones. This is the goal of the chapters that follow.

The most practical, effective, and politically acceptable standard on which to base a politics of mobility for the twenty-first century is not "the End of Automobility" but "the Automobile, Plus." Such a politics tries to preserve for most Americans the immense and undeniable benefits of car ownership. It welcomes rather than denigrates the advent of less polluting, more efficient cars. It also offers carefully crafted alternatives to the car for certain trips and certain locations. It allows individuals and communities to choose freely from an expanded range of choices rather than seeking to impose regimented bureaucratic patterns of travel behavior. In addition, a successful politics of mobility focuses on developing programs that can be implemented by our decentralized federal, state, and local institutions. It relies as much as possible on policies that work with market forces and private enterprise rather than against them. Above all, a successful politics of mobility must have commonsense appeal to citizens. They must see it as a means to help them meet their specific personal needs now and in the future, not as an elitist crusade to save the planet.

2

PROMOTING HIGHWAYS

Trust Funds and Taxes

Many critics see 1956, when the highway trust fund was created, as the year that U.S. transportation policy went "off the track." In his book arguing the case for high-speed rail, Joseph Vranich writes:

> The highway trust fund institutionalized the automobile in America more than any other single factor. [It was] more important than any supposed economic superiority of the auto. . . . The federal government will match funds for highway programs, but such grants are non-existent or puny for rail programs. Thus, the federal bias toward highways fosters a state bias toward highways.[1]

Vranich joins a long line of the auto's enemies who have decried the federal highway trust fund as the key institutional and political underpinning of America's car culture for over forty years.[2] Indeed, it is the "jewel in the crown" of the highway lobby's success at the national level.[3] But it was not the trust fund that made the auto dominant. It was the auto-highway mode's inherent political and administrative advantages as an object of promotion policy.

With or without the federal highway trust fund, the auto-highway mode would have received sufficient public support from general federal revenues, state government trust funds, toll authorities, and other sources to attain a dominant position vis-à-vis rail and transit in metropolitan area passenger transportation. The advantages the highway mode enjoyed as an object of promotion policy existed before 1956, and they will continue to exist whatever happens to the federal highway trust fund. Recognizing this is the foundation of any politically realistic effort to redesign highway policies for the future.

The fit between the characteristics of a transport mode and the capabilities of public authorities at the local, state, and federal levels is a key factor determining a transport mode's ability to compete for public support. As a new transportation technology emerges, local and state governments see the advantages of fostering its growth. Their goal is to ensure that enough investment in the new mode is attracted so that their community can prosper as much as possible. The initial kind of political conflict engendered by promotion policy is between one town or state and another. Which one will get the new canal, the new rail line, the new superhighway? Historians have noted how nineteenth-century state and local governments and their business communities engaged in "rivalistic state mercantilism" or "metropolitan mercantilism" by promoting investments in new transportation facilities to conquer markets, divert trade, and flourish at the expense of their neighbors.[4]

If the scramble to promote the new mode ultimately results in a *modal shift*, whereby a previously dominant transport mode is overtaken by the publicly promoted newer technology, that is just "progress." Such publicly promoted modal shifts were a well-established pattern as early as the mid-nineteenth century. Canals overtook primitive turnpikes, and railroads in turn surpassed canals. A similar modal shift occurred in the twentieth century in connection with automobiles. The "good roads movement" (which had become the "highway lobby" by the 1930s) developed a promotion regime that made motor vehicles and highways the dominant mode of urban and intercity land transport even before 1956.

The opportunities offered in the promotional stage of a new transport technology typically generate a *modal growth coalition* of (1) localized business interests, particularly land developers hoping to capitalize on the improved access offered by the new mode; (2) investors attracted by the public incentives offered and the potential profits from financing, building, owning, and operating specific transportation facilities; (3) politicians eager to boost the local economy, help their political careers, and perhaps get a "piece of the action" for themselves one way or another; and (4) workers seeking jobs building and operating the new mode. These interests may quarrel from time to time over the division of benefits, but none fundamentally opposes any of the others' existence or their right to benefit from their investment or labor. They work out what might be termed a *modal benefits regime*, a set of rules and practices embodied in public law to regularize the distribution of benefits among the members of the growth coalition.

The typical benefits regime created during the promotion phase of a mode's growth stresses mechanisms for providing more-than-ample public incentives to bring the new mode to the local community. Public subsidies, direct investments, loan guarantees, land grants, exclusive franchises, earmarked "user fees," and ingenious tax incentives have been used singly and in combination to make sure that progress comes quickly. The distribution formula also allows private interests and investors to capture as much of the financial benefits as possible.

The Advantages of Highways for Promotion Policy

In American history governments have promoted many different modes of transport. But none has been promoted so successfully and so steadily as autos and highways. This success can be ascribed, not to some vast and nefarious conspiracy, but to the following inherent advantages of the auto-highway mode.

Legitimacy as a Public Endeavor. Governments, particularly county and municipal governments, had always assumed substantial financial and administrative responsibility for roads and streets within their borders.[5] There was very little ideological conflict over whether the public sector should take financial responsibility for roads. Railroads and transit companies, even when receiving public aid early in their promotion stage, were intended to eventually be self-supporting private enterprises. After the often bitter battles during the regulatory policy stage of their development, private rail and transit firms were the objects of great suspicion and had little hope of public subsidies for many decades.

Incrementalism. When governments first started to upgrade roads (initially in response to demands from bicyclists, then from automobilists), they did not have to go from a rutted dirt track to the interstate highway system before the roads could be used. A relatively small amount of investment yielded large improvements in capacity and comfort. Grading, better drainage, gravel, then asphalt surfaces, a few sign posts, the occasional traffic light at busy intersections—suddenly counties and states had a useful all-weather highway system opening up the countryside. Today a city contemplating a new rail transit network must count on spending billions building a complex system before the first rider even passes the turnstile.

A Good Fit with the Federal Intergovernmental Structure. Local governments initially took responsibility for improving roads for the automobile. When the limitations of localism became apparent, states and then the federal government took on a role that, far from superseding local authorities, actually reinforced their capabilities. A complex system of intergovernmental transfers of money and expertise was developed to retain most of the jobs and contracts at the grass-roots level. Federal highway aid virtually pioneered the modern style of intergovernmental relations.

Appeared More Complementary than Competitive to Other Modes. In the early decades of this century, automobiles, trucks, and improved roads were seen as natural feeders to the rail system, not as rivals. Transcontinental highways and long-distance trucking were fantasies. The political activities of the rail industry concentrated on more traditional threats, such as rival rail companies, unions, and overzealous regulators. In fact, the railroads even sponsored "Good Roads Trains" to tour the country to drum up support for better highways. In cities new road and street capacity was often seen as a boon to transit, helping to get streetcars and then buses out of snarled traffic. And as airports moved farther and farther away from downtown, it became cheaper and faster to improve highway access from the center city and the suburbs than to build new rail lines from the center city.

Broader Impact on Land Use and Land Values. A railroad increased the value of the land immediately adjacent to its stations, but did relatively little for land along the track but far from a stop. A new two-lane highway increased the accessibility, hence the value, of all the land along its length. It opened up more opportunities for everyone, from roadside fruit stand owners to developers of housing subdivisions. Its initial impact was more "democratic" than that of a rail or transit line, because it spread the "unearned increment" of "speculative" increases in land value more widely.

Key Element in Economic Growth and Social Change. Like railroads, the engine of heavy industry (coal, steel) in the late nineteenth century, the automobile was a crucial component of economic growth in the twentieth century. Not only did it drive heavy industries (steel, petroleum, rubber), but it supported an even faster growing service sector: filling stations, tourist cabins, trailer parks, and roadside restaurants, and later drive-ins, motels, shopping malls, and suburban office parks.[6]

Separation of Infrastructure from Rolling Stock Investments. A relatively small public investment in highway infrastructure underwrote a much larger private investment in cars, trucks, fuel, repairs, insurance, and other operating costs. Highway system rolling stock investments were decentralized into millions of small private decisions to buy cars and trucks. Since private railroad and transit systems had to pay for both infrastructure and rolling stock, they had more incentive to cut costs by skimping on both investments. Later, after enactment of public subsidies to rail and transit systems, infrastructure investment decisions tended to involve large sums and be politically controversial.

"Self-Financing" through Highway User Fees. Some roads, bridges, and tunnels could be financed by tolls, the most basic kind of user fee. But for roads where tolls were not appropriate, taxes levied on motor fuels were earmarked exclusively for roads. This created a second-order "highway user fee." Dedicating these gas taxes to highway "trust funds" became the political, financial, and ideological key to a successful highway promotion regime. It legitimized a special status for highway spending that was protected from the vagaries of budgetary ups and downs, and it enabled public and private stakeholders in highway promotion to hammer out a durable benefits regime. The enormous success of the highway promotion benefits regime and its legitimizing ideology have fascinated critics and supporters alike.

The Highway Promotion Regime: Intergovernmental Transfers and Trust Funds

Many people mistakenly assume that the highway coalition is a monolith, a constellation of groups bound together with a strong common interest, whose disputes are minor, if they exist at all. Nothing could be farther from the truth. Highway groups have had and continue to have serious conflicts of interest with each other. At times the coalition has been at such loggerheads that highway policymaking has been almost paralyzed. Rural interests pushing for farm-to-market roads fought with cities over spending on urban highways. Truckers clashed with motorists' organizations over which vehicles do most damage to roads and who pays their fair share of highway repair costs. Western elected officials advocating "free" roads opposed eastern governors and legislatures supporting toll road authorities. Petroleum companies wanting low gas taxes battled automobile manufacturers and road builders supporting higher gas taxes and more road spending. The enduring strength of the highway coalition has not been the absence of conflict among its members, but its model benefits regime, which enabled public policy to continue to promote highways while the coalition members carried on their disputes on the side.

Basic Principles

The highway promotion benefits regime has two basic principles: the intergovernmental transfer principle and the trust fund principle. The former has four main tenets:

—The states and the federal government share authority to plan, finance, and operate the nation's roads.

—The states and the federal government share authority to tax motor fuels.

—State highway departments build the roads; the federal government dispenses financial aid, sets regulatory standards, and coordinates planning.

—Highway funds are distributed among the states according to a "fair share" formula devised by the U. S. Congress.

The intergovernmental transfer principle is founded on a fundamental compromise between federal politicians and bureaucrats and their state-level counterparts. Together the federal and state governments have developed a professional, sophisticated, and mutually reinforcing partnership for planning, funding, building, and maintaining the nation's highways.[7] The compromise held that there would be no separately owned federal and state highway systems. Even highways designated "U.S." or (later) "Interstate" are partly financed by and wholly administered by the state in which they are located. Federal officials coordinate planning and set standards in consultation with state officials, but the vast majority of employees and contracts needed to build and maintain the roads come from the state and local levels.

The second element of the highway benefits regime, the trust fund principle, has four tenets:

—Gas tax revenues should be dedicated exclusively to highway infrastructure needs.

—Gas tax rates should be no higher than needed for the roads.

—The vast majority of post-1956 road construction should be "free" roads financed from trust fund revenues, not tolls.

—Highway spending decisions should be made jointly by the executive and legislative branches of government, but the highway trust fund financial balances should not be used for other purposes such as fighting inflation or reducing budget deficits.

Like the intergovernmental transfer principle, the trust fund principle represented a political compromise, in this instance between tax-paying groups (such as petroleum refiners, trucking companies, and motorists' associations) and spending groups (such as state highway departments, road building firms, engineering consultants, cement and asphalt suppliers, and construction unions). The tight link between highway taxation and road spending fits well with Americans' ideas concerning a social contract between citizens and government, that is, between taxpayers and spending authorities. This Lockean outlook holds that citizen-motorists will agree to pay gas taxes every time they fill their tanks, but only if the public revenues thereby generated are used to build roads that will make highway travel easier and more economical. This social contract between the road user and the government ensures a stable flow of funds to the public sector departments and the private road construction interests by prohibiting the diversion of revenues to other public needs.

Equally important, exclusive dedication sets an upper limit on how high the road-use taxes can be. They should generate only enough public revenue to pay for the roads and no more. Fifty years ago a distinguished transportation expert, Charles L. Dearing, wrote that diversion of highway revenues "in effect constitutes a breach of faith with road users. Either the user rates have been fixed so high that they produce more revenue than is required to maintain the plant in satisfactory condition, or the plant is being permitted to deteriorate because of the diversion of road funds to other purposes."[8]

The trust fund principle was embedded in a powerful web of legal and institutional protections of highway spending at the state level. Throughout the late 1920s and 1930s, motorists' groups, automobile manufacturers, gasoline refiners, and dealers fought for dedication as a way of capping gasoline taxes. Kansas and Missouri passed amendments to their state constitutions dedicating gas tax revenues to highways in 1928.[9] Today twenty-eight states have a gas tax earmarking provision in their state constitution or their legislative statutes. Eleven others dedicate their highway receipts to a special transportation fund that includes highways as its major component.[10]

Policy Monopoly and Pressures for Change

The benefits regime created by the intertwining of the two principles exemplifies what Frank Baumgartner and Bryan Jones call a "policy monopoly." Similar to the terms "iron triangle," or "policy subsystem," a policy monopoly refers to the ability of a group to gain more or less uncontested control of policymaking in a particular area. Adversaries of the policy monopoly can try to undermine it by redefining its image from a positive to a negative one, enabling them to engineer a "mobilization of criticism." It is "the generation of new ideas [that] makes policy monopolies unstable in the long run." American policymaking thus tends to experience "long periods of relative stability or incrementalism interrupted by short bursts of dramatic change." Baumgartner and Jones call this style of policy change "punctuated equilibrium."[11]

In recent decades the anti-auto vanguard has done its best to undermine the ideological support enjoyed by the highway promotion regime, while the groups representing rival modes (for example, urban transit or intercity passenger rail) have sought to get access to the revenues in the highway trust fund for themselves. And, of course, the pro-highway coalition (the "road gang") has strenuously fought to protect its position. Efforts to undermine or preserve the highway benefits regime can best be understood in terms of how changes in the distribution of costs and benefits affect the pattern of political conflict over highway policy.

James Q. Wilson's classic typology explains how a policy's distributive impact can shape politics. He notes that the costs of a policy may be widely distributed or narrowly concentrated. Benefits also may be wide or narrow in their distribution. Relating the patterns of costs and benefits yields four different types of politics: client politics, interest group politics, majoritarian politics, and entrepreneurial politics.[12]

Client politics results when benefits are narrowly concentrated but the costs are widely dispersed. A small, easily organized group has every incentive to lobby for its benefits. But since the costs of the policy will be spread over a large number of people, the mass of taxpayers have little incentive to organize in opposition. The countless industries that enjoy subsidies, quotas, and special protections are examples of client politics.

Interest group politics occurs when both the costs and the benefits of a policy are narrowly concentrated. Each side has an incentive to reap the benefits for itself and shift the costs to others. For example, during the drafting of the Interstate Commerce Act of 1886, railroads, farmers, oil companies, and other interests scrambled to win favorable regulatory rates under the new legislation.

Majoritarian politics arises when costs and benefits are widely distributed. No small, definable group expects to receive a disproportionate share of the benefits or burdens of a policy. Examples are the adoption of social security and the establishment of a peacetime draft.

Sometimes a policy "will confer general (though perhaps small) benefits at a cost to be borne chiefly by a small segment of society." Since the incentive to organize is strong for opponents but weak for its beneficiaries, it is surprising that legislation of this type of policy is ever adopted. It requires the efforts of a skilled policy entrepreneur, who can "mobilize latent public sentiment . . . put the opponents of the plan on the defensive . . . and associate the legislation with widely shared values."[13] Auto safety legislation is an example of *entrepreneurial politics*.

The highway promotion benefits regime initially fused elements of majoritarian and client politics. This accounted for much of its "durability."[14] The majoritarian elements were embodied in the intergovernmental transfer principle that sought to make all of America's vast territory accessible by auto travel and to ensure economic growth across the whole nation. At first the highway trust fund was presented as a majoritarian policy, gathering widely dispersed costs (the pennies per gallon taxes paid by millions of motorists) and disbursing benefits widely to build the national network of "free" roads. But the trust fund principle also stimulated client politics, since the direct financial benefits were focused narrowly on road contractors, materials suppliers, engineering firms, and highway department bureaucrats. In terms of providing motivation for political organization, a multi-million-dollar road construction contract for a highway builder is an order of magnitude more important than access to a new highway for the average motorist. As long as the trust fund principle was broadly accepted, its client politics operated smoothly and unobtrusively behind the majoritarian elements, like a road project being built behind a large "Your Highway Taxes at Work" sign. But once the trust fund was seriously challenged by antihighway groups, trust fund politics became interest group politics, with clearly delineated groups (such as the transit lobby) struggling to shift benefits to themselves and impose costs (higher gas taxes) on their opponents.

The Politics of Federal Taxes on Motor Fuel

The history of federal gasoline taxes illustrates the highway promotion regime's ability to resist pressures for change. It also reveals how well the compromise between the antitax elements and the pro-spending elements of the highway coalition is holding up under the stresses of changing conditions and changing values.

Two issues must be decided with regard to federal taxes on motor fuel. How high should the taxes be? And what should be done with the proceeds? Acceptance of the trust fund principle as the answer to the second question also provides the answer to the first. Thus the highway promotion regime established two politically intertwined but distinct policy positions. One reserved a secure revenue stream to the intergovernmental highway spending bureaucracy and its associated private road-building interests. The second held down taxes on motor fuel and protected the petroleum, trucking, and auto interests from being taxed on motor fuel to promote the general welfare. Once the link between the fuel tax ceiling and the financial needs of highways is broken, the politics of protecting each of the two separate positions might take quite different paths.

Since 1919 state governments had been levying gas taxes, but it was not until 1932 that the federal government got involved. In 1932, the last year of the Hoover administration, the U.S. Congress imposed the first federal gas tax at one cent per gallon. The receipts went into the depression-depleted general treasury, not into any sort of highway trust fund. Since then federal gas taxes have been increased seven times. There have been many other attempts to raise the tax, of course, but only these have succeeded (see table 2-1).

Wartime Increases in the Gas Tax

The first two gas tax increases in 1940 and 1951 are easy to explain politically. Although the federal treasury certainly needed funds to meet the demands of World War II, the cold war, and a shooting war in Korea, the

Table 2-1. *Federal Gasoline Tax Increases, 1932–93*

Year	Amount (cents)	Recipient	President and party	Majority party in Congress
1932	0.1	Treasury	Hoover (R)	House (D) Senate (D)
1940	0.5	Treasury	Roosevelt (D)	House (D) Senate (D)
1951	0.5	Treasury	Truman (D)	House (D) Senate (D)
1956	0.1	Highway Trust Fund	Eisenhower (R)	House (D) Senate (D)
1959	0.1	Highway Trust Fund	Eisenhower (R)	House (D) Senate (D)
1982	0.5	Highway Trust Fund	Reagan (R)	House (D) Senate (R)
1990	0.5	Highway Trust Fund and Treasury[a]	Bush (R)	House (D) Senate (D)
1993	4.3	Treasury	Clinton (D)	House (D) Senate (D)

a. Each received 2.5 cents.

most that national politicians were prepared to ask American motorists to pay toward these problems was two cents per gallon. The one cent gas tax was increased by half a cent in 1940 as World War II loomed on the horizon. Another half cent increase was added in 1951 during the Korean War.

Clearly, federal taxation of motor fuel was a sensitive political issue from the very beginning. One cannot ascribe these remarkably low gas tax rates to the effect of the federal highway trust fund, since that did not come into existence until 1956. But the notion of earmarking gas taxes for highways to legitimize their imposition was present in the political culture as early as the 1930s. For example, the federal highway bill of 1934, known as the Haydon-Cartwright Act, authorized the denial of federal highway aid to states that diverted their own highway revenues to nonhighway uses.[15] In the late 1940s and early 1950s, highway groups publicized the ratio between federal gas tax receipts and federal highway aid disbursements in a given year, and they were severely critical when federal highway aid fell significantly below revenues. Although there was no legal mechanism to enforce the link between federal highway revenues and federal highway spending, there were significant political pressures to do so.

Gas Tax Increases in the Interstate Era

When President Dwight D. Eisenhower took office, there seemed to be consensus in the highway community as well as the public at large that traffic congestion had reached unacceptable levels. The problem that had stymied state and federal officials since the war's end was finding a politically acceptable way to finance new road construction. In 1954 President Eisenhower appointed a special committee headed by General Lucius D. Clay to examine the issue and make recommendations for the best way to get interstate highway construction moving forward at a much faster clip.[16] The Clay committee rejected the concept of basing the interstate system on tolls. It recommended the creation of a Federal Highway Corporation that would finance interstate highway construction by floating thirty-year bonds. The revenues from the federal gasoline tax were dedicated to bond repayment. The committee estimated that no increase in the gasoline tax would be necessary under its plan.[17]

But the Clay committee's plan ran into a great deal of opposition. State highway officials opposed a Federal Highway Corporation as a threat to their own authority and independence. Senator Harry Byrd (Democrat of Virginia), chairman of the Senate Finance Committee, rejected long-term federal borrowing and insisted on a pay-as-you-go plan that would avoid interest charges. That meant that more current revenues would be needed, and the most suitable source was clearly a hike in the federal gasoline tax. This was fine with the construction industry, which wanted a dramatic increase in federal road spending, but farmers' organizations and petroleum companies wanted to abolish the federal gas tax altogether. Motorists' organizations also opposed an across-the-board gas tax hike. They wanted heavy trucks to pay a steeply graduated tax for using (and damaging) the roads. The truckers complained that this was blatant discrimination that would hurt their business and hinder the economy. A rising chorus of objections and special pleadings soon bogged down the debate in Congress, and no action was taken on a new highway bill in 1955.

During the legislative session the following year, gentle prodding from the administration produced a compromise that brought all the stakeholders on board. To satisfy Senator Byrd and skittish state officials, the administration dropped bonding and the Federal Highway Corporation in favor of a pay-as-you-go system based on the popular and proven (at the state level) formula of dedicating gas taxes and other highway revenues (taxes on tires and motor oil) to a new federal highway trust fund. For the spending side of the highway coalition, the federal government promised to increase its share of the cost of building interstate highways to 90 percent. The federal share of noninterstate highway construction remained at 50 percent, but the absolute amount of funds available was substantially increased "for balance." The truckers found they could live with an extra penny per gallon fuel tax; in return, Congress stopped the toll road movement in its tracks and put off consideration of graduated truck taxation by referring it to a technical study committee (the first of a long series of studies).

Thus was the benefits regime for highway promotion policy modified and solidified: it provided something for all the established stakeholders (see table 2-2), while giving the public what it seemed to be asking for. Raising the level of federal aid for interstate highways left state highway departments with "only 10 percent of the [financial] responsibility but 50 percent of the authority." The companies, suppliers, and unions who would build the new roads were very enthusiastic. "The key to success," notes one historian, was that the deal promised "plenty of new roadway for everyone . . . and asked truckers to pay only modest tax increases."[18]

As construction of the interstate segments accelerated in the late 1950s, it became clear that the cost of the system had been seriously underestimated. But the immediate political and economic benefits of the construction contracts were also quite evident. In 1959, unlike in 1956, the highway coalition had no political difficulties raising the federal gas tax. It went up another one cent per gallon to a total of four cents.

The Coalition's Last Hurrah: The 1982 Gas Tax Increase

The 1960s and early 1970s were halcyon years for the highway coalition. But by the late 1970s it was starting to feel a financial squeeze. Highway construction and maintenance costs were increasing much faster than the already high rate of inflation, and revenues flowing into the highway trust fund had leveled off as newer fuel-efficient cars burned less gasoline per mile traveled. There was not enough money in the intergovernmental fiscal transfer pipeline to keep construction activity going at its most productive pace. The spending side of the highway coalition and its congressional allies began to prepare the ground for a tax increase some time after the 1980 presidential election.

These preparatory efforts were focused on hearings convened in August and September 1980 by Democratic senator Jennings Randolph of

Table 2-2. *The Highway Coalition: Tax-Paying and Spending Groups*

Tax-paying groups
  American Trucking Association
  American Automobile Association
  American Bus Association
  Highway Users Federation
  American Petroleum Institute
  Rubber Manufacturers Association

Spending side groups
  American Association of State Highway and Transportation Officials
  American Public Works Association
  National League of Cities
  U.S. Conference of Mayors
  National Governors Association
  American Public Transit Association
  Associated General Contractors
  American Road and Transportation Builders Association
  National Ready Mix Concrete Association
  Portland Cement Association
  National Asphalt Pavement Association
  American Consulting Engineers Council

West Virginia, longtime chairman of the Senate Environment and Public Works Committee. Their ostensible purpose was to consider a routine highway appropriations bill. Their real goal was to air the views of all the major groups on both sides of the highway coalition and to begin to reconcile differences over details of a future tax increase. Senator Randolph was quite candid on this point:

> Now, why are we holding these hearings in the year 1980? It is not for window dressing. We can do nothing this year. We understand that. But we needed to begin now to be ready for the introduction of legislation ... next year based upon what you gentlemen, speaking for your organizations, are testifying to today.[19]

The spending side representatives who testified were prepared to support immediate steps to achieve a significant revenue increase. William Bulley, the president of the American Association of State Highway and Transportation Officials (AASHTO), acknowledged that the trust fund needed "increased levels of receipts from present sources" and proposed shifting the basis of the gas tax from a per gallon rate to a percentage of the wholesale price of gasoline.[20] In an era of rapidly increasing wholesale gas prices this would have entailed a sizable increase in the tax. Private construction groups were ready to go further. The chairman of the American Road and Transportation Builders Association recommended keeping the four cent per gallon tax but adding on top of it a tax amounting to 4 percent of the wholesale price. At then current prices this would have meant at least an eight cent per gallon revenue yield.[21]

Groups that would have to pay the higher taxes, such as the American Automobile Association (AAA) and the Highway Users Federation, acknowledged the need for more spending. They indicated they would not bitterly resist a tax increase as long as it remained dedicated to highway spending. But first ways to limit the size of the tax increase should be explored. The AAA suggested "that any new taxing program include some recognition of the effects of heavy axles and miles traveled," and it recommended a weight-distance tax for trucks over 26,000 pounds gross vehicle weight. It also wanted the tax exemption for gasohol removed.[22] The Highway Users Federation wanted to draw down the cash balance of the trust fund before raising taxes.[23]

Highway supporters like Senator Randolph were reasonably optimistic about the political prospects of the increase. True, it had been over twenty years since the federal gas tax had been increased. And several attempts by "outsiders" to increase the gas tax failed between 1975 and 1980. Still fresh in their minds was the fiasco of President Jimmy Carter's decisively rejected attempt to impose an oil import fee to be collected only on gasoline.[24] Their tax, however, was not a scheme to promote energy conservation. It was a responsible public finance measure supported by the groups that would administer and benefit from the tax and understood by the groups that would have to pay it. None of the revenues would be diverted to the general fund. All that was needed was for the winner of the presidential election, whoever he was, to approve the tax increase and it would be assured of success.

Or so they thought. However, the Reagan administration did not take office intending to increase the federal gas tax. In an appearance before the Senate Committee on Environment and Public Works before his confirmation, Andrew ("Drew") Lewis, the president's nominee to be secretary of transportation, was asked by Senator Randolph: "What would be your reaction to a proposal to increase the present gasoline tax?" Lewis equivocated. He acknowledged that "maintaining the highway trust fund in the dollar amounts we need is a very serious problem." But he went on to mention the Reagan administration's "very strong commitment to reduction in taxes." Even though the gasoline tax "comes closer to a user tax than most taxes," Lewis responded, until he had a chance to review the budget in detail, he would "prefer not to answer that question."[25]

By the end of his first year in office, Secretary Lewis had been won over by the highway coalition. Not only were the funds needed for the highways, there was already widespread bipartisan congressional support for a gas tax increase. A few well-aimed compromises could solidify support from the main interest group stakeholders on the tax-paying side as well. The only problem was that President Reagan and his advisers did not agree with the idea. Secretary Lewis realized he would have to "sell" the tax increase to the White House.

He began by solidifying the transit lobby's support. He promised to create a mass transit account in the highway trust fund that would receive 20 percent of the revenue from a five cent per gallon tax hike (the "transit penny"). This convinced many big city Democrats and liberals to support the measure despite their concern over the effects of the tax on the poor.[26] Next Secretary Lewis turned to the perennial dispute between the truckers' and the motorists' groups over whether heavy trucks were paying their fair share of highway costs. A study completed in January 1982 concluded that heavy trucks were not, in fact, paying for their share of damage to the highways. Lewis recommended increasing highway-use taxes for heavy trucks (above 33,000 pounds gross weight), with taxes on the heaviest trucks (80,000 pounds) rising to $1,600 in 1984 and to $1,900 in 1988. This would be in addition to a five cent increase in the tax on diesel fuel.

Naturally, the trucking industry was unhappy with his proposals. But Lewis offered the truckers a quid pro quo. He supported legislation to set federal truck weight and length standards. Federal standards would eliminate the problem of the so-called "barrier states" (Illinois, Missouri, and Arkansas) whose stricter weight and length restrictions created a midcontinent barrier around which heavily laden trucks had to detour.[27] The rest of the highway coalition, except for the American Automobile Association, was firmly behind the fuel tax hike. Even the AAA recognized the need for more revenues to finish the interstate system and keep the roads in good repair. It concentrated its opposition on the diversion of the one cent per gallon to the transit sector, insisting that highway-generated user tax revenues remain strictly dedicated to highways.

Yet Lewis and the congressional highway coalition still could not get White House approval for a tax hike. As late as his September 28, 1982, news conference, President Reagan seemed adamantly opposed to higher gasoline taxes. When asked specifically if he would "rule out" a gasoline tax increase he responded: "Unless there's a palace coup and I'm over-taken—(laughter)—or overthrown, no, I don't see the necessity for that."[28] The November 1982 congressional elections provided the necessity. The Republicans lost more seats than usual for off-year elections, and the rec-ord high level of unemployment the country was experiencing was blamed for the party's poor performance. The president's advisers concluded that he needed to do something to show positive cooperation with Congress on the jobs problem.

Secretary Lewis's hard work selling the tax hike package during the preceding year had put the White House in the position of simply having to send a signal to Congress that the president would accept the increase. The legislative process could then move forward with relative dispatch during the "lame duck" session between the election and the Christmas recess. So in the last week of November, Reagan was able to endorse the tax increase by relabeling it a "user fee." When asked about the apparent conflict with his September statement, he replied that he meant he "would not support a gas tax increase to provide general revenues."[29] Since this money was ear-marked for badly needed road repairs and transportation infrastructure in-vestments, it was acceptable.

Even after President Reagan gave the green light, the administration had to overcome one final hurdle: a filibuster by Republican antitax con-servatives in the Senate—a harbinger of ideological problems to come. The House had already passed its version of the bill by a vote of 262 to 143, with a majority from both parties voting for the tax hike.[30] But three Repub-lican senators—Gordon J. Humphrey of New Hampshire, Don Nickles of Oklahoma, and Jesse Helms of North Carolina—delayed passage for sev-eral weeks. Finally, the Senate majority leader, Republican Howard Baker of Tennessee, invoked cloture to cut off the debate.[31]

The Gas Tax Bandwagon and the Budget Deal

When George Bush succeeded Ronald Reagan as president, specula-tion began about another increase in the federal tax on motor fuel. Because of the "oil glut" and falling crude oil prices, Americans were paying less for their gasoline after the 1982 gas tax increase than before it.[32] This led a growing number of people to conclude that the gas tax was "in play" in na-tional politics and not just something to finance the roads.

Bankers and financiers, such as Alan Greenspan and Paul Volker, the chairman and past chairman respectively of the Federal Reserve Board, believed that a gas tax hike would be an easy way to increase revenues to combat the budget deficit. Environmentalists, such as Jessica Mathews of the World Resources Institute, believed that a substantial increase in the tax was vitally needed to combat air pollution and global warming. Economists, such as the Brookings Institution's Robert Crandall, saw a gas tax increase as a more efficient tool of energy conservation than cumbersome federal regulations on automobile fuel economy.[33]

The *New York Times*, the *Washington Post,* and *Time* climbed aboard the bandwagon with editorials endorsing a substantial increase in the gas tax.[34] The Japanese government called for higher gasoline taxes as a means of restoring America's competitiveness in international trade.[35] The chief executives of Chrysler and Ford motor companies stated that they supported a gas tax increase.[36] The chairmen of the House Ways and Means Committee and the House Budget Committee expressed their view that a gas tax increase should be a key part of a compromise package of revenue hikes and spending cuts to reduce the federal deficit.[37]

This drumbeat of support from "outsiders" alarmed the highway coalition. The Democratic chairman of the House Subcommittee on Surface Transportation, Representative Glenn M. Anderson of California, introduced a resolution opposing a gas tax increase for deficit reduction purposes. By March 1989 the number of cosponsors of Anderson's resolution had risen to 165, including members of both political parties, and drew public support from organizations as diverse as AASHTO and the NAACP. A coalition of groups calling itself Fuel Users for Equitable Levies (FUEL), chaired by William Berman of the American Automobile Association, spearheaded the public relations and lobbying campaign against gas tax increases for budget balancing.[38]

Nevertheless, when administration officials met with Democratic congressional leaders to negotiate a package of spending cuts and "revenue enhancements," an increase in federal gas taxes was prominent among the measures up for negotiation. After prolonged haggling, the conferees finally agreed on a complicated bundle of spending cuts, budget process rule changes, and tax hikes, including a ten cent per gallon increase in the federal motor fuels tax on gasoline and diesel fuel. Half of the proposed fuel tax increase was to be deposited in the highway trust fund, and half used for deficit reduction. A rebellion by conservative Republican House members against the whole agreement and last-minute lobbying by the trucking industry lowered the fuel tax increase in the final bill to five cents per gallon. But for the first time since 1956, federal gasoline tax revenues (two and a half cents of the five cent per gallon increase) were being diverted from the trust fund, while highway aid was stagnating.[39]

The "Nickel for America" Campaign

The spending side of the highway coalition regrouped for a counterattack in 1991. By September 30th of that year, the federal programs on surface transportation aid needed to be renewed. In the House the job of drafting and managing the bill fell to Representative Robert Roe, a New Jersey Democrat who became chair of the House Public Works Committee after members ousted Anderson for not being aggressive enough in defense of the committee's turf. Roe announced he would include another five cent per gallon gasoline tax increase in his surface transportation reauthorization bill. This time all the revenues would be dedicated to the highway trust fund. He promoted his tax proposal as "a nickel for America." Roe's political strategy was classic: use the new revenues to fund a dramatic increase in highway spending and promise key legislators "demonstration projects" in their districts to help overcome their reluctance to vote for another gas tax hike so soon after the political battle for the 1990 increase. At one point the bill included 458 special demonstration projects worth some $6.8 billion, compared with 152 projects worth $1.3 billion in the 1987 surface transportation bill.[40]

Still smarting from the Republican right's criticism of the 1990 budget deal, the Bush administration announced that it would veto any transportation bill that contained a tax increase. The climate in Congress also had changed. Support for a gas tax increase in the Senate was lukewarm at best. In the House Roe's gas tax proposal ran into serious opposition, despite support from Democratic Speaker Thomas Foley of Washington.

The House Ways and Means Committee asserted that only the net revenues from the tax hike could be credited to the highway trust fund according to the 1990 budget agreement. The difference between gross and net revenues reflected the tax credits and deductions claimed by importers and refiners. Ways and Means calculated that net revenues were 1.25 cents per gallon below gross revenues. Annually, this meant a drop from an anticipated $6.6 billion in new revenue to only $4.7 billion, necessitating a scaling back of the politically important demonstration projects. In addition, the Appropriations Committee strongly objected to the Roe bill's plan to classify the revenue from the tax increase as a "mandatory" spending program, like social security entitlements, and hence exempt it from domestic discretionary spending caps.[41]

Many vocal groups, from urban interests seeking flexible funding for transit to "donor states" that wanted to get back more of the federal gas taxes their motorists paid, had input on the transportation bill. Roe's old-fashioned pork barrel approach seemed curiously ineffective, almost anachronistic. In the end Roe and the highway coalition had to abandon the "nickel for America" tax hike. In order to save something from all their efforts, the final bill, the Intermodal Surface Transportation Efficiency Act (ISTEA) of 1991, extended the period covered by the transportation authorization bill from five years to six. It also extended the 2.5 cents of the 1990 gas tax increase dedicated to the trust fund from its scheduled expiration in 1995 until 1999, to help pay for the increased spending levels of the six-year bill.[42]

The Intermodal Surface Transportation Efficiency Act

The changes that were made in the spending provisions in the ISTEA transportation funding bill were seen as further symbols of the highway coalition's declining power. While Roe's efforts in the House had attracted most of the lobbying attention of the traditional highway spending groups, the antihighway forces stole a march on them in the Senate. Leading the push to open up highway spending for broader uses was Democratic senator Daniel Patrick Moynihan of New York, an intellectual who had been a Fulbright scholar at the London School of Economics and had directed the Harvard-MIT Joint Center for Urban Affairs. Moynihan had harbored vanguard-like views on the federal highway program since the late 1950s.[43] He had been elected to the Senate in 1976, and by the time the surface transportation funding bill was due for renewal in 1991, he had become chairman of the Senate Subcommittee on Water Resources, Transportation, and Infrastructure, the subcommittee handling the highway bill. With effective lobbying and public relations support from the newly formed anti-auto coalition, the Surface Transportation Policy Project, Moynihan was able to incorporate elements of the vanguard's agenda in the Senate's version of the bill.[44]

The words most often used to describe ISTEA's innovations were "flexible funding" and stronger "intermodal" planning mandates. They seemed to promise local officials a greater possibility of switching funds from highway programs to nonhighway programs, such as transit, and to other "enhancements," such as bike and pedestrian paths, landscaping, and historic preservation. The law authorized a 155,000-mile National Highway System to be funded at $21 billion over six years, a block-grant-type Surface Transportation Program to be funded at $23.9 billion, and a Congestion Mitigation and Air Quality (CMAQ) program to be funded at $6 billion.[45] The role of metropolitan planning organizations (MPOs) was strengthened vis-à-vis state departments of transportation, and planners at all levels were required to pay more attention to the impact of transport investments on air pollution (see chapter 6).

ISTEA was a significant symbolic achievement for the antihighway forces. Its practical effects on transportation funding and planning have been mixed, however. Many who had hoped for rapid and significant shifts of funds from highways to transit were disappointed. They did not see much "flexing" of funds taking place and felt that expectations had been "raised too high by the rhetoric. . . . [O]n balance, ISTEA . . . represents business as usual."[46] On the other hand, observers of the metropolitan transportation planning process concluded that "ISTEA has brought a great deal of change to MPO's . . . [and] greater attention . . . to air quality, intermodal issues, long range planning, and intergovernmental coordination."[47] The increased complexity of planning infrastructure investments reflects so many goals (air quality, promoting public transit, historic preservation, wetlands protection, environmental justice) that moving cars can get lost in the shuffle. As one observer has noted, in the early years of the federal aid highway program "the clear goal was to get the farmer out of the mud. From 1956 on, the clear goal was to build the interstate system. There is no real goal now."[48]

Clinton and Partisan Polarization of Gas Taxes

When Bill Clinton took office in January 1993, it was the first time the Democrats had won control of the White House and both houses of Congress since the end of Jimmy Carter's presidency. It could almost be said that Clinton took up where Carter left off—with a complicated plan to increase taxes on energy, especially petroleum products. The Clinton administration's plan was motivated by financial and environmental concerns. Clinton wanted to generate revenues to reduce the federal budget deficit, and he wanted to lessen Americans' energy consumption. The initial scheme that was presented to Congress involved creating a new broad-based energy tax based on the Btu (British thermal unit) content of different fuels. The tax rate for petroleum would have been much higher than for coal or natural gas. None of the revenues would have gone to the highway trust fund.

Members of Congress bickered over the different regional and sectoral impacts of the proposed new tax, and their search for exemptions, loopholes, and changes soon bogged down the president's bill in the legislative process. For weeks the press featured stories with headlines such as "The White House Struggles to Save Energy Tax Plan; Political Heat Is Intense; Powerful Lobby Groups Work to Cripple or Kill Proposal Aimed at Cutting Deficit."[49] The House did pass a version of the president's bill based on the BTU content of fuels, with a rate that would have translated into an eight cent per gallon increase in gasoline taxes. But important members of the president's own party in the Senate rejected the House's BTU-based tax and substituted a simple increase in the motor fuels tax of 4.3 cents per gallon. Since the object was deficit reduction, not highway construction, none of the revenues from the new tax hike were dedicated to the highway trust fund.[50] The president's whole package squeaked through Congress by the narrowest of margins, with Vice President Al Gore casting the tie-breaking vote in the Senate. Not a single Republican in either chamber voted in favor of the bill, making the Clinton gas tax increase the most polarized and partisan federal gas tax increase in history.[51]

How partisan the gas tax had become was again demonstrated when it briefly became an issue in the 1996 presidential election. Gasoline prices suddenly spiked upward during the spring of 1996. The Republican candidate, Senator Bob Dole of Kansas, sought to gain political momentum by calling for a repeal of Clinton's gas tax hike.[52]

Federal gasoline taxes have not always been a highly charged partisan issue. Conflicts over the Eisenhower-era increases were interest-based battles that cut across party lines, and they were resolved by compromise among the stakeholders. No one campaigned against Ike (or any members of Congress in the 1950s) on the grounds that the candidate raised gas taxes! When President Reagan agreed to the largest gasoline tax increase in U.S. history, a majority of both parties in both houses of Congress still supported it.

The 1990 Bush increase showed that gas tax politics was driven by the political interests of executive and legislative leaders rather than by the financial needs of the highway bureaucrats and the road builders. Representative Roe's aborted "nickel for America" effort demonstrated that the highway coalition could not even get a dedicated tax increase through the House of Representatives in connection with a major multiyear transportation authorization bill. Clinton's gas tax increase saw partisan polarization of the issue at its peak. Many Democrats discarded the trust fund principle and voted for a nondedicated tax, while Republicans voted unanimously against the bill.

The Highway Benefits Regime: Restoration or Revolution?

Although the highway benefits regime has weakened since its heyday in the 1950s and 1960s, the political appeal of the trust fund idea, like the Cheshire cat's smile, lingers on. The trust fund is still quite useful to the tax-paying elements of the highway coalition and to antitax politicians in general. It helps them resist every gas tax increase that is not earmarked for the trust fund. It also helps them keep at bay increases that are earmarked, because they can argue that the multi-billion-dollar "surplus" in the fund should be spent down before any new tax is considered.

For the spending side of the highway coalition, the trust fund concept remains a rallying point. Leading the charge in Congress was Republican representative Bud Shuster of Pennsylvania, a classic pork-barrel, pro-highway politician.[53] He was made chairman of the House Committee on Transportation and Infrastructure following the 1994 congressional elections, when the Republicans became the majority party in Congress. In a bill he labeled the Truth in Budgeting Act, Shuster pushed his pet idea of taking the highway trust fund "off budget." Shuster's aim was to give the trust fund a semblance of the autonomy it enjoyed when it was created in 1956.[54] After a long and bruising turf fight with Transportation Appropriations Subcommittee chairman Frank Wolf and Budget Committee chairman John Kasich, Shuster succeeded in getting the House to pass his bill by a vote of 284 to 143.[55] The Senate did not pass its version of the off-budget bill, but Representative Shuster remained single-mindedly committed to restoring the trust fund's original autonomy.

Such a restoration was a daunting challenge. In the 1950s and 1960s both federal spending and federal revenues grew rapidly, and there was little sense of a zero-sum competition for appropriations. The decentralized budgetary process allowed authorizing committees to play the lead role in setting spending priorities. When Congress adopted a new budgetary process in 1976, it began to shift the balance of power between appropriating and authorizing committees. The appropriations committees and the new budget committee could indirectly control spending from trust funds through their use of "obligation ceilings."

In 1985 the Gramm-Rudman-Hollings Balanced Budget and Emergency Deficit Control Act mandated five annual across-the-board reductions in spending until the budget deficit reached zero. In principle, even holding highway spending constant would require decreased spending in other programs. The agreement between Congress and President Bush, formalized as the Omnibus Budget Reconciliation and Budget Enforcement Acts of 1990, made it more important than ever to weigh highway spending against other spending priorities. Highway trust fund spending was classified as domestic discretionary spending and subjected to the overall spending caps laid down in the act.[56] Any increase in highway spending had to be offset by a reduction somewhere else. In addition, the pay-as-you-go provision of the act declared that even increases in revenues from higher gas taxes could only be used to offset reductions in other taxes or to offset increases in "direct" spending programs such as medicare. Gas tax hikes could not be used to pay for more domestic discretionary (that is, highway) spending.[57]

Finally, the changing role of the federal highway program has reduced the importance of a trust fund mechanism. Completion of the interstate system led to the loss of a central programmatic focus for federal aid to highways. The political discipline imposed by the challenge of building a vast continental superhighway system had slowly evaporated over the years. Upgrading existing roads or funding repairs, necessary though they may be, do not require the kind of self-restraint by politicians and interest groups that the interstate effort did in its growth years. Now squabbles break out in Congress between donor states and recipient states over how to get back in federal aid ever higher percentages of the federal gas tax revenues collected within their boundaries. Committee chairmen load each highway bill with more and more pork-barrel demonstration projects. The 1982 Surface Transportation Act contained ten demonstration projects worth $362 million. By 1987 there were 152 projects worth $1.4 billion. Passed in 1991, ISTEA had 538 projects valued at $6.23 billion, and the estimated worth of the "pork" in the 1998 transportation authorization bill was $9 billion.[58] Small wonder, then, that groups representing other transportation modes, from bike path advocates to Amtrak supporters, feel emboldened to try their hand at getting a slice of the trust fund pie.

If restoration of the Eisenhower-era complete policy monopoly is not likely, is there a new highway benefits regime in the works to replace the old one? The forces undermining the old regime are quite disparate, and there is wide disagreement on the principles that might form the basis for a new highway regime. The two leading possibilities—the intermodal regime and the devolution regime—reflect contrasting interests and ideologies and tend to polarize the forces of change to the point where the status quo, weak though it may be, remains the least objectionable option.

The basic notion behind an intermodal regime has been around for years.[59] It calls for merging the several existing modal trust funds into a single transportation fund that would finance investments in highways, railroads, public transit, waterways, and, perhaps, airways. President Clinton's first secretary of transportation, Federico Pena, offered the most elaborate version of the intermodal regime and single trust fund in connection with the administration's "reinventing government" initiative. Secretary Pena submitted a bill to Congress in April 1995 that proposed a major reorganization of the Department of Transportation.[60] Six existing modal agencies (the Federal Highway Administration, the National Highway Traffic Safety Administration, the Federal Transit Administration, the Federal Railroad Administration, the Maritime Administration, and the Research and Special Programs Administration) would be merged into a single Intermodal Transportation Administration. Pena also proposed the creation of a new transportation trust fund that would replace the separate highway and aviation trust funds, although without commingling their revenues. For surface transportation, however, the new trust fund would have shifted "all transit and most rail programs to trust fund financing" through a new unified transportation infrastructure investment program (UTIIP). The largest part of UTIIP funding (initially budgeted at $21 billion) was allocated to state and local governments by formula. They could then spend the money according to their own transportation priorities. New York could spend more on transit, while Wyoming could put all its allocation into roads. The second, or federal, part of the UTIIP contained $442 million for roads on federal lands, $219 million for research, $1 billion for Amtrak's Northeast Corridor, and $1 billion in federal discretionary grants to projects of regional or national significance.[61]

Pena's reinvention plan was extremely ambitious. Although it paid lip service to "home rule" in the state and local formula portion of UTIIP, it was essentially a strong centralizing plan vis-à-vis the modal administrations and their congressional allies. The highway coalition feared it would make gas tax revenues the "milk cow" not just for transit but for Amtrak and for state plans to launch high-speed rail programs as well. In strictly political terms the legislation came too late. The Republicans had won control of Congress, and they gave the proposal an "underwhelming" reception. It was allowed to die when it became clear that it had no chance of passage.[62]

The roots of the devolution regime go back to the early Reagan years. In his 1982 State of the Union address on the "new federalism," President Reagan proposed turning back to the states all federal aid highway and transit programs, except the interstate highways. One-half of the existing federal gas tax would also be turned back to the states to pick up if they chose.[63] Since the federal gas tax rate at the time was only four cents per gallon, state officials had little enthusiasm for a proposal to pick up dozens of federal grant programs for only two cents per gallon. Reagan's proposal went nowhere in Congress, but the devolution theme resurfaced from time to time, especially in conservative, anti-Washington circles. In 1996 Republican senator Connie Mack of Florida announced he was sponsoring "turn back" legislation similar to Reagan's proposal. His plan would keep 6 cents per gallon for the interstate system, roads on federal land, and disaster relief, and turn the remaining 12.3 cents per gallon of the 1996 federal gas tax rate back to the states. Mack's devolution proposal received support from George Voinovich, the Republican governor of Ohio, who complained to the House Budget Committee that his state sends $1 billion in gas taxes to Washington each year but gets back only $635 million. He pointed to Clinton's 4.3 cents as the biggest "diversion."[64]

Some conservatives are attracted to devolution because they believe that ending federal aid to most highway programs would end federal regulations and mandates on state highway departments. Without burdensome federal regulations (for example, environmental impact statements, minority set-asides, and intermodal planning mandates), they believe state highway programs would cost less, and state gas taxes could be lowered. At least twenty-eight states currently have some kind of highway trust fund, so devolution of most of the federal government's gas taxing power would help keep the practice of exclusive dedication at the center of gasoline tax policy.

Despite these attractions, devolution does not appear to have enough political support to constitute the basis of a new benefits regime. Close observers of the Washington transportation policy scene continue to believe that devolution "will not fly with the Congressional committees that created the highway and transit programs in the first place."[65] Bud Shuster did not fight to take the highway trust fund off budget in order to turn control of its revenue stream over to state politicians.

With the completion of the interstate system, the promotion phase of highway policy is over. But the legal and institutional structures of the old benefits regime continue to shape debate over future directions in highway policy. The highway coalition's policy monopoly has been weakened, but its embedded political influence is far from vanquished. The coalition prefers to continue pushing for more spending from the existing trust fund revenues rather than risk the uncertainties of a new devolution regime. Environmentalists and enemies of suburban sprawl oppose devolution. They want to use the intergovernmental transfer principles of the current regime to force states and metro areas to enact restrictions against auto use. The advocates of urban transit and intercity passenger rail want to get more revenue from the trust fund side of the current regime.

This lack of broad support for bold new departures was clearly evident in the politics that accompanied ISTEA reauthorization in 1997 and 1998. Donor states pushed for formulas that would enable them to recoup 90 percent or more of their gas tax contributions to the trust fund. These and other conflicts bogged down progress so much that a six-month extension of the old bill was needed, taking the process into 1998. There was not even accord on what to call the bill. It seemed to be a contest for a name with the cutest acronym. The Senate's name was relatively sedate, ISTEA II. The administration submitted a proposal it called NEXTEA, the National Economic Crossroads Transportation Efficiency Act. Bud Shuster's House committee initially dubbed its version BESTEA, the Building Efficient Surface Transportation and Equity Act. The name finally chosen by the House-Senate conference committee was the Transportation Equity Act for the Twenty-First Century—TEA-21.

Despite their differences, legislators in both houses did have one common interest: increasing transportation spending.[66] As administration officials warned that transportation spending would "bust" the balanced budget agreement, the House and Senate transportation committees put together the most expensive transportation bill ever.[67] Representative Shuster used the last-minute negotiations on the bill for a final push to take the trust fund off budget. In the end the trust fund remained officially on budget, but Shuster negotiated a complicated compromise arrangement to put a "fire wall" between trust fund revenues and other government spending programs.[68]

Under the terms of TEA-21, most surface transportation spending will be considered as a separate, mandatory spending category similar to social security and medicare, rather than being lumped in with other domestic discretionary spending.[69] Budgetary outlays for the highway and transit programs from the trust fund are considered "guaranteed" and will be set at roughly the level of the previous year's gas tax receipts. The bill specifies funding levels for each year through fiscal 2003 and contains a provision that would automatically adjust spending if trust fund revenues exceed (or fall short of) its estimates. It left about 10 percent of transportation spending in the nonguaranteed domestic discretionary category.

To pay for their increased transportation spending, lawmakers had to find "offsets" from other domestic programs. They chose to deny veterans' disability payments for smoking ailments not related to military service. This tradeoff is precisely the kind of sticky political compromise that the original trust fund was created to prevent. Although Representative Shuster's committee put the total amount of funding authorized by TEA-21 at $218 billion over six years, the administration may oppose spending that much. An administration spokesperson cited the bill's achievement of a "record, guaranteed $198 billion in surface transportation investment while protecting our commitment to a balanced budget and to President Clinton's other vital priorities." Observers believed that wording signaled the administration's intention to hold transportation spending to guaranteed levels only and not seek any additional discretionary funds.[70]

Thus squabbles over transportation spending between Congress and the administration, and between the authorizing and appropriating committees, are certain to continue. Eisenhower-era autonomy for the trust fund has not been fully restored. But the basic highway benefits regime based on the two principles of intergovernmental transfers and the trust fund lives on, *faute de mieux*. It will not be replaced by either an intermodal regime or a devolution regime during the six-year life of the bill. Given the lack of consensus on a replacement, the prognosis for the medium-term future of highway policy is more of the same, rather than a bold decision to strike out in a new direction.

3
REGULATING THE AUTO INDUSTRY
Washington versus Detroit

The classic economic regulation of transportation in the late nineteenth and early twentieth centuries was intended to offset the presumed monopoly power of giant railroads and urban traction companies. The economic goals of regulation were concrete: control freight rates, rebates, and passenger fares; regulate entry and exit; and establish a fair rate of return on capital. The Interstate Commerce Commission was created in 1887 to oversee the railroads, and state public utility commissions were created to oversee the urban traction industry. These institutions were not designed to give public authorities proactive powers to guide future rail development or to balance the public interest among competing modes. They were designed to protect shippers and passengers from abuse of power by railroads and street car monopolies, and to protect companies from "predatory" competition from each other. The politics of this kind of regulation was interest group politics.

The automobile manufacturing industry, purveyors of the nation's main mode of transportation after 1920, was essentially unregulated until the mid-1960s. Detroit was free to sell cars and trucks of any design it chose. Its decisions on product design, new investments, and marketing strategies did not need to take account of auto industry–specific public policy regulations because there were none. Despite occasional suggestions that the antitrust enforcers look into the industry's oligopolistic structure, or complaints from auto dealers about their treatment by the big auto companies, industry executives spent little time worrying about government regulations.[1] They saw their "industry of industries" as hugely successful and as making vital contributions to the general welfare in peace and in war. In the 1950s and early 1960s almost everyone seemed to agree with the dictum attributed to Charles Wilson, the president of General Motors: "What's good for GM is good for the country."[2]

As the 1960s progressed, a novel type of regulatory policy, "new social regulation," emerged from "an uneasy marriage between the New Deal and the New Left."[3] The goals of social regulation went beyond renegotiating the benefits formula between capital and labor. Its proponents sought to transform the regulatory process itself, to open up government to more democratic forms of citizen participation. In this more participatory political process, "business would have to vie for influence with public lobby groups that functioned as itinerant representatives of the citizenry."[4] By insisting on new ways of making citizens' voices heard (more public hearings, greater recourse to courts), the new social regulation created a "public lobby" regulatory regime that could not be captured by the industries being regulated.

In automobile regulatory policy the goal of social regulation was not to shift concrete economic advantages from one set of organized interests to another, but to protect the general public from the diffuse dangers of unsafe automotive design and worsening air quality caused by auto emissions. The National Highway Traffic Safety Administration, created in 1967, and the Environmental Protection Agency, created in 1970, are institutional legacies of the new social regulation, as are the many requirements for public hearings, advisory committees, and environmental impact statements. These institutions were the fruit of entrepreneurial politics, with costs narrowly concentrated on auto manufacturers and benefits dispersed widely over the entire auto-buying public.

Before the dramatic arrival of the new social regulatory policy, the U.S. automobile industry was an apparently unshakable oligopoly. The "Big Three" American producers offered a narrow range of vehicle choices ("competition by tail fin"), and the market was guided by the "price leadership" of General Motors. Under the placid surface, however, flowed growing public dissatisfaction with the cars produced by Detroit and with their "second order" consequences for safety, air quality, and energy consumption. The success of the Volkswagen was an indicator of consumer unrest in the marketplace. The success of books critical of Detroit products and its mind-set indicated unrest of a more political nature. By the time the most stringent new social regulations began to affect Detroit's product design, capital spending, and market mix decisions, Japanese imports threatened economic disaster for U.S. auto companies.

What should government do to ease the transition from a crumbling domestic oligopoly to a globally competitive marketplace? Were the recently promulgated regulations dragging Detroit under? Was the answer deregulation in the form of a rollback of federal regulatory requirements? Or was it better to protect American companies and jobs from foreign competition by means of tariffs, quotas, or local content requirements?

The Reagan administration sought a "restoration" of profitability to Detroit and of amicability in government–auto industry relations. Trade protection and executive efforts at deregulation were its tools. The impetus for technology-forcing regulations was slowed greatly. Yet the problems of the automobile's negative externalities did not go away. During the 1990s, policymakers have been seeking the right balance of carrots and sticks to enlist the industry in a program of technology development that will resume progress toward cleaner, safer cars.

This chapter examines the roller-coaster ride of regulation and deregulation that Detroit and Washington have been on together since the mid-1960s. Consumers want vibrant competition in the auto marketplace. Environmentalists want the development of new automotive technologies that "tread lightly on the earth." Auto companies want regulations flexible enough to allow them to take advantage of profitable market opportunities. Labor unions want a large domestic industrial capacity in automobile production. And safety advocates want as much protection as possible for U.S. consumers. The challenge of the twenty-first century is to find a creative balance among these competing interests.

Policy Entrepreneurs and the Politics of Adversarialism

James Q. Wilson reminds us that entrepreneurial politics occurs when a proposed policy seeks to confer general though perhaps modest benefits broadly across society and concentrate the costs on a small segment of the population. Those who must bear the costs of the policy have a strong incentive to organize in opposition to it. Therefore, this type of politics requires the efforts of a skilled political entrepreneur who can mobilize latent public sentiment, either by creating scandal and suspicion in the media or by capitalizing on a crisis. The entrepreneur puts his opponents on the defensive and associates his proposed plan with widely shared values, performing a feat of political jujitsu by defeating the "vested interests" on behalf of the public interest.[5]

The lack of regulation of Detroit had created a kind of political vacuum waiting to be filled when the public's perception of the automobile industry changed. With no established programs, there were no federal or state bureaucrats, and no committee or subcommittee chairs who had an incentive to defend a status quo that they had created. Chapter 2 explained how the effort to move away from the established benefits regime in highway policy was impeded by a policy subsystem populated with entrenched bureaucrats, turf-conscious subcommittees, and powerful interest groups. Compared with regulating highway policy, regulating Detroit in 1966 was a political *tabula rasa* on which entrepreneurial policy activists and politicians could inscribe their personal agendas and enact their pet ideas.

The unregulated automobile policy equilibrium was punctured like a balloon in 1966 when General Motors hired a private investigator to dig up potentially embarrassing material on Ralph Nader, a relatively obscure lawyer and author of a critical book about a GM product, the Corvair.[6] Nader discovered GM's investigation and revealed it to Democratic senator Abraham Ribicoff of Connecticut, whose subcommittee had been holding hearings on auto safety. Soon GM president James P. Roche was publicly apologizing to the subcommittee, the Congress, and the American public for such heavy-handed tactics. The effect of the disclosure of GM's snooping and its public apology was electric. "An issue that had been slowly heating up boiled over. . . . [S]enators tripped over each other in the stampede to express their outrage. The press response was equally powerful. . . . A pro-Nader, pro-safety, pro-federal intervention feeling swept the country."[7] The major landmarks on the road to regulation are summarized in table 3-1.

Of course, Ralph Nader was not the only policy entrepreneur interested in regulating Detroit. A number of politicians had sensed that Detroit's days as an unregulated industry were coming to an end and were eager to be out front in the process. Senator Ribicoff had been pursuing the auto safety issue since his days as governor of Connecticut. Daniel Patrick Moynihan, who in 1965 was an assistant secretary of labor, had publicized his views on the problems of the automobile society and worked for years

Table 3-1. *Regulatory Initiatives Affecting the Automobile, 1963–93*

Year	Initiative
1963	Congress passes Clean Air Act, first federal legislation on air quality.
1965	Congress authorizes emissions standards for all new motor vehicles.
1966	Senator Abraham Ribicoff holds hearings spotlighting Nader-GM confrontation. The National Traffic and Motor Vehicle Safety Act authorizes National Highway Traffic Safety Administration to set safety standards and issue recalls. The Department of Health, Education, and Welfare sets first automobile emissions standards for 1968.
1968	First emissions standards take effect.
1970	The first Earth Day is celebrated; automobiles are buried as a symbol of protest. Clean Air Act of 1970 requires 90 percent reduction in emissions by 1975–76. Environmental Protection Agency is created.
1975	Energy Policy and Conservation Act creates corporate average fuel economy (CAFE) standards: 27.5 miles per gallon required by 1985.
1977	Clean Air Act of 1977 authorized two more years to meet 1975 emissions standards; set stricter standards but gave EPA discretion to waive if technology was not available.
1978	First CAFE standard (at 18.5 miles per gallon) takes effect.
1985	Reagan administration reduced CAFE standard to 26 miles per gallon for 1986–88 model years.
1989	Bush administration set CAFE standard at 27.5 miles per gallon for 1990 and subsequent model years.
1990	Clean Air Act Amendments of 1990 required further emissions reductions, reformulated gasoline and cleaner fuels, longer warranties on pollution control equipment.
1993	Partnership for a New Generation of Vehicles launches cooperative research for new propulsion technologies.

to develop an agenda for federal policy toward the auto.[8] Freshman senator Ted Kennedy of Massachusetts was willing to publicly confront GM over the fact that it spent about $1.25 million on safety in a year when its total profits were over $1.7 billion in 1964.[9] Even President Lyndon Johnson sought to portray the 1966 highway safety bill as another feather in his Great Society cap.[10]

Nader was the key, however. His status as an outsider, his acerbic and combative personality, and his enormous media celebrity imparted a particularly adversarial style to the whole process of regulating the automobile. Nader used the media to embarrass, discredit, and virtually demonize Detroit. His David and Goliath victory made him the archetype of the modern policy entrepreneur. He touched a nerve in American society and gave rise to a new style of politics in America—entrepreneurial, adversarial politics. By institutionalizing his adversarialism, Nader took pains not to become just a flash in the pan. He began a series of consumer-oriented research and reform projects in his Center for the Study of Responsive Law and finally in a permanent "public interest" lobby group, Public Citizen. Soon there were many young "Nader's Raiders" and "Naderite" reform groups pressing for auto regulation across a broad front.[11]

Detroit, however, was at least as responsible as Nader for its sudden fall from grace. "Inept and insensitive" are the kindest, gentlest words one can use to describe the auto companies' handling of public relations after the upsurge in regulatory demands.[12] Even the pro-business press recognized that auto executives had developed insular, anti-intellectual, and even antipolitical attitudes as they came up through the ranks in the forties and fifties, and that these attitudes were excruciatingly slow to change.[13] Suddenly, auto industry executives found themselves confronted with political "issue networks" on the safety, emissions, and energy problems of the automobile.[14] These networks gave the industry's bitterest critics, once relegated to impotent obscurity, the chance to use the Congress to tell the heads of multi-billion-dollar corporations how to redesign their own products! Detroit's self-defense seemed to play into the hands of those who sought to portray it as an insensitive, undemocratic dinosaur.

In 1971, five years after apologizing to Nader, Roche voiced these blunt views on industry critics:

> These critics whose aim is destructive are following the basic tactic of divisiveness. . . . Their ultimate aim is to alienate the American consumer from business. . . . They tell the consumer he is being victimized. . . . Businessmen are greedy. . . . Advertising is false. Prices are padded. Labels are inaccurate. . . . The criticisms themselves are a form of harassment. . . . They tend to mislead the courts and government into other forms of business harassment [that] have added significantly to the cost of doing business. . . . Adapting products to new regulations . . . meeting daily harassments, answering criticism, defending against public attack, all these carry costs.

Roche was then chairman of the board of General Motors. In this speech he went on to complain that the critics were a "covert danger we can no longer ignore." He seemed to stop just short of labeling them "communists."[15]

This was not language that would build bridges to moderate members of the safety and environmental communities and convince the public that the auto companies genuinely wanted to improve the safety, energy, and emissions performance of their vehicles. What Detroit executives found so hard to accept was the loss of autonomy in determining their products and their markets. Joan Claybrook, a Nader associate, went on to become the director of the National Highway Traffic Safety Administration and later the head of Public Citizen. She explained what happened to Detroit in this way:

> Social regulation took decision making out of the hands of corporate managers and *socialized* it. . . . [T]here were a whole number of changes in the way business did business, but decision making was the key. Public interest groups essentially democratized the decision process and put something other than profit into the equation.[16]

The New Social Regulatory Regime

This political entrepreneurialism reflected the adversarial climate and the frustrating fact that the automobile seemed to be closely linked to major problems threatening America's well-being. Rapid movement toward solutions was needed. The principles of the new social regulatory regime can be summarized as follows.

First, auto manufacturers have made billions by imposing heavy external costs on the American public by vehicle designs that are less safe, less fuel efficient, and more polluting than they could be. Strong public regulatory standards must be imposed to compel auto makers to develop the technologies and vehicle designs to reduce the negative externalities of their products.

Second, technology-forcing regulatory standards for automobiles, backed by the threat of stiff financial penalties against auto manufacturers, should be set as high as outside experts deem feasible.[17] The objections of the wealthy auto companies that the cost of compliance is too high should be discounted in advance. In most cases where the object of the regulatory standard is to reduce the risk of damage to human safety and health, the standard that achieves the greatest reduction in the risk of accident, injury, or public health damage should be chosen, without regard for benefit-cost trade-offs.

Third, the administrative agencies that set standards and monitor compliance must be closely monitored by public interest watchdog groups to guard against their "regulatory capture" by the auto companies. To facilitate this public interest oversight, statute and case law will grant public interest groups standing in federal court to sue the administrative agency on behalf of the public. But if automakers appear to be genuinely unable to meet a given regulatory deadline, Congress will grant them an extension rather than permitting the imposition of huge fines or the shutting down of assembly lines.

In light of the vanguard's fervent predictions of the coming death of the automobile industry, the regulatory regime's assumption that the industry would continue to prosper is ironic. Detroit, of course, loudly proclaimed that each new regulation would be prohibitively expensive, would price many car buyers out of the market, and would put thousands of workers out of jobs. But the most vociferous of the "Naderite" proponents of regulation simply assumed that Detroit was lying about the costs of regulation, as it did about so many other things.

Clearing the thicket of contradictory "cost of regulation studies" is beyond the scope of this chapter.[18] Clearly, complying with the regulations entailed costs that the industry would not have had to bear otherwise. But it was not the cost of regulation per se that caught up with Detroit and called the assumption of permanent prosperity into question. It was the changing economics of international competition in the auto manufacturing sector. Detroit, despite its complaints, could cope with Washington. By the end of the 1970s, however, there were serious doubts as to whether it could cope with Tokyo.

The Road Not Taken: Positive Public Leadership

Executive branch officials in the Carter administration began to realize that the adversarial relationship between Detroit and Washington was promoting conflict and litigious hostility instead of progress toward public goals. Recent initiatives in other transportation-related areas suggested that it did not have to be that way. Examples include the federal financial rescue of Lockheed Aircraft Corporation in 1971, the preservation of passenger trains by the creation of Amtrak in the same year, and the reorganization of seven bankrupt northeastern railroads into Conrail in 1976.[19] In each case the government intervened to preserve vital components of the nation's transportation system. In 1979 the Chrysler Loan Guarantee Act gave further evidence that the government could get a major auto company, its creditors, dealers, and unionized workers, to agree to short-term sacrifices for the long-term good of all.

The Chrysler Loan Guarantee

That year Chrysler was the fourteenth largest industrial corporation in the United States. It employed 97,000 U.S. production workers in forty-six plants in eight states.[20] Supporters argued that if it were allowed to go under, competition within the auto industry would be further reduced. Moreover, the costs of government payments for unemployment, welfare, and pension obligations, plus the loss of income taxes, would far exceed the cost of federal assistance. The opponents of the "bailout" were worried that it would set a bad precedent for other companies: "Don't worry about bad management decisions. Hire a lobbyist to get the government to bail you out."

Late in December the Chrysler Loan Guarantee Act of 1979 was passed by votes of 241 to 124 in the House and 43 to 34 in the Senate.[21] The federal government agreed to issue loan guarantees for up to $1.5 billion; the major constituencies of the corporation agreed to make their own concessions worth about $2 billion. The law required unionized workers to make wage, benefit, and work rules concessions worth $462.5 million, and nonunion workers to give up some $125 million. U.S. banks and other creditors were required to contribute $500 million in new loans and debt deferral. Foreign creditors had to contribute $150 million, and state and local governments $250 million. Chrysler's suppliers and dealers were told to contribute $180 million.

Chrysler itself was required to raise $300 million in cash by selling off assets. It was also required to raise another $50 million by selling new stock. The act prohibited the company from paying any dividends on its common and preferred shares as long as there were guaranteed loans outstanding. Finally, the act created the Chrysler Loan Guarantee Board headed by the secretary of the treasury, with the chairman of the Federal Reserve and the comptroller general as full members, and the secretaries of Labor and Transportation as nonvoting members. The Board was in charge

of seeing that the act's terms were carried out and that all of the concessions were forthcoming.

In the Chrysler experience "the central discovery for federal officials
was the payoff from putting conditions on public help."[22] Although the ostensible goal of the Loan Board was simple, to keep Chrysler in business,
officials could not help but notice how their ability to offer financial help
made the company more receptive to public priorities such as meeting corporate average fuel economy (CAFE) standards and improving labor's rep-
resentation in company deliberations.[23]

The intervention at Chrysler struck some policymakers as a potential
model for future government-industry relations in the whole auto industry, one which would end adversarialism without returning to the days of
"What's good for GM. . . ." It put the public interest "in the driver's seat"
and gave public goals more prominence in the management of a major
auto company than ever before in peacetime. It was an intriguing possibility for remodeling the social regulatory benefits regime. As events un-
folded, the new style of public leadership in the auto industry was never
brought into existence; nevertheless, it is worth exploring this "road not
taken" in order to highlight the contrast between its potential and the policies of the Reagan administration. Reagan put an end to adversarialism in
a very different way.

The Goldschmidt Plan

In 1980 the American auto industry plunged into the worst sales slump
in its history. A cyclical downturn in auto sales accompanied a jump in the
sales and market share of Japanese imports. The results were devastating to
the auto manufacturers and the communities that depended on them. New
car sales fell to their lowest levels in twenty years. Ford's North American
operations hemorrhaged cash; the company lost $2 billion in 1980. That
year even GM was feeling the financial pinch, losing over $92 million on
North American operations. More than 259,000 workers were laid off from
auto companies and close to half a million more unemployed among the
components suppliers.[24] The auto-producing heartland experienced depres-
sion-era economic devastation. Meanwhile, the import share of the U.S.
auto market, only 17.7 percent in 1978, jumped to 26.7 percent in 1980.
Japanese imports alone made up 21.2 percent of total U.S. auto sales, and
Japanese cars were selling at an annual rate of 1.9 million units.[25] Some

auto industry spokespersons still blamed regulation for much of their economic difficulties, but many analysts were convinced that Detroit faced serious price and quality disadvantages compared with their Japanese competitors.[26] Pressure for trade protection built steadily through the election year of 1980 (see table 3-2).

In this crisis the Chrysler rescue model was very much on people's minds in Washington. Secretary of Transportation Neil Goldschmidt led an effort to remake the contentious relationship between the government and the auto industry by expanding the scope of a *quid pro quo* deal to the whole industry. The centerpiece of Goldschmidt's plan was not loan guarantees, but international trade protection from Japanese import competition for a five-year period. The plan was to establish a three-way bargain among the government, the auto companies, and the United Auto Workers' Union to restructure the basic relationships in the industry. This "tripartite" approach suggested mutual concessions by the companies and the union to promote increased productivity and a rapid return to international competitiveness. The union would agree to wage restraint. Management would promote profit-sharing programs to reward the workers for their help when the companies returned to profitability. The government would negotiate a temporary import quota with Japan, replace its adversarial regulatory process with a negotiation process, redefine antitrust laws, and increase support for worker retraining and community redevelopment.

In addition to this central compact, Goldschmidt proposed a deal on fuel economy regulation. Since the period of trade protection would be ending around 1985, just as the CAFE goal of 27.5 miles per gallon was reached, Goldschmidt offered to change the style of energy conservation regulation. Rather than raising the CAFE standards by legislation, government and industry would negotiate future fuel economy targets. The government would ensure that fuel prices rose in a steady and predictable fashion by means of a "standby" gasoline tax. Should market prices become erratic, this tax could be imposed to guarantee fuel economy incentives.[27]

Goldschmidt's plan would have been a major extension of the government's influence over the structure of the auto industry and its markets. It recognized that a rapid return to prosperity for the industry was very important to the national economy. But it refused to see prosperity as the only goal worth pursuing. Indeed, it held that a return to economic success could be enhanced by pursuit of other public goals, particularly energy conservation.

Although President Carter did propose a standby gasoline tax (which, in the end, was rejected), he never officially endorsed any program of trade

Table 3-2. *Trade Protection Initatives Affecting the Automobile,*
1980 and 1981

Year	Initiative
1980	
February	UAW president Douglas Fraser travels to Japan to urge Japanese auto makers to invest in U.S. plants.
March	House Ways and Means subcommittee begins hearings on the automobile trade problem.
May	U.S. Customs Service reclassifies Japanese truck imports as assembled vehicles, not parts; tariff increases from 4.5 percent to 25 percent.
June	Ford Motor Company and UAW petition International Trade Commission (ITC) for relief from Japanese imports.
July	President Carter meets auto company leaders in Detroit; announces plan for "partnership" to help industry, but does not mention trade protection.
September	Ronald Reagan, campaigning at a Chrysler plant in Detroit, says he would attempt to convince the Japanese that the deluge of their cars in the United States must be slowed.
November	Ronald Reagan elected president. After election, ITC rejects Ford-UAW petition for import relief.
December	House passes resolution authorizing president to negotiate an orderly marketing agreement on autos with Japan. Senate blocks resolution.
1981	
January	Senate trade subcommittee holds hearings on auto trade issue.
February	Senators Danforth and Bentsen introduce a bill to impose an annual 1.6 million car limit on Japanese imports for three years.
March	President's cabinet council meets to decide issue of auto import quotas. General Motors joins Ford and Chrysler in calling for import relief.
April	U.S. Trade Representative William Brock goes to Tokyo for consultations with Japanese government and auto industry.
May	Japanese Ministry of International Trade and Industry announces it will voluntarily restrain Japanese auto exports to the United States for three years.

restraint. Instead, he traveled to Detroit in July 1980 to meet with leaders of the auto companies and announce a more modest program of government help for the industry.[28] The package included small regulatory changes and tax advantages for manufacturers, $400 million in guaranteed loans for retail auto dealers, and additional aid for unemployed auto workers and communities hurt by the auto slump.

Carter avoided advocating any kind of protectionism even after his opponent appeared to open the door to trade restraints. Campaigning at a Chrysler plant in Detroit in September, Ronald Reagan said he would attempt "to convince the Japanese that . . . the deluge of their cars into the U.S. must be slowed while our industry gets back on its feet."[29] In response, the most Carter would do was order the U.S. International Trade Commission to speed up its hearings on a Ford-UAW petition for trade protection. Only after his defeat in November did the lame duck president authorize Transportation Secretary Goldschmidt to publish the report outlining the tripartite approach and trade protection proposals.

Nothing came of them. Bruised by his rejection at the polls and still preoccupied with negotiations to free the American hostages in Iran, Carter washed his hands of Goldschmidt's plan for a new style of public leadership in the auto sector and returned to Plains, Georgia. He left the problems of Japanese auto imports and the future of relations between Detroit and Washington to his successor to decide.

Ronald Reagan and the Politics of Restoration

In December 1980 Representative David Stockman of Michigan, soon to be the new director of the Office of Management and Budget, and Representative Jack Kemp of New York prepared a memo urging President-elect Reagan to reverse a decade of regulatory policy. They called for an "orchestrated series of unilateral administrative actions to defer, revise, or rescind existing and pending regulations where clear legal authority existed." They also recommended a one-year moratorium on new rulemaking. In their view "McGovernite no-growth activists" had spent the Carter years preparing a "ticking regulatory bomb." They anticipated an "outpouring of rule-makings, interpretive guidelines, and major litigation . . . [that] will sweep through the industrial economy with near gale force" to produce an "economic Dunkirk."[30]

Regulatory Rollback

The counsel of his supporters and his own instincts impelled the new president to usher in a period of "restoration," a return to a more industry-supportive relationship between Washington and Detroit. Few were surprised when the White House announced on April 6, 1981, that it was ordering a series of actions to roll back thirty-four regulations affecting the auto industry. They were described in a press release as "Actions to Help the U.S. Auto Industry." The White House estimated the package would save the industry $1.4 billion within two years.[31] One of the actions canceled a notice of proposed rulemaking on higher CAFE standards in the post-1985 period that the National Highway Traffic Safety Administration had issued in the waning days of the Carter administration. President Reagan's budget for fiscal 1982 called for a 50 percent cut in NHTSA's budget.[32] Similar reductions were slated for the Environmental Protection Agency. Since authorization for the Clean Air Act terminated in 1981, the new administration sent Congress a draft reauthorization bill that doubled allowable tailpipe emissions levels and eliminated the durability requirements for pollution control equipment on motor vehicles.[33]

Following the rollback of regulations in its first few months, the Reagan administration pursued three strategies: wage a war of attrition against leftover "regulatory zealots" in the federal bureaucracy, make regulatory decisions favorable to the auto companies, and convince Congress to overturn key regulatory statutes from the sixties and seventies. In the first two endeavors the Reagan administration was largely successful, but Congress did not support its legislative proposals.

Typical of the first strategy was the Reagan administration's treatment of the National Highway Traffic Safety Administration. It eliminated the agency's Fuel Economy Research Office and shipped its technical records out to the Transportation Research Center in Boston, Massachusetts. It relaxed regulations on the information that auto manufacturers were required to supply to NHTSA, thus hampering efforts to monitor their progress toward fuel efficiency. The fuel economy rulemaking staff was cut from eighteen employees to three, and the office was collapsed into a division called Market Incentives. According to testimony given in 1983 by former NHTSA administrator Joan Claybrook: "Of the 27 full-time professionals assigned to do this work . . . none . . . have been promoted in the last 2 1/2 years. Several were RIF'ed, more than 10 were downgraded, several retired early to avoid the embarrassment of being downgraded or RIF'ed, and others have left the agency."[34]

In addition, the administration used the discretion given to it by statute to make regulatory decisions favoring Detroit. Beginning in the 1983 model year, GM and Ford began to fall below the CAFE standard. But neither company was assessed any penalties because of carryforward credits they had accumulated in earlier years. Fuel economy standards for light trucks, which were lower than for cars to begin with, were lowered further. After Reagan's reelection in 1984, NHTSA reduced the model year 1986 CAFE standard from 27.5 miles per gallon to 26.0 miles per gallon. Subsequently, it lowered the standards for model years 1987 and 1988 to 26.0 miles per gallon.[35]

Persuading Congress to modify regulatory legislation was another matter. One of the Reagan administration's key attempts was in the area of fuel economy legislation. In February 1987 the White House sent to Congress a draft bill that formally proposed repealing the CAFE standards and all their penalties. Commerce secretary Malcolm Baldridge testified on behalf of the bill and said that CAFE standards distort the market and pose special difficulties for U.S. full-line manufacturers. Moreover, Baldridge said, "the objectives of the standards have largely been achieved. U.S. manufacturers have virtually doubled the fuel economy of their product since 1975." CAFE is no longer necessary because "oil price decontrol has made the price of gasoline an effective, market-based control on fuel economy."[36]

The Democratic Congress was having none of it. Interestingly, an important factor weakening the administration's case for repeal of CAFE was the lack of unanimous support from within the auto industry. Chrysler, the only U.S. auto company that fully met the fuel economy standards, opposed a rollback because it would make life easier for its two domestic rivals. They held an advantage in the large-car market. Chrysler claimed that it had spent billions to develop its front-wheel-drive fuel efficient fleet to comply with the law:

> If . . . the companies which would break the law are released from their obligation to pay fines, they can use that money for future models and features that Chrysler cannot afford because we spent our money on fuel economy. This is a de facto penalty for Chrysler. Or to put it another way, Ford and GM will flunk the standards, and Chrysler will pay the fine. How ironic.[37]

Deregulation was completely in keeping with expectations, but many of Reagan's most ardent supporters were surprised and disappointed when the new administration followed up regulatory rollback with a shamefaced protectionist intervention intended to interfere with free trade in the automobile sector.

The Voluntary Export Restraint Agreement

Upon taking office, Reagan gave the job of handling the automobile import problem to an "auto task force" of cabinet officers and key advisers.

It soon became apparent that there was a split among the members over the issue of protection.[38] Supported by the secretaries of commerce and labor, Secretary of Transportation Drew Lewis was the leading proponent of restricting Japanese imports. The opponents of trade restraint included the treasury secretary, OMB director Stockman, and the chairman of the Council of Economic Advisers. William Brock, the special trade representative, and Alexander Haig, secretary of state, were primarily interested in which one of them would take the lead in whatever negotiations with the Japanese might be required.

Pressure for restricting Japanese imports was already intense and continued to build in early 1981. Two respected senators, Republican John Danforth of Missouri and Democrat Lloyd Bentsen of Texas introduced a bill to limit Japanese auto imports to 1.6 million cars per year for the next three years. Ford and Chrysler had been calling for import restrictions all throughout 1980. But during the many months of the great auto slump, GM had refused to endorse a policy of trade protection. Then in mid-March, just as the debate within the Reagan administration was coming to a head, General Motors changed its tune. GM's chairman, Roger Smith, went on CBS's *Face the Nation* to announce that he believed the U.S. government should negotiate voluntary import restrictions with the Japanese. The Japanese would go along, he said, because "in the long run their interests would be served and free trade protected." Smith said he was usually opposed to government intervening in business, but in this case "the big rule" is "to stop something that could damage the country."[39] GM's change of position made some form of voluntary trade protection the unanimous preference among the Big Three auto companies.

Calls for help from big business were just the thing to appeal to Reagan. David Stockman describes how Drew Lewis and other protectionists persuaded Reagan to accept the voluntary restraint agreement as a means of undoing the damage to the industry from government-imposed regulations. In Stockman's view it was "the triumph of politics" over proper economic thinking. Stockman quotes Reagan as saying, "Yes, we believe in free trade, but there's something different here. Government regulation is responsible for this."[40]

The auto task force met with President Reagan on March 19 to ratify a compromise fashioned by presidential counselor Edwin Meese. Meese came up with what he thought was an "antiseptic, Republican, and voluntary" formula under which "our hands would be clean."[41] The U.S. ambassador to Japan, Mike Mansfield, would be instructed to "talk turkey" in private and warn the Japanese that they must "voluntarily" restrain their exports. Otherwise, the Congress would pass the Danforth-Bentsen bill. The president specifically declined to threaten a veto of the bill in advance.

Although the Japanese government was more reluctant to accept voluntary restraints than was expected (U.S. Special Trade Representative William Brock had to go to Tokyo to hammer out last-minute details), on May 1, 1981, it announced that it would limit exports of Japanese autos to the United States at the level of 1.68 million vehicles for two years, rising to 1.85 million in the third year. The possibility of a fourth year of restraint was mentioned but not definitely settled. The stated purpose of the restraint was to allow the U.S. auto industry a breathing space in which to restore its financial health and regain its competitiveness. Because the deal was formally presented as a unilateral and voluntary Japanese decision, the U.S. government had nothing officially to do with it, and no grounds for demanding any concessions from Detroit. Thus the auto companies were given the *quid* of substantial protection from Japanese imports without having to offer any *quo* in return.

How effective was the voluntary restraint agreement in restoring prosperity to the auto sector, and how much did it cost American consumers? The answers to these questions have been widely debated.[42] Between 1980 and 1985 the average imported car increased in price (in 1983 dollars) by $2,736, or 29.6 percent.[43] The International Trade Commission estimated that the VRA increased the average price of Japanese imports by $831 in 1983 and by $1,338 in 1984.[44] In addition, the agreement raised the cost of autos made in the United States. The Congressional Budget Office estimated the VRA-induced cost increase in domestic cars at $310 in 1983 and $430 in 1984.[45] Virtually all economists believe that the agreement boosted the profits of Japanese and American auto makers at the expense of American consumers. The estimates of the extra annual cost imposed by the agreement on American consumers run from a low of $1.1 billion to above $5 billion.[46]

The VRA helped to slow the growth of Japanese import penetration of the U.S. auto market in terms of units sold (see table 3-3). Japan's export sales to the U.S. auto market in terms of dollars continued to expand rapidly as a result of higher prices for each unit sold, as well as continuing sales of imported parts and components. In addition, foreign auto makers not subject to export restraints (for example, Hyundai of Korea) expanded their auto shipments to the United States to meet the demand for less expensive cars at the lower end of the market.

Table 3-3. *Japanese Imports as a Percentage of Passenger Car Sales in the United States, Selected Years, 1971–95*

Year	Total sales of passenger cars in the United States	Sale of Japanese imports	Japanese imports as a percentage of total sales
1971	10,242,205	578,977	5.7
1975	8,624,448	807,931	9.4
1980	8,979,194	1,905,968	21.2
1982	7,982,143	1,801,969	22.6
1985	11,042,287	2,217,837	20.1
1990	9,300,211	1,719,384	18.5
1995	8,634,998	981,462	11.4

Sources: American Automobile Manufacturers Association, *Motor Vehicle Facts and Figures 1996* (Washington, D.C.: 1997), p. 20.

The voluntary restraint agreement convinced the Japanese Ministry of International Trade and Industry that the rules of the game had changed for auto imports to the United States. MITI began to push direct investments in auto assembly and production plants in America in order to dampen protectionist political pressures.[47] Japanese auto companies have made extensive investments in the United States since the 1981 agreement. Seven Japanese auto firms made over $3.8 billion worth of initial investment in "transplant" automotive assembly facilities in seven different American states (see table 3-4). In 1995 these transplants produced nearly 1.7 million vehicles in the United States. With the addition of just under a million imported vehicles, the Japanese auto companies sold 2,553,378 of the total of the 8,634,998 passenger cars in America in 1995. That gave Japanese manufacturers a combined share of 29.6 percent of the U.S. passenger car market.[48]

The Lessons of the Reagan "Restoration"

Even in a globalizing multinational automobile industry, no government can permit offshore producers to capture a major portion of its domestic market purely through exports. World-class manufacturers must also be local manufacturers. American auto makers learned that lesson in the 1920s and 1950s. The Japanese learned it in the 1980s. Their presence

Table 3-4. *Japanese "Transplant" Auto Assembly Facilities in the United States*

Company	Plant site	Start-up date	1995 production
Honda	Marysville, Ohio	1982	552,995
Nissan	Smyrna, Tenn.	1983	333,234
Toyota-GM	Fremont, Calif.	1985	228,920
Toyota	Georgetown, Ky.	1988	381,445
Mazda-Ford	Flat Rock, Mich.	1987	149,562
Mitsubishi-Chrysler	Normal, Ill.	1988	218,161
Subaru-Isuzu	Lafayette, Ind.	1989	80,660

Sources: James A. Dunn Jr., "Automobiles in International Trade: Regime Change or Persistence?" *International Organization* 41 (Spring 1987): 246; and American Automobile Manufacturers Association, *Automobile Facts and Figures 1996* (Washington, D.C., 1997), p. 9.

as manufacturers in the United States has helped make the American auto sector more competitive. The Big Three's oligopoly is a thing of the past.

In 1995 the Big Three's market share was only 62.8 percent, and GM's share was down to 33.9 percent.[49] Imports and transplants accounted for one in three cars sold. There were somewhat fewer workers employed in the automobile manufacturing sector, as automation progressed and lessons in "lean production" were learned from the best practice of Japanese producers. The United Auto Workers' Union has declined with the industry's oligopoly. It represents a shrinking percentage of domestic auto workers, mainly because workers at Japanese-owned transplant factories in the South have been persuaded not to unionize.

The Reagan administration decided to ride the economic benefits of steadily declining energy prices and not worry about U.S. dependence on oil imports or auto emissions any more. Its regulatory rollback measures did more than simply eliminate bureaucratic red tape. They sent an unmistakable signal to Detroit and its customers that the federal government was no longer going to press them on these issues. Decisions taken about fuel economy standards in the 1980s influenced the shape of the motor vehicle market in the 1990s. Before Reagan many analysts believed that federal regulations would soon produce a much narrower range of vehicles. They saw U.S. motorists confined to small "econoboxes" and two-person "city cars." Instead, U.S. car buyers have reaffirmed their preference for larger cars, vans, and sport utility vehicles. A 1997 Ford Expedition weighs 4,800 pounds and is heavier than a 1965 Cadillac. But the popular sport utility vehicles of the nineties are not like the tail fins of the fifties. They have not been forced on a helpless public by arrogant oligopolists. The American driving public has plenty of small fuel-efficient cars to choose from. They simply prefer larger, less fuel efficient vehicles, and they have the means to afford them. Regulation has not yet been able to change that basic preference. It would seem that, like Pogo, "We have met the enemy and he is us!"

Between Regulation and Partnership: The Politics of Propulsion Systems

When George Bush took office in 1989 and proclaimed his desire to be "the environmental president," the executive branch's antiregulatory stance softened. President Bush signaled his willingness to compromise on the environment by sending a clean air bill to Congress that was much tougher than anything the Reagan administration had proposed. After an enormous amount of debate and a good bit of compromise, the president signed the Clean Air Act of 1990, which among other things renewed the regulatory pressure on the auto industry over emissions standards. Title II of the act specified a 35 percent reduction in hydrocarbon emissions and a 60 percent reduction in nitrogen oxides, beginning in some cars in 1994 and in all cars by 1998. It mandated use of reformulated fuels in areas failing to achieve air quality standards. By 1998 pollution control equipment in all new cars had to have a ten-year, 100,000-mile warranty. The law also mandated that the auto companies produce a fleet of low emission vehicles (LEVs) for sale in California, specifying 300,000 vehicles by 1998.[50]

Bill Clinton's election as president in 1992 raised expectations of a renewed push toward the goals of cleaner, more fuel efficient automobiles. Democrats controlled both the executive and legislative branches for the first time in twelve years. Vice President Al Gore had well-publicized views on the need to alleviate the auto's impact on the environment. President Clinton planned to make some kind of energy tax the centerpiece of his effort to raise revenues for reducing the budget deficit. It appeared that the stage was set for a renewal of federal activity in auto regulatory policy. But, as was to become his pattern, Clinton confounded expectations. He disappointed many of his supporters and startled his opponents by embracing the basic tenets of their position, while redefining the problem in a way that made possible a broadly acceptable, if superficial, political solution.

The Partnership for a New Generation of Vehicles

On September 29, 1993, President Clinton and Vice President Gore joined the heads of the Big Three auto companies in the White House to announce the Partnership for a New Generation of Vehicles (PNGV). The stated goal of the partnership was a joint research program to develop a passenger vehicle that was three times more fuel efficient than a 1994 intermediate size car by the year 2004. The general atmospherics were as important as the specific goal. They were designed to signal the arrival of a new era in Washington's relations with Detroit. It would be an era of cooperation rather than confrontation, but it would not ignore the need for improvements in automotive fuel efficiency and emissions reductions as the Reagan restoration had.

The announcement had something of the look of a treaty between sovereign powers. The administration described the partnership as "an all-out effort . . . a technological venture as ambitious as any America has ever attempted . . . comparable to or greater than that involved in the Apollo project."[51] It was viewed as "a model for the new partnership between government and industry envisioned by President Clinton." It would provide a "peace dividend" by making the resources and expertise of the Defense Department, the Energy Department's national labs, and technology from the "star wars" programs available to meet this peacetime challenge. The interdepartmental management hurdles would be overcome by putting the principles of the vice president's National Performance Review to work in an interagency team led by Mary Good, undersecretary of commerce.

The language that the industry negotiated in the "communiqué" pointed out that "this is not a government project with government goals. It allows American business to set a path . . . and define areas where government support can be most helpful. . . . Unlike the Apollo or Manhattan projects . . . success in this venture means practical vehicles sold by U.S. auto companies in competitive markets." The new partnership "replaces controversy with cooperation, breaking decades of gridlock between industry and government." Today both government and industry share "a vision of . . . competitively priced, high performance, low pollution, safe vehicles" that will "ensure that the freedom and convenience of personal vehicles continue to be available to all Americans and to people around the world." The industry would organize its participation in PNGV through the U.S. Council for Automotive Research (USCAR), an organization formed in 1992 by

Chrysler, Ford, and General Motors to carry out and monitor "pre-competitive" research on energy and environmental matters.

The PNGV had no requirement that the new generation of vehicles actually be mass produced and sold, but the hope was that enough of the new technology could be incorporated into cars coming off future assembly lines to make substantial improvements in overall energy consumption and emissions levels. Thus the country would benefit from lower oil imports and lower levels of greenhouse gases and other pollutants without the need for an old-fashioned fight over new regulatory standards. Harmony would replace adversarialism, and a technological fix would preserve mass automobility while protecting the environment.

As the project got under way the government and industry established a set of intermediate goals. Researchers would survey potential new technologies and select the most promising ones by the end of 1997. Auto companies would fabricate concept vehicles embodying the selected innovations by 2000 and prepare preproduction prototype vehicles by 2004. Technologies that received prominent mention in the early PNGV literature were compression ignition direct injection (CIDI) engines, four-stroke direct injection spark ignited (4DISI) engines, gas turbines, Stirling engines, fuel cells, ultracapacitors, lithium-ion batteries, flywheels, and sophisticated electric power converters and electronic controllers. Some of the proposed innovations provided grist for the industry's publicity mills and generated interest in the industrial research and engineering communities.[52]

How soon will new technology make its way into production-line cars? Some herald the arrival of dramatically different types of cars in the not too distant future.[53] Perhaps the most optimistic forecaster is well-known energy activist Amory Lovins. He believes the PNGV has unleashed forces that "well before 2003 . . . can bring to market cars efficient enough to carry a family coast-to-coast on one tank of fuel." These "hypercars" will result from designing cars "more like airplanes and less like tanks." They will be ultralight, superslick aerodynamic vehicles made of composite materials and powered by innovative hybrid-electric systems. They will make their own electricity on board by a small gasoline engine (or perhaps a fuel cell) that would produce electricity, not drive the wheels. That will be done by four small electric motors at each wheel. Regenerative braking will supply even more electricity.[54]

In addition to solving most of the energy and environmental impact problems of the motor car, these innovations would revolutionize the way cars are manufactured. Hypercars will be "more like computers with wheels than . . . cars with chips." The steel-stamping, tool and die, industrial-mechanical capabilities will become obsolete, replaced by composite molding, software designing, electronics skills. Such "wrenching changes," warns Lovins, could be "catastrophic for millions of individuals and tens of thousands of companies." Although these trends have been developing steadily in recent years, the auto industry preferred to ignore them and "milk old skills and tools for decades." Lovins hopes that the Partnership for a New Generation of Vehicles "will stimulate instead a winning, risk-managed strategy: leapfrogging to ultralight hybrids."[55]

The National Research Council is much less optimistic than Lovins on the progress made by the PNGV. A standing committee of the council with responsibility for oversight of the PNGV issued reports in 1994, 1996, and 1997. The 1997 report was by far its most critical assessment of the program's deficiencies.[56] It noted that cooperation was being impeded because essential data to validate key models are considered proprietary by the auto companies. Development of some technologies, such as the CIDI engine, was slowed by uncertainty about federal exhaust emission requirements after 2004. Overcoming a number of barriers will require "very significant technical breakthroughs," and not enough work is being done to achieve them. The most fundamental problem, however, is money. The fiscal 1997 budget did not include a "definable funding line" to support research and development activities by the PNGV, and there is "no way to rely on such funding in subsequent years," the report said. The Defense Department, the Transportation Department, the National Aeronautics and Space Administration, and the EPA "need to be more supportive and integrated into the PNGV research program." Unless severe problems of funding and resource allocation "are resolved expeditiously, they will preclude the program from achieving its present objectives."[57]

In other words, the PNGV is not at all like the Apollo project. It does not even have its own line item in the federal budget. Its interdepartmental funding is shaky because when an agency's own funding is being cut back, it has little incentive to direct scarce resources to an interagency, public-private program. Balanced budget and tax cut politics obviate any new Apollo-type programs. Clinton's free trade stance and the success of the Japanese transplant strategy leave the administration with little leverage for Goldschmidt-style tripartite leadership. Republican control of Congress since 1994 severely limits the possibility of a renewed regulatory thrust coming from policy entrepreneurs in the legislative branch.

The Clinton administration is making a virtue of necessity by putting a favorable spin on what it sees as an unavoidable regulatory pause. PNGV provides some short-term political benefits. It enables the administration, and especially the vice president, to tell environmentalists that something is being done about the auto-related problems Gore wrote about so eloquently in his book *Earth in the Balance*.[58] It gives executive departments an observation point from which to monitor the progress of automotive R&D and judge what is technically feasible. But it is not a crash program to enable a "giant leap for mankind" into a new frontier of auto technology.

Some auto adversaries fear that the PNGV could function as a brake on the development of truly revolutionary "hypercars" of the kind predicted by Amory Lovins. The role of the Big Three as the government's key partner could give the industry at least a suspensive veto on innovations. They are not likely to push hard for new technologies that would put them at a competitive disadvantage vis-à-vis insurgent producers. Daniel Sperling, a strong supporter of electric cars, believes that "so long as automakers feel no regulatory pressure . . . the movement of technology from the lab to the marketplace will be slow."[59] From adversarial "technology-forcing" regulations of the seventies, Washington and Detroit have moved to "technology-monitoring" cooperative R&D of the nineties. How much new technology the PNGV actually develops (and how fast it is incorporated into production vehicles) remains to be seen.

State Leadership: California's Mandate for Zero Emission Vehicles

Washington is not the only governmental venue that can play a role in promoting new automotive technology. State governments with serious air pollution concerns are also sources of movement toward a new regulatory benefits regime. California has faced particularly severe air pollution problems and has been the most activist state in promulgating regulations to address them. The *New York Times* noted that the California Air Resources Board (CARB) "lays down the toughest regulations, forces the biggest changes, and generally blazes the path for everyone else, including the United States Environmental Protection Agency."[60]

Since 1970 California has set emissions standards for vehicles sold in California that are stricter than the federal government's, leaving the federal forty-nine-state standard to catch up in due time. In 1990 the California

Air Resources Board issued what was perhaps the most far-reaching technology-forcing automobile regulation ever promulgated in the United States—the so-called "ZEV mandate."[61] Auto companies that wanted to continue doing business in California had to have 2 percent of their sales made up of zero emission vehicles by 1998, with the percentage of ZEVs rising to 10 percent by the year 2003.

Needless to say, the auto companies were strongly opposed to this mandate, arguing that it would require them to introduce electric vehicles (the only ones that could possibly meet the ZEV standard by the 1998 deadline) prematurely, thus jeopardizing electric technology's reputation with the public. More to the point, they complained that the mandate would require them to sell electric cars at a big loss and that they would have to raise prices on their internal combustion engine cars to compensate. The possibility that other states or the federal government might follow California's lead made the ZEV mandate even more anathema in Detroit, and the industry used all its influence (stopping short of private detectives!) to persuade the state to change the regulation. It was rumored that they were negotiating with Governor Pete Wilson to build or reopen auto assembly plants in California in return for easing the mandate.[62]

In 1996 CARB relented on the rigid sales mandate and postponed the 1998 deadline until 2003. With the seven largest auto sellers in the state (GM, Chrysler, Ford, Honda, Mazda, Nissan, and Toyota), it signed separate memorandums of agreement that made the introduction of electric vehicles voluntary, but required the companies to continue to invest in the development and demonstration of battery-power and electric vehicles. The car makers agreed to produce a combined total of 3,750 advanced battery-powered vehicles in the 1998–2000 period and to submit information on their ZEV development and introduction plans to the Board. To help make up for the loss of air quality entailed by the postponement of the ZEV mandate, the companies promised to begin producing in 2001 cleaner cars nationwide.[63]

The California Air Resources Board, for its part, tried to promote the development of ZEV infrastructure (by removing barriers to ZEV introduction in the fields of auto insurance, finance, and battery recycling; by advocating building-code modifications for recharging circuits and the retraining of police, firefighters, and medical emergency teams for electric vehicle accidents). In addition, other local and regional California authorities are providing incentives for customers to choose zero emission vehicles over internal combustion engines. For example, the South Coast Air

Quality Management District (AQMD) offers a $5,000 buy-down for each new ZEV sold or leased on its territory that is produced below the luxury tax level. The money goes directly to the auto manufacturers to induce them to lower the retail price of their electric vehicles. Funds are available for approximately 1,200 ZEVs. The AMQDs in Sacramento, San Diego, San Francisco, Santa Barbara, and Ventura also have $5,000 buy-down incentive programs, although with considerably less funding as yet. The California Air Resources Board also publicizes the fact that the federal government has a tax credit worth up to 10 percent of a ZEV's purchase price.[64] Massachusetts and New York had been on the verge of following California in adopting a ZEV mandate until the postponement. Although the two eastern states are unlikely to achieve anything more rapidly than California, they will not be far behind.[65]

The Results of Regulation: The Politics of Evaluation

American automobiles are undeniably safer than they were before regulation began in the mid-1960s.[66] They are also less polluting and more fuel efficient.[67] But when the analysis of regulatory impact gets more sophisticated, endless technical and political disputes arise.

Which regulations are the most cost effective? Should the auto makers' estimates of the cost of compliance with regulations be accepted? What are the estimated health benefits of reducing new-car emissions 99 percent below the baseline vehicle instead of 96 percent, compared with the costs? What about the problem of human behavior subverting regulatory intent? How many drivers will take increased risks because their cars have mandatory seat belts and air bags? How many will neglect the maintenance of the pollution abatement equipment as their car gets older? And what about regulations' negative interactions? Catalytic converters make cars less polluting, but also less fuel efficient. Making cars lighter saves fuel, but it also reduces the protection of occupants in a crash with heavier vehicles. Finally, could nonregulatory policies achieve the same goals more efficiently? In other words, could changes in product liability law do more to promote safety than NHTSA regulatory standards? Could an increase in gasoline taxes save more energy than an increase in the CAFE standards?

The complexity of trying to answer these questions has pushed evaluation research to arcane levels. Bureaucrats from regulatory agencies and lobbyists from the opposing advocacy coalitions bombard politicians, the courts, and the public with cost-benefit studies, multiple regression analyses, and econometric scenarios that are almost incomprehensible to anyone not tuned into the jargon within the issue network. The major impact that these weighty analyses seem to have is to offset each other and reinforce a precariously balanced policy equilibrium.

The CAFE Controversy

The controversy over the costs and benefits of federal fuel efficiency standards exemplifies how hard it is to evaluate the impact of regulations on the auto sector. Enacted in 1975, the corporate average fuel economy standards called for a gradual increase in the sales-weighted fuel efficiency of each company's new-car fleet from about 14 miles per gallon in 1975 to 27.5 miles per gallon in 1985. The standards promised to eventually save drivers money on fuel costs. The compliance deadlines were phased in over a full decade to allow time for the manufacturers to adjust their designs and sales strategies. The secretary of transportation had the flexibility to lower the standards by up to 1.5 miles per gallon in the event of hardship on the auto companies. UAW members were protected by separate imported and domestic fleet calculations. CAFE seemed like a good example of a win-win regulation.

During the mid-1980s, supporters of CAFE standards declared them a winner: "automobile and light truck efficiency improvements since 1973 constitute a major triumph of national energy policy." They estimated that if fuel efficiency had not improved over 1975 levels, motorists would have used 35 billion gallons more gasoline in 1987 they than actually did. Over the period 1975 to 1987, the value of the gasoline saved amounted to $260 billion in 1987 dollars.[68] Not content to rest on their laurels, these CAFE supporters wanted to raise the standards even higher. They believed as early as 1983 that a CAFE standard of 33 miles per gallon was readily attainable by 1990. Some felt that a standard in the range of 40 to 45 miles per gallon was feasible with the right mix of proven, existing technologies.[69]

But by the mid-1980s the auto companies and the Reagan administration were not the only ones who had turned against CAFE standards. Independent analysts debunked the achievements of the standards and called attention to their unintended negative consequences. Perhaps the best-known of these critiques was by Robert Crandall. In *Regulating the Automobile,* Crandall and his coauthors argued that the fuel efficiency improvements from 1978 to 1982 were not attributable to CAFE standards at all, but to the "sharp increase in the price of gasoline and declining real income growth."[70] The authors conducted what they termed "a test of fuel economy without standards" in the form of a series of equations based on such factors as fuel costs, new-car prices, and estimates of the elasticities of production costs. They concluded that "the improvement in fuel economy for the industry was very close to what would have been expected without the CAFE standards." They went on to recommend that "if future improvements in fuel efficiency were desired, the most direct way to obtain them would be to raise gasoline prices by increasing the federal tax."[71]

Crandall later called attention to other drawbacks of the CAFE standards. In an article with John Graham, he argued that because CAFE had promoted lighter vehicles, it could be "indirectly responsible" for between 2,000 and 4,000 deaths each year.[72] In 1995 Pietro Nivola and Crandall ascribed even more "serious shortcomings" to the CAFE system. First, "mandatory improvements in fuel efficiency may reduce the marginal cost of driving, perversely inducing increases in vehicle miles traveled." Thus CAFE may be contributing to highway congestion and air pollution by making it cheap to drive. Second, CAFE standards apply only to new vehicles, which account for about 7 percent of all vehicles and a mere 4 percent of gas consumption each year. Therefore, they may contribute to keeping older, more inefficient, and more polluting cars on the road. Third, since the light truck CAFE standards are lower than those for automobiles, they encourage people to buy more of these fuel inefficient vehicles than if a stiff federal gas tax kept pump prices high. Nivola and Crandall recognize that a major increase in the federal gas tax may be difficult to implement. Even so, they recommend abolishing the "flawed scheme" of CAFE standards, so representative of the "myopic" regulatory thinking of the seventies and with such an "awkward" interface with contemporary policy problems.[73]

In CAFE's defense, one could argue that it is unrealistic to contrast the CAFE regulatory standards so unfavorably with the presumed benefits and efficiencies of a steep increase in the gas tax. What are the chances that the Congress would raise U.S. gasoline taxes high enough to offset the effect of abolishing CAFE? Chapter 2 described some of the difficulties presidents and legislators have had in trying to raise gas taxes by pennies per gallon. A dollar per gallon increase is a Mount Everest challenge in a sys-

tem that has trouble scaling foothills. Although many regulations are undoubtedly far from the best of all possible policies, prudence dictates that
they not be abandoned cavalierly with no alternative firmly in place. Is it
evidence of policy prudence that even under the Republican-controlled
Congress from 1994 to 1998, no serious effort was mounted to abolish
CAFE? Or is it evidence of policy deadlock?

Toward a Postpetroleum Benefits Regime?

The cycle of regulation and protection in the past thirty years has left
government-industry relations far short of the goals of the Naderite forces.
Their hope was (and still is) to give social goals equal weight with profit in
the auto manufacturers' decisionmaking. Only the most sanguine observer
would judge that such equality has been attained. Many of the design improvements for safety, emissions, and especially fuel economy that were
envisioned by auto adversaries in the 1970s are far from being realized. For
example, smog-producing auto emissions are still a serious problem. Gary
C. Bryner, a well-informed scholar of environmental politics, judges that
the Clean Air Act of 1990 is "only a partial, modest effort" that needs to be
strengthened.[74]

But a new auto emissions problem that is much more intractable than
conventional smog has been "discovered" by environmentalists and the
vanguard of the auto's enemies: global warming. The combustion of petroleum and other carbon-based fuels produces carbon dioxide. This gas is
completely harmless to humans who breathe it, but it contributes to the
"greenhouse effect" that traps heat from the sun's rays, preventing it from
radiating back into space. The higher the level of carbon dioxide in the atmosphere, the more heat will be trapped, leading to the phenomenon of
global warming. This in turn could have very harmful effects: the melting
of the polar ice caps, rising sea levels, the inundation of many low-lying
coastal areas, and large changes in global weather patterns. Significantly
lowering greenhouse gas emissions from autos will require either drastically reducing the amount of auto travel or shifting the auto's propulsion
system from combustion of petroleum fuels to a different form of energy,
or both.

At some point in the twenty-first century, an automotive system completely dominated by heavy vehicles powered by internal combustion engines may become politically undesirable. The emergence of a popular

consensus on the dangers of global warming, or a dramatic hike in world oil prices from increased demand (perhaps from China), or unforeseen developments could trigger such a change. If and when it happens most Americans will not want their only mobility choices to be bicycles or buses, and auto makers certainly will not want to have only public transit vehicles to manufacture. The ultimate rationale for both the federal government's PNGV program and California's ZEV initiative was to make sure that drivers and manufacturers never had to face such unpalatable choices.

These federal and state initiatives, modest as they are, begin to reveal the broad outlines of a new benefits regime for the auto industry. Its goal will be to redesign the car and reform or replace its basic propulsion technology, the internal combustion engine (ICE). The benefits will be collective, social benefits: cleaner air, less greenhouse gas emissions, and less national dependence on oil imports. The costs will be concentrated initially on corporations heavily invested in the ICE and purchasers of non-ICE vehicles (assuming they are significantly more expensive in the early stages of their product cycle).

A regulatory regime that does little more than impose costs on auto producers stimulates great political resistance and results in less than optimal technologies being chosen. This has been the experience with technology-forcing regulations in the past thirty years. Instead, the new regime might use stringent regulations sparingly and rely on incentives that are more characteristic of promotional policy than regulatory policy. And why not? The goal of the regime is a fundamentally new menu of automotive technologies.

Following are some of the principles of this "postpetroleum" benefits regime. First, it will not try to revolutionize the present distribution of internal benefits (profits for auto producers, personal transportation for auto drivers). Rather, its goal will be to ease the transition from conventional internal combustion engine technology to new propulsion systems with dramatically fewer negative externalities.

Second, the new regime will focus on individually owned and operated vehicles that can function safely and swiftly on existing streets and highways. Fully automated highways, personal rapid transit capsules, and the like will not be major elements in the postpetroleum transition.

Third, to launch the new technologies, the new regime will rely more on public investments (for example, the provision of refueling and recharging facilities for vehicles with non-ICE propulsion systems) and public incentives (for example, subsidies, buy-downs, and tax credits for purchase of new technology cars) than on command and control mandates, deadlines, and fines on auto manufacturers.

Fourth, during a relatively long transition period a mix of new technologies will compete with each other and with dramatically improved ICE vehicles for consumer acceptance, market niches, and investor support.[75] The new regime will allow market forces as much play as possible in determining which new technologies will be widely adopted.

Fifth, the federal government, in conjunction with automotive equipment manufacturers, will concentrate its funding on basic research in new technologies. It will establish a national framework for state regulatory and promotional efforts in order to ensure the economic health and competitiveness of the American auto sector. It will also establish limited demonstration programs, new flexibility provisions in federal transportation aid programs, and tax incentives to promote the new technologies.[76] It is unlikely, however, that there will be a ZEV equivalent of the interstate highway program. States and local authorities, at their own pace and in response to local circumstances, will provide the infrastructure, legal environment, and minimum regulatory standards needed to encourage the new technologies in their territories.

Vehicles of the Future

What kinds of vehicles will emerge under the new benefits regime?[77] The long-time contender for the postpetroleum prize is the electric vehicle (EV). Electric cars emit no pollution whatsoever. All of the major car makers have built prototype electric cars, and EV supporters are convinced that tens of thousands could be put on the road within a few years. Some of the biggest supporters of electric vehicles are large electric utility companies. They point out that they have a lot of surplus generating capacity at night, when most people would want to recharge their cars.[78]

The biggest barrier holding back electric vehicles is battery technology, which limits how fast and how far they can travel. Once the battery research now under way leads to batteries that are cheaper, more powerful, longer lasting, and more quickly rechargeable, the road for EVs will be wide open, its supporters say.[79] They call for more public support of EV development in the form of publicly financed programs to recycle used batteries and to provide convenient recharging facilities away from home. They also advocate programs to encourage large fleet operators, like the U.S. Post Office, to begin operating significant numbers of electric vehicles. If a breakthrough in conventional battery technology cannot be achieved, conventional batteries might be supplemented by other "promising" means of storing electricity such as ultracapacitors or high-tech flywheels.

Some observers and inventors are convinced that hybrid vehicles will offer more advantages than pure electrics until the battery problem is solved. Hybrids have an electric motor propulsion system for use in town and a small internal combustion engine that can extend the range of the car by recharging the batteries for out-of-town trips. Although hybrids are not zero emission vehicles, they would be considerably cleaner than conventional vehicles.

Another contender to replace the internal combustion engine is the hydrogen fuel cell vehicle. Using hydrogen fuel cells to generate electricity on-board, the vehicle would emit no pollution or greenhouse gases. One drawback is the need to develop large hydrogen manufacturing and transport facilities. Until this is accomplished, and until fuel cell technology is perfected, hydrogen would be considerably less attractive commercially than most other fuels.[80]

In addition to new propulsion systems, cars themselves may be redesigned. Proponents of "future cars" believe that current automobiles are too large and too powerful for most of their "missions." It is a huge waste of energy for American motorists to make short trips to the convenience store in a 4,000-pound sport utility vehicle and to drive alone to work everyday in a 3,200-pound four-door sedan. Ninety-five percent of the energy used in these trips goes to moving the unnecessary metal and unneeded passenger and cargo space. Redesigning vehicles to be smaller, lighter, and built for short trips by one or two persons will help overcome some of the remaining performance gap between the internal combustion engine and postpetroleum propulsion systems. The new power trains and the new vehicle designs will complement each other and be able to provide service comparable to traditional ICE-powered vehicles for most of the short, single-occupant trips motorists make. In a society where most families own multiple vehicles, it will become easier (and perhaps eventually cheaper) to make their second or third cars "neighborhood electric vehicles" (or "city cars" or "urban cars") for daily chores, while keeping the old ICE wagon for special trips like family outings.[81]

Conclusion

The new regime is a long way from being established. How fast it might develop is hard to predict. It will depend on the salience of public concern over global warming, the price and availability of petroleum, and the political and technological responses of businesses deeply vested in current oil and internal combustion technologies.

The auto's enemies are working hard to raise public consciousness about global warming, but they face real challenges when it comes to translating public concern into effective public policies (see chapter 7). In addition, the vanguard has long proclaimed that the world's petroleum resources are dwindling and that automobiles will soon be "running on empty."[82] They continue to argue that renewed U.S. dependence on oil imports, uncertainty about the size of "undiscovered resources" of oil, and an inevitable hike in world oil prices by the Organization of Petroleum Exporting Countries (OPEC) could create another energy crisis within a decade.[83]

The United States is again becoming more dependent on oil imports. In 1985 net imports of petroleum products were 4.3 million barrels per day and accounted for 27 percent of U.S. oil consumption. In 1996 net imports had nearly doubled to 8.4 million barrels per day and 46 percent of U.S. consumption.[84] But if one looks at North America and the Western Hemisphere as a whole, the picture is more balanced. The United States' partners in the North American Free Trade Agreement, Mexico and Canada, are two of its top oil suppliers. Another Western Hemisphere source, Venezuela, also provides more than a million barrels per day. Of the six sources that account for 80 percent of U.S. oil imports, only Saudi Arabia is in the Middle East (see table 3-5). North America is much less dependent on potentially unstable Middle Eastern oil imports than its trading partners in East Asia or Western Europe.

What about the prospects for depletion of the world's oil reserves? At the end of 1994, the world's "proved reserves" of oil—that is, the amount that is "recoverable in future years from known reservoirs under existing economic and operating conditions"— was 1,114.7 billion barrels. Annual world production was 22.6 billion barrels. Thus the ratio of reserves to annual production was 49.2. The U.S. Energy Information Administration is at pains to point out that this statistic *"does NOT imply* that the world's reserves will be exhausted in 49.2 years."[85] Exploration and discovery of new oil add to the reserves every year. And it should be pointed out that the

Table 3-5. *The Top Six Sources of U.S. Crude Oil Imports, 1996*
Thousands of barrels per day

Source	Exports to U.S.
Venezuela	1,305
Saudi Arabia	1,248
Mexico	1,207
Canada	1,068
Nigeria	592
North Sea	509
Rest of world	1,553

Source: Department of Energy, Energy Information Administration, *Petroleum 1996* (1997), p. 76.

world's level of proved reserves is higher now than it was in the oil crisis decade of the 1970s.[86]

Thus a shift away from petroleum-powered internal combustion engines is likely to be driven more by politics than by geology or geography. Public policy incentives, mandates, and regulations will be more influential in speeding the introduction of new auto propulsion technology and new fuels than will dwindling oil supplies.

The thousands of firms, large and small, that are the backbone of the automobile-petroleum complex will fight to ensure that whatever incentives and mandates are adopted will enable them to make the transition without too much disruption. In addition to political resistance, their most effective strategy will be to develop new variants of the internal combustion engine that push fuel economy and emissions performance to levels that reduce the societal advantage of new technologies.[87]

To be sure, the anti-auto vanguard continues to oppose the very notion of automobility. It questions the wisdom of investing huge sums of scarce public resources in a new vehicle fleet and infrastructure for individual automobiles, even if they are no longer petroleum powered and polluting. It argues that investing the funds in collective means of transport will provide even greater social benefits than simply swapping an ICE car for an electric one. These claims and the possibility of a major rejuvenation of the modal adversaries of the automobile—buses, subways, light rail transit, and high-speed intercity passenger trains—are addressed in the next two chapters.

4
RESTORING URBAN TRANSIT
Between Protection and Rejuvenation

Protection is a familiar policy in American politics. Industries from agriculture to textiles have sought to protect their farms, firms, and workers from the effects of international competition, surplus capacity, and changing technology. In transportation, protection involves slowing the decline of a mode that is losing money and market share to other competitors. It tries to prevent the liquidation of key enterprises and the cessation of service. The distribution of costs and benefits from protectionist policies is relatively easy to calculate because the stakeholders are well known and they simply want to continue the status quo. The politics of protection is client politics, with the clients concentrating benefits on themselves and costs on the general taxpayer.

The political dynamics of seeking protection in a transportation mode can often push policy in the direction of rejuvenation. If the benefits of the old transit system are worth preserving, and if the competition—the private automobile—is constantly improving, one cannot protect transit very long unless something significant is done to improve its competitiveness. Why increase subsidies to a decrepit old system when, with a little imagination and boldness, a newer, faster, higher tech one can be had that will have a better chance of luring back the riders? Rejuvenation, then, requires improvement in physical function and improvement in competitiveness. Its goal is renewed growth and expansion. It seeks to entice more people to ride transit. A rejuvenation policy is more ambitious and more expensive than a protectionist policy because changing the balance of attraction between competing modes requires much greater improvement in vehicle speed and amenities, stations, security, levels of service, convenience, and articulation with other modes and facilities.

Rejuvenation's more ambitious goals require a more ambitious and elaborate public interest paradigm than protection. Since more public funds will be required, the public must be convinced that it is getting something worth the investment. Some may argue that former passengers apparently no longer value the benefits of transit enough to pay for them. To this objection the proponents of rejuvenation respond that the benefits of transit are not only the internalized individual ones reflected in the ticket price, but also external collective benefits to the whole community. A bus, subway, or train ride is more than simply moving Mr. Smith from point A to point B. It means one more auto removed from the crowded highways at rush hour, less precious petroleum consumed, lower air pollution. This makes the whole community a stronger, cleaner, better place to live. Public transportation is a vital public service like fire and police protection, garbage collection, or education. Proponents of rejuvenating transit must convince the public that it provides collective benefits that are real, worth paying for, and unobtainable by some other less expensive means. Rejuvenation's public interest paradigm becomes a vitally important part of its political success.

Rejuvenation is expensive. Except in those rare periods when government is perceived as having surplus resources, the public money to foster rejuvenation must come from higher taxes or from funds diverted from other programs. Calls for higher taxes soon alert antitax groups and fiscal conservatives to scrutinize spending programs for flaws, waste, and abuse. Shifting funds from other programs, particularly from another mode's specially earmarked pot of money (for example, the highway trust fund), can turn relatively calm client politics into a classic interest-group-politics battle. It can make bitter political enemies of the very groups transportation planners need to work with if their hopes of improving metropolitan mobility are to succeed.

A Policy Window for Public Transit:
Building a New Benefits Regime

The 1960s was a time when the federal government was perceived as having money to spend. It was the era of the New Frontier ("pay any price, bear any burden") and the Great Society (America can afford both guns and butter). Even the Nixon administration in the early days was willing to explore innovative domestic policies like a guaranteed income. Confidence in government's ability to solve societal problems was high, especially in Washington, D.C. Calls for new government programs often began with the mantra "if we can put a man on the moon, why can't we. . . ?" Policy windows opened in many areas including, somewhat surprisingly, urban public transportation. It was surprising because the federal government had never taken any interest in urban public transport. Urban transit was considered a private business. If any public action was required in the area, it was for local government to take. Even more surprising was how long the policy window stayed open. By the time it was slammed shut in the early 1980s, a new benefits regime had been established and a new lobby had been formed to protect it.

The impetus for this policy innovation did not come from the urban transit industry but from big city mayors and railroad executives concerned about declining service and growing financial losses on commuter rail lines.[1] At the time the urban transit sector was dominated by privately owned bus companies that were still, as a whole, making a profit, although the companies were shrinking service and cutting costs to balance their books. In most medium-size cities and smaller towns, this was seen as inevitable, and public officials did not feel any particular pressure to do something about it. Nor did the bus companies ask them to. But elected officials representing America's large cities sensed the beginnings of "urban blight" and were already searching for ways to involve the federal government in "urban renewal." Mass transit had been closely associated with the growth and prosperity of American cities from the 1890s to the 1920s. It seemed logical that improving transit would help the cities. Protection and rejuvenation of public transit were not goals in and of themselves. Rather, they were part of the broader goal of protecting and rejuvenating the big cities, particularly the central business districts that were the focus of the transit systems. Federal politicians plunged ahead with little pressure and not much guidance from the bus-oriented urban transit industry.

President John F. Kennedy, familiar with the travails of transit in Boston and Washington, D.C., and aware of the importance of urban voters and political organizations in the Democratic coalition, was glad to sound reveille for federal initiatives to rejuvenate transit. His administration sponsored a report calling for increased federal involvement in preserving and improving mass transportation. The report introduced the idea that transit should be viewed, not as a private business, but as "a public service which often cannot be a profit making enterprise."[2]

In early 1963 Democratic senator Harrison Williams of New Jersey introduced a bill calling for $500 million in federal aid to urban transit. Kennedy supported the bill and sent a message to Congress stating that "our national welfare . . . requires the provision of . . . modern mass transit to help shape as well as serve urban growth."[3] In the aftermath of Kennedy's assassination, and as an early installment on President Lyndon B. Johnson's Great Society, Congress passed a modified version of Senator Williams's bill. The bill, the Urban Mass Transportation Act of 1964, became the cornerstone of the nation's urban transit policy and the framework of a new benefits regime for the urban transit sector.[4]

"Federal initiative *preceded* local concern about the future of transit in most communities," correctly notes historian David Jones. "Congress was . . . 'out front' of local officialdom and transit management in embracing the proposition that transit should be financed as a public service rather than as a private enterprise."[5] Given the proactive stance of politicians in developing federal transit policy and the confidence in government that characterized the times, it is hardly surprising that the transit benefits regime they fashioned was concerned less with efficiency and cost effectiveness than with jobs, contracts, and other tangible benefits for established constituent groups.

The Principles of the Transit Benefits Regime

The main principles of the new benefits regime can be summarized as follows.

First, federal transit aid funds will be given to local public agencies, not to private firms. Thus the money should not be seen as bailing out failing private businesses but as helping provide an essential public service.

Second, unlike highway funds, federal transit aid will be given directly to local or metropolitan-level public agencies, not to state governments.

States that operate transit systems (for example, New Jersey and Delaware) are exceptions. Public agencies in a single state can receive no more than 12.5 percent of the total transit aid funds disbursed in a given year.

Third, no project receiving federal transit aid can lay off workers, reduce their wages, or worsen their working conditions.

Fourth, federal aid will consist mainly of capital grants. Smaller amounts will be available for planning, training, and research. (After 1974 federal aid for operating subsidies was authorized by Congress.). Local governments will be required to match federal grants.[6] Local governments that had not been extending any money to transit must do so as a condition of receiving federal aid.

Fifth, to receive federal aid, public transit agencies must comply with federal regulations regarding, for example, improved comprehensive transportation planning, citizen involvement in planning, environmental impact statements, affirmative action, and handicapped access.

The Struggle to Make Transit an Intergovernmental Entitlement

The increasing availability of federal appropriations after 1964 (and especially after 1970) nurtured the growth of a strong transit lobby. George M. Smerk, the leading student of the legislative politics of federal transit aid, notes that in the early and mid-1960s the urban transit industry "was relatively amateurish and seemed ineffective . . . in lobbying Congress."[7] The sector itself lacked coherence, and its lobbying reflected this. The bus industry was represented by the American Transit Association (ATA), which was not inclined to seek help from the federal government because the majority of its members were private businesses suspicious of the strings likely to be attached to federal subsidies. Commuter railroads, in more serious financial difficulty, and the subway firms, which by then were all publicly owned, had established the Institute for Rapid Transit (IRT). Its members were in big cities and were willing to be more active in supporting the mayors' case for transit aid in Congress. Most railroads were also members of the Association of American Railroads. Some commuter railroads preferred to work through the AAR, which was trying to get railroads out of the passenger transport business as fast as possible.

Federal transit programs were initially located at a relatively low bureaucratic level in the Department of Housing and Urban Development. In

1968 transit assistance moved over to the newly created Department of Transportation, where it moved up to become the Urban Mass Transportation Administration (UMTA)—on a bureaucratic par with the Federal Highway Administration. UMTA remained considerably smaller in terms of personnel and funding, however. In 1991 UMTA was renamed the Federal Transit Administration.[8]

As money flowed from Congress to UMTA and then out across the nation, transit interests and constituencies came together into a reasonably coherent policy community. Early on the mayors and congressional Democrats had brought the transport workers' unions into the fold by giving them the labor protection the unions demanded as the price for their support. Other interests came on board as they saw that they might get a "piece of the action." These interests eventually included stockholders in financially shaky private transit firms, rail equipment and bus manufacturers, engineering and public works construction firms, as well as consultants, urban planners, expansion-minded public sector bureaucrats, and last (and in some ways least), consumer advocates and representatives of the riding public. The coming of age of the transit lobby was formalized in 1973, when the ATA and the IRT merged to form the American Public Transit Association (APTA). It quickly became the principal voice of the public transit community.[9]

Undecided by the Urban Mass Transportation Act of 1964 was the question of a dedicated source of funding for federal transit aid. How intergovernmental highway interests flourished with support from the federal highway trust fund was not lost on the evolving urban transit lobby. State highway officials did not have to scramble for each annual allotment of federal aid, and the 90 percent federal share of interstate highway projects made them almost irresistible to state and local officials, prompting them to choose expensive highway projects over more modest transit improvements.

Throughout the 1970s the increasingly professionalized transit lobby, determined to shape federal policy, pursued two main goals: stable funding for transit and local flexibility between highways and transit. As early as 1969, Senator Williams had introduced a bill to create an urban transit trust fund based on earmarking receipts from the federal excise tax on automobiles.[10] The Nixon administration, which in 1970 announced a huge increase in its budget for transit aid, opposed a transit trust fund and shortly thereafter repealed the federal excise tax on autos as part of its new economic policy. But the transit lobby kept pressing for a stable source of funding and targeted the federal gasoline tax as the most likely source. This set the stage for a decade of pressure-group guerrilla warfare between the transit lobby and the highway coalition. At issue was the transit lobby's interest in diverting money from the highway trust fund to the growing intergovernmental transit sector.

Of course, the anti-auto critics wanted nothing better than to take funds from the auto-highway complex and give them to transit. But it was not anti-auto ideology alone that impelled the transit lobby to tackle this citadel of auto power. In cities across the country, groups of citizens tried to stop urban highway projects that were destroying homes and neighborhoods. These freeway revolts alarmed mayors, governors, and members of Congress from urban areas. If demonstrations and lawsuits caused federal highway construction dollars to stop flowing into their constituencies, projects worth hundreds of millions of dollars and thousands of jobs would be lost.[11] Urban politicians are interested in any program that promises to keep federal funds flowing down the intergovernmental pipeline to their areas. They provided a strong base from which the transit lobby could seek to keep federal trust fund money coming in but redirect it to the transit mode.

The transit forces fired a shot across the highway coalition's bow in 1972. Taking aim squarely on the highway trust fund, they persuaded the Senate to pass a highway funding bill that permitted trust fund money to be used to purchase buses and subway cars. The House refused to agree to this, and consequently no highway bill was passed that year. As federal aid funds began to run low in 1973, pressure for a compromise built up. The Federal Aid Highway Act of 1973 was a turning point in the transit lobby's struggle to win recognition for their mode.[12]

While it did not break the trust fund wide open and put transit on an equal footing with highways, it was a major step in the direction of institutionalizing federal transit aid as an intergovernmental entitlement. It permitted states and cities to use a portion of their "urban systems account" highway appropriation for mass transit capital equipment purchases in 1975 and 1976. The act also allowed states to trade the value of a segment of interstate highway that they did not choose to build for an equal amount of general fund money to be used for mass transit projects. Finally, the 1973 act increased the proportion of federal aid from two-thirds to three-quarters of the net cost of a mass transit capital project, and it authorized 100 percent federal funding of technical studies grants for transit planning.[13]

The very next year the National Mass Transportation Assistance Act of 1974 authorized federal transit aid monies (from the general fund, not from the highway trust fund) to be applied to operating deficits.[14] In addition, the act increased overall funding levels, providing a six-year commitment to funding projects, and established a distributional formula based on population and population density for allocating aid directly to urban areas. Continued hard lobbying resulted in further improvements in the urban transit assistance program's intergovernmental position. In the Surface Transportation Act of 1978, the federal percentage of transit projects funded under the interstate transfer program was raised to 85 percent, and the formula grant programs were expanded, refined, and extended.[15]

In 1982 the transit lobby achieved a long-sought symbolic victory: the creation of its own trust fund. Actually, what it got was a mass transit account within the federal highway trust fund. The highway coalition had pushed hard that year for an increase in the federal motor fuels tax in connection with the highway reauthorization bill. The highway forces knew that, with Democrats still in a majority in the House of Representatives, transit was in a position to do what it had done in 1972—"maximize its nuisance potential" to create an interest group deadlock and prevent them from getting the tax increase they needed.[16] In a compromise brokered by Transportation secretary Drew Lewis, the highway coalition agreed to the creation of a mass transit account within the highway trust fund. The new transit account would receive the proceeds of the "transit penny," one cent of the five cents per gallon gasoline tax increase. In return, the transit lobby agreed to actively support the gas tax increase. This settlement passed into law as the Federal Public Transportation Act of 1982, enacted as Title III of the Surface Transportation Act of 1982.[17] Since then every gas tax increase that has been dedicated to the highway trust fund has earmarked 20 percent of its revenues for the mass transit account.

Closing the Window: Fiscal Retrenchment and the Privatization Challenge

The 1982 creation of the mass transit account crowned a decade of success for the transit lobby. It was a bittersweet victory, however. A countercurrent of resistance to transit spending was growing as was a jaundiced view of transit's public interest arguments. The 1980s saw both a politically driven financial retrenchment and an intellectual challenge to transit's public service paradigm.

Between 1970 and 1980 federal aid to transit increased 1,600 percent (from $230 million to $3.9 billion), while ridership increased only 18 percent.[18] The financial deficit of the transit sector, $90 million in 1968, had grown by 1980 to $7.8 billion. The average transit operation in 1980 could cover only 41 percent of its operating expenses (to say nothing of its capital expenditures).[19] Labor costs rose dramatically, while labor productivity declined sharply. Consequently, transit operating expenses rose by 319 percent, compared with the overall consumer price index increase of 147 percent. Fares, on the other hand, rose only by 67 percent.[20] Thoughtful analysts of public transit policy had to acknowledge the seriousness of the sector's financial and productivity problems.[21]

During Jimmy Carter's presidency, the executive branch made an effort to restrain the growth of federal transit spending and to increase transit productivity and nonfederal sources of finance, including public-private partnerships.[22] When Ronald Reagan took office, executive branch skepticism about transit became outright hostility. "Why should someone in Sioux Falls pay taxes so that a bureaucrat in Washington, D.C., can ride to work on transit?" was the president's most-quoted line about transit. If cities wanted to subsidize their transit system, let them do it with their own money. The administration would be glad to turn over responsibility for transit to state and city governments. Meanwhile, Reagan's initial agenda for urban transportation policy was fiscal retrenchment across the board.

Budget director David Stockman recommended phasing out all operating subsidies by 1984. He declared a policy of "no new starts" for rail projects and froze federal transit spending at 1981 levels.[23] The Democrats, the National Conference of Mayors, the American Public Transit Association, and the transit workers' unions prepared for a hard fight in Congress to resist the administration's budget-slashing efforts.[24] After the first two budget cycles, a stalemate emerged. The distributive political pressures in Congress were too strong for it to accept a no-new-starts policy. Operating subsidies would shrink, but not nearly as fast as Stockman had wanted. But the rapid growth in federal transit aid that took place in the 1970s was clearly over as long as Reagan remained in office.[25]

The Public Service Paradigm: Benefits versus Costs

The public service paradigm had been politically helpful in promoting transit rejuvenation in its early stages. Successive promises to restore central cities, reduce congestion, serve the mobility-disadvantaged, fight pollution, and save energy broadened support for transit assistance to a wide spectrum of groups. But the intellectual underpinning of the paradigm had an important weakness that gradually became apparent. Transit supporters were unable to develop readily comprehensible and persuasive methods of social accounting to measure the external benefits that public subsidies for transit produced. There were too many divergent, even conflicting, goals. For example, should planners try to provide service to underserved, light-density suburban areas, or should they attempt to maximize ridership for a given level of subsidy? Moreover, no clear guidelines helped rank the many different goals.[26]

It was one thing to *assert* that transit was producing a long list of external benefits and that it should not be held to conventional standards of profit and loss. It was another thing to *demonstrate* this convincingly to a skeptical audience of politicians and taxpayers. This difficulty was recognized by the authors of a comprehensive survey of efforts to improve and simplify transit benefits measurement. They concluded that "attempts to create a single measure of transit benefits . . . are subject to significant problems of double counting and require assumptions that are difficult to justify." Such a single measure could be "misleading and . . . create more problems than it solves." Despite all the efforts at quantification, "transit decision making is dominated by intangibles [such as] community pride, health effects of pollution, potential for urban redevelopment, equity . . . and [transit's] option value."[27]

There are external benefits from investment in transit, and numerous sophisticated methodologies have tried to measure them. In addition, innumerable benefit-cost studies have been done in support of specific transit projects.[28] But the complexity of these procedures and studies has been a mixed blessing at best. Hefty tomes lining the shelves of planners' offices (and hefty fees lining the pockets of the consultants hired to produce them) did little to resolve political debates over the value of transit subsidies. Once a political asset, the public service paradigm became a stumbling block. The public could understand the "bottom line" fiscal deficit far more readily than abstract analyses of external benefits.

The Privatization Challenge

George V. Hilton was one of the first transit critics to point out that the typical transit enterprise receiving federal aid was a local monopoly structurally dependent on the classic radial city in which most jobs and many key retail and service functions were centralized in the downtown.[29] David Jones, less antitransit than Hilton, nonetheless agreed with him that the organizational form and operating procedures of public transit agencies dated from the period 1890 to 1920 when cities were compact and centered on downtown.[30] In those days few people had cars and thus tended to use transit not just for the peak-hour journey to work but also for off-peak and recreational travel. Wages for urban workers were depressed by high levels of immigration. Unions were weak, inflation was virtually nonexistent, and private capital eagerly sought opportunities in the rapidly growing market for urban electric traction.

That era ended long ago. Hilton claims that urban electric traction was unable to attract new capital investment as early as the panic of 1907! Jones puts the climacteric somewhat later, at the end of World War I when wage inflation and auto competition hit the industry hard. Both agree that by the 1960s the old compact city was well on its way to becoming a decentralized metropolis. This kind of city was ill suited not only to efficient, profitable transit operations, but to any kind of effective transit service at all. Federal transit subsidies rescued an anachronistic style of operation and prevented Schumpeter's "winds of creative destruction" from doing their necessary work.

The Reagan administration accepted this line of thought and issued the "privatization challenge" to public transportation. Its goal was to restore as much competition as possible to the transit sector. This would be accomplished gradually according to what might be called the privatization paradigm.

First, local officials would create a regional transportation commission, an institution distinct from the public agency or enterprise that operated the transportation system.[31] The commission would have the power to decide which public transportation service needs would be met in a city or region. Then the political authorities responsible for funding public transportation services would begin to introduce competition into the sector. Gradually they would put more and more services out for competitive bidding. Weekend and evening bus service could be contracted out to independent bus or taxi companies. Elderly and handicapped paratransit service also could be privatized. Even some peak-hour fixed route bus service might be susceptible to contracting out. This kind of strategic privatization, far from "skimming the cream" off the most profitable traffic, would actually be skimming the deficit, because it would enable the main public transit enterprise to buy fewer buses and hire fewer drivers.[32] Having more transit services managed in the private sector would not only enhance efficiency. It would also put pressure on the main public transport enterprise to become more productive. Transit workers' unions would become more willing to accept productivity-enhancing work rule changes such as part-time drivers and crosstraining in multiple job categories. Managers would be more cost conscious, more customer driven, and better able to tailor service to individual market niches.

Despite its theoretical merits, the privatization paradigm has practical and political limitations. How much change can be achieved through privatization? The capital-intensive parts of urban transit systems—the subways, the commuter rail lines, the elevated people movers, even the light rail lines—are difficult to privatize.[33] Even if public authorities took over responsibility for providing the "infrastructure" of tunnels, bridges, tracks, signals, and stations, while putting the management of the rolling stock under private enterprise, the amount of true competitive pressure this would introduce would be minimal.

Stiff political resistance to privatization by affected interests can be expected. Transit workers' unions are obvious candidates to lead the fight. But public sector managers are likely to join them. They have seen that salaries, perks, pensions, and expense accounts tend to rise in proportion to the size of the operation being managed. No wonder they are reluctant privatizers. Organized passenger groups will fear fare hikes and service cuts. Politicians will be glad to raise a variety of objections, from the union-busting issue to the racial minorities issue. (Blacks and Hispanics are well represented among the passengers and the workers in large urban transit enterprises.)

In fact, these political weaknesses in the paradigm prevented the Reagan administration from successfully imposing most of its privatization plans on reluctant local transit operators around the nation. A case in point is the "hostage bus" confrontation between the Urban Mass Transportation Administration and the New Jersey Transit Corporation.[34]

Frustrated at its inability to persuade Congress to make the deep funding cuts it wanted, the Reagan administration sought to change transit policy as much as it could by purely executive branch efforts. Reagan's second appointee to the post of UMTA administrator, Ralph Stanley, became the point man for this attempt. Stanley launched his privatization campaign at a conference in Teaneck, New Jersey, in October 1984, in the midst of the president's reelection campaign. To observers, especially those from

New Jersey, Stanley seemed to be targeting the Garden State and its large public transit agency for high-profile treatment.

The New Jersey Transit Corporation (NJT) was founded in 1979 by consolidating bus properties across the state. By the mid-1980s it had become a publicly owned, statewide operator of bus and train service with 9,000 employees and an annual budget of over half a billion dollars. A conduit for capital subsidies to the state's remaining private bus companies, it made regulatory decisions on their routes and service levels. In addition, it competed with the privates on certain routes.

Some of the private operators saw Stanley's privatization thrust as an opportunity to get a better deal from New Jersey Transit. They asked UMTA, through its New York regional office, to require NJT to restructure its relations with the private bus companies and contract out more of its routes to them. Stanley responded by informing NJT of other plans. With regard to its pending grants for 250 new buses, he would only approve funding for the 205 buses slated to go to private carriers and would hold up the 45 that were for New Jersey Transit itself until more progress was made toward privatization. Further, he held up a "letter of no prejudice" by which UMTA would give NJT credit as the local match for an additional 250 buses already purchased with funds from the Port Authority of New York and New Jersey.

New Jersey refused to accept the 205 buses for the private carriers unless UMTA released funds for the 45 public buses. This created an impasse: each side held the other side's buses hostage. Eventually, and with much Machiavellian maneuvering, the impasse was resolved. But the crisis was an ironic turn of events for an administration purportedly eager to get the federal government off the backs of states and local communities.

The political shock waves from Stanley's "browbeating" of New Jersey Transit in the name of privatization spread across the nation's transit community, and the transit lobby struck back in the political arena. The American Public Transit Association issued a study rebutting many of the administration's assumptions about cost savings from privatization. The study suggested that the Urban Mass Transportation Administration modify or abandon many of its new regulations concerning privatization.[35] In 1986 the transportation subcommittee of the House Appropriations Committee investigated charges that UMTA was "conditioning" approval of grant applications on progress toward its administratively mandated privatization and contracting out goals. Congress then decided to specifically prohibit UMTA from requiring that a fixed percentage of an agency's business be contracted out.[36] Thus UMTA was put on notice that its administrative attempt to push privatization had very clear limits. It was acceptable for Administrator Stanley to promise salary increases of 3 percent to his ten regional administrators if they promoted privatization aggressively in their districts. But it was definitely not acceptable for transit agencies and transit riders to be threatened with the loss of federal aid to which they were entitled by the rules and formulas that Congress had enacted.[37]

Ralph Stanley left his post as UMTA administrator at the end of May 1987 to head a private company seeking to build a toll road in Virginia. His departure signaled the end of UMTA's aggressive administrative push for privatization. In the future it would concentrate on small demonstration grants and developing information on local success stories. There is an important lesson to be learned from the experience. Federal transportation policies are essentially incentive systems. When a federal initiative is perceived as bringing new resources to the table, state and local officials are likely to accept the initiative and redirect their own programs toward its goals. But when a controversial federal policy provides no new resources and is widely perceived as undermining both the central mission of a transit agency and an established benefits regime, resistance is inevitable. In our loosely jointed political system, with its separation of powers and its decentralized federal structure, resistance is also likely to be successful.

Evaluating the Results of the Transit Benefits Regime

After thirty years of policymaking and implementation, what are the accomplishments and the shortfalls of the federal government's attempt to protect and rejuvenate urban transit? A good place to begin this evaluation is with the balanced judgment of George M. Smerk. He notes that transit policy can be called "a winner" insofar as it provided hardware and fixed facilities, stimulated the preservation of urban mass transportation, and raised the public consciousness about mass transportation. On the other hand, if the standard of judgment is whether transit won "an increasing proportion of urban travel, . . . [had] a major impact on shaping cities in a more rational or efficient pattern, or in significantly mitigating the burden of congestion on a nationwide basis, the federal transit program has been a failure." In other words, the protection part of the policy has succeeded but the rejuvenation part has not—at least not yet.[38]

On Smerk's first point, there can be little dispute. The U.S. transit industry is larger and better equipped than it would have been without the subsidy programs. From its modest beginnings in 1961, the federal transit assistance program poured $82.2 billion into the transit industry through fiscal 1995.[39] This money (and matching funds contributed by state and local governments) bought 92,992 new buses, and 8,609 new rail cars and locomotives (through 1993). Over 322 miles of new rail transit lines were constructed and put into service, many in cities that had been without rail transit such as Washington, D.C., Miami, Atlanta, Baltimore, Buffalo, Detroit, and Los Angeles.[40] Hundreds of bus maintenance facilities have been dramatically upgraded from decrepit trolley barns to modern bus garages. Because of their requirements for local matching funds, federal subsidies stimulated many localities and states to enact or increase their own subsidies. By 1993 state and local subsidies were running at $8.7 billion in operating assistance and $2.4 billion in capital funding annually, a total that was more than twice the level of federal assistance.[41]

Subsidies from all levels of government reversed the long postwar decline in transit sector employment. Table 4-1 shows that from 242,000 employees in 1945, total transit sector employment declined to a low of 138,040 employees by 1970. Since then total transit employment has more than doubled, reaching 302,758 by 1993. Even more impressive, from a certain point of view, total employee compensation (salaries plus benefits) has risen more than fourfold since 1975, from $2.8 billion to $12.3 billion.

Thus the original "clients" have done quite well for themselves under the public service benefits regime. Federal financial support rose rapidly during the 1970s and stimulated the growth of state and local subsidies as well. Capital for new equipment was funneled into the system to help overcome years of private disinvestment. Operating subsidies permitted the hiring of many new employees whose salaries rose faster than inflation. Career opportunities blossomed, especially for managerial and technical personnel. There are hundreds of new, well-paying jobs as bus drivers, train conductors, mechanics, office staff, planning personnel, and executives in every city of a certain size in the country, and many of these jobs have gone to minorities and women. No wonder urban politicians support public transit subsidies, especially when the money comes from the federal and state treasuries!

But if big city politicians find the benefits regime for transit quite attractive, economists, both transit critics and supporters, are less sanguine.

Table 4-1. *Employees, Salaries and Wages, and Labor Costs in*
U.S. Public Transportation, Selected Years, 1940–93

Year	Number of employees	Salaries and wages (millions of dollars)	Total labor costs (millions of dollars)[a]
1940	203,000	360.6	n.a.
1945	242,000	632.0	n.a.
1950	240,000	835.0	n.a.
1955	198,000	864.0	n.a.
1960	156,400	857.3	n.a.
1965	145,000	963.5	n.a.
1970	138,040	1,274.1	n.a.
1975	159,800	2,236.1	2,849.3
1980	187,000	3,280.9	4,634.0
1985	270,020	5,843.1	8,711.4
1990	272,830	7,226.3	11,212.3
1993	302,758	7,935.6	12,328.0

Source: American Public Transit Association, *Transit Fact Book*, various years.
n. a. Not available.
a. Salaries and wages plus fringe benefits.

They agree that the regime contains a number of perverse incentives and uneconomic special protections.[42] The labor protection imperatives for organized labor embedded in section 13(c) of the Urban Mass Transportation Act of 1964 make it difficult to introduce modern labor-saving innovations and work practices. Extending transit to the suburbs and small towns expanded transit's political base, but it also increased expenses faster than it increased ridership. Concentrating aid on public authorities and public agencies introduced additional rigidities that further inflated costs and made it harder to do what market-driven companies do best: hold down costs, improve efficiency, and fit the supply of their product or service to the demand. Finally, the political distributive requirements (limiting states to a maximum 12.5 percent of total funding) could not overcome the fact that most transit riders are concentrated in a few large metro areas where population densities and travel patterns are most conducive to transit.

One analyst compared the capital cost and ridership projections of new rail systems in Atlanta, Baltimore, Miami, and Washington, D.C., with the figures for the proposed Second Avenue subway line in New York, which was never built for lack of funds. The new subway line in New York would have been far more cost effective per rider than any of the other systems. He concluded that "somewhere, something is wrong with the process" that builds "marginally successful, or unsuccessful new heavy rail systems in cities which are unsuited for them" while underfunding the one city with the highest level of transit use.[43]

Indeed, Don H. Pickrell, an economist at the Department of Transportation's National Transportation Systems Center, found that local officials "grossly overestimate" rail transit ridership and underestimate rail construction and operating costs for proposed projects in their communities in order to compete for federal discretionary transit assistance. Pickrell examined eight urban rail projects built in the 1970s and 1980s and compared pre-approval cost and ridership estimates with actual costs. Only the extensive metrorail system in Washington, D.C., experienced ridership that was more than half of the forecast level. Capital spending overruns ranged from 17 percent for Sacramento's light rail line to more than 150 percent for Washington's Metro. Pickrell also examined the bureaucratic and political factors that tend to produce such overoptimistic forecasts for urban rail projects. Local officials get committed to a project and pressure their planning staffs and consultants to produce optimistic estimates in order to have a better chance to compete for federal dollars. If federal officials are skeptical, local leaders use their congressional delegations' pork barrel power to earmark the funds for the new rail system in their districts.[44]

The cost of transit restoration may be higher than necessary, but that is not necessarily a damning indictment. Smerk rightly points out that ridership is the key test of the policy's success. Without increased ridership, none of the external benefits (congestion relief, pollution reduction, energy savings) that are the policy justification for public service subsidies can be achieved.

Table 4-2 presents the trends in ridership and vehicle miles between 1940 and 1993. With a lag of several years after the beginning of substantial federal subsidies, the postwar decline in ridership was arrested. Since the mid-1970s, total patronage has returned to near its 1965 level—that is, about where it was before the federal assistance program began. Note, however, that the total vehicle miles operated in 1993 exceeded the vehicle miles operated in 1965 by 1.3 billion, and the number of transit employees exceeded the level in the mid-1960s by some 157,000 persons. Indeed, the total vehicle miles in 1993 were slightly higher than in 1950, when there were more than twice as many passenger trips!

Another way of looking at transit's performance is in terms of market share: what proportion of travel by all surface modes is made by urban public transit? In 1992 transit's share of total national surface transportation

Table 4-2. *Public Transportation Passenger Trips and Vehicle Miles,
Selected Years, 1940–93*

Millions

Year	Total passenger trips	Total vehicle miles
1940	13,098	2,596
1945	23,254	3,253
1950	17,246	3,007
1955	11,529	2,447
1960	9,395	2,142
1965	8,253	2,008
1970	7,332	1,883
1975	6,972	1,989
1980	8,235[a]	2,093
1985	8,636[b]	2,790[b]
1990	8,799	3,241
1993	8,362	3,387

Source: American Public Transit Association, *Transit Fact Book*, various years.

a. Series is not continuous between 1979 and 1980. Beginning in 1980 "unlinked passenger trips" are given based on data collection procedures defined by the Urban Mass Transportation Act of 1964, section 15.

b. Series is not continuous between 1983 and 1984. Includes demand-responsive transit and smaller and rural systems not counted before 1984.

passenger miles was 1.06 percent.[45] This included travel in rural areas as well as urban travel. When only passenger miles traveled in urban areas are considered, transit's market share increases. It stood at 2.3 percent in 1994 (see table 4-3). Both ways of measuring transit's market share show that it has been declining over the years. Decline is inevitable, of course, if a mode can only hold its own or produce small increases in passenger miles, while the total amount of travel steadily increases almost exclusively because of the great rise in automobile travel in the decentralizing American metropolis.

Rail Transit and the New Polymorphous Metropolis: The Case of Los Angeles

The key problem facing transit—especially rail transit—is low-density suburban sprawl. Virtually everyone has access to a car. Los Angeles, with its famous freeways and broad boulevards, has long been considered the prototype of the auto-dominated American region. Yet in 1980 politicians

Table 4-3. *Urban Transit and Urban Automobile Passenger Miles, Selected Years, 1945–94*

Year	Passenger miles		Transit as a percentage of total passenger miles
	Urban transit	Urban automobile	
1945	130	240	35.1
1950	90	403	18.3
1955	60	515	10.4
1960	48	627	7.1
1965	43	786	5.2
1970	41	1,089	3.6
1975	38	1,341	2.8
1980	40	1,288	3.1
1985	40	1,400	2.7
1990	41	1,533	2.6
1994	40	1,667	2.3

Sources: For 1945 to 1975, see Alan Altshuler with James P. Womack and John R. Pucher, *The Urban Transportation System: Politics and Policy Innovation* (MIT Press, 1979), table 2.2, p. 22. For 1980 to 1994, the transit passenger miles are from Depatment of Transportation, Bureau of Transportation Statistics, *National Transportation Statistics 1995* (1995), table 6, p. 64. Urban automobile passenger miles for 1980 to 1994 were calculated by the author using the methodology described in Altshuler, Womack, and Pucher, *Urban Transportation System*, appendix C. Data for the calculations were drawn from DOT, Federal Highway Administration, *Highway Statistics*, various years, table VM-1. Vehicle occupancy rate figures used in the calculations were taken from DOT, Bureau of Transportation Statistics, *Transportation Statistics Annual Report 1995* (1995), table 3-4, p. 61.

and planners in the Los Angeles region pushed through a one-half-cent local sales tax dedicated to transit. Their thirty-year "Integrated Transportation Plan" called for spending $183 billion in local, state, and federal money between 1990 and 2010 on new subways, light rail and heavy rail lines, electric trolleys, and new technology buses. The project hoped "at long last to align Los Angeles alongside Paris, London, New York, and Boston."[46]

In 1989 the state legislature promised up to $18.5 billion in new state spending for transportation in the 1990s. California voters approved Proposition 108, the Passenger Rail and Clean Air Bond Act of 1990, which authorized $1 billion in bonds for capital investment in new rail lines. Proposition 116 provided nearly $2 billion more for rail investment.[47] These state and local funds, when combined with federal transit assistance funds, put politicians in the Los Angeles area on a fabulous "money train."[48] Public contracts to construction and engineering firms and new construction jobs in the region quickly followed.

In the 1990s, however, mounting problems began to plague the ambitious rail construction projects: negative publicity about cost overruns, financial scandals, construction glitches, and disappointing ridership on the new rail lines.[49] Several different agencies plan and operate rail transit efforts in the Los Angeles area. Public perception of organizational disarray and duplication of effort resulted. This led to the creation in 1993 of the Los Angeles County Metropolitan Transportation Authority (MTA), which merged the Southern California Rapid Transit District and the Los Angeles County Transportation Commission.

The new MTA had hardly been formed when it "hit the wall" financially, largely because of the escalating construction costs of the new rail lines and higher than expected operating expenses. The light-rail Blue Line from Los Angeles to Long Beach, which opened in 1990, cost $877 million to construct, or about $40 million per mile. In 1992–1993 it covered only 10 percent of its operating expenses from the fare box. This amounts to a subsidy of over $11 per trip for each and every passenger. The Green Line's construction costs escalated from a projected $254 million to over $725 million. The initial four-mile segment of the proposed twenty-two-mile Red Line cost an estimated $300 million per mile. Opened at the end of 1993, it carried some 15,000 daily riders. But the operating subsidy per passenger trip was estimated at $21, the most expensive per mile subsidy in the country.[50]

Public support for new rail investment sharply declined. Rail bond issue propositions were defeated at the polls in 1992 and 1994. In addition, a referendum to increase taxes on gasoline to fund mass transit was defeated by a vote of 81 to 19 percent in 1994.[51] The burden of heavy operating subsidies and the formidable construction costs required to complete the system began to give pause to even many transit supporters. A U.S. Department of Transportation official was quoted as saying, "The costs are completely off the map. We could spend the entire federal allocation for mass transit in the U.S. in L.A. for the next ten years and still not finish the rail system."[52] The cost problems and the difficulties of finding funding led the new MTA's board to sharply scale back the old long-range plan.[53] By early 1995 the MTA plan called for spending only $60 billion, with only 96 miles of rail line and 300 buses, and more reliance on high occupancy (HOV) lanes on freeways, ride sharing, and telecommuting.[54]

To the financial woes of the MTA were added unrelenting political and legal pressures. Two former transit employees who claimed they were fired in 1989 for blowing the whistle on fraud in contracting won $1.2 million in a settlement of their suit.[55] In December 1995 the CBS program *60 Minutes* broadcast a devastating portrait of the MTA's performance. Los Angeles mayor and MTA chairman Richard Riordan led a majority of the MTA board to fire the chief executive officer, Franklin E. White. White had presided over the throttling back of the money train. Riordan complained that the transit system was a "national embarrassment" that was just "flying from crisis to crisis."[56] In September 1996 MTA officials approved a sweeping plan to give higher priority to bus service, paving the way for settlement of a lawsuit that had charged the agency with neglecting poor and minority bus riders in order to construct expensive new rail lines for affluent commuters.[57]

Congress also got in the act. The chairman of the transportation subcommittee of the House Appropriations Committee, Republican representative Frank Wolf of Virginia, told the MTA it needed to emphasize busways rather than subways.[58] Federal Transit Administration officials threatened to stop the flow of funds unless the MTA put its financial house in order. Local politicians whose districts had no rail projects complained about wasting funds on rail projects while congestion mounted on the freeways; while politicians whose districts were benefiting from rail projects pointed out that scaling back on construction could cost the area hundreds of millions in federal transit assistance.[59]

Mayor Riordan brought in Julian Burke, a reputed corporate turnaround specialist, to head the MTA and put the agency's finances back in order. Early in 1998 Burke persuaded the MTA board to suspend work on three major rail links—the Eastside, Mid-City, and Pasadena lines—for six months in order to reassess their financial prospects. Some board members feared the suspension might be a prelude to cancellation of the lines. Others felt the action did not go far enough and threatened to sponsor a ballot initiative to cut off sales tax funding for subway construction. Mayor Riordan did not want to definitively write off the extensions, but he said that even "with the most optimistic views of funding from Washington, we can't really build the subway extensions for a number of years. To continue to spend a lot of money on it now is virtually wasted money."[60]

If the rail system was truly vital to residents in the Los Angeles area, it is unlikely that such problems would have been allowed to delay improvements in mass mobility for decades. But the rail system is not vital to, or even well suited to, the region. The mismatch between public transit's capabilities and the changing structure of American metropolitan areas has been studied by Peter Gordon and his colleagues.[61] A professor of urban

planning at the University of Southern California, Gordon argues that most
U.S. metro areas have decentralized so dramatically that only a shrinking
share of their jobs remain downtown where commuting workers can be
well served by rail. Even though downtown Los Angeles continues to
grow, its regional weight is declining. In 1960, 60 percent of the region's
office space was located downtown; in 1989 its share was down to 14 percent "and still falling."[62] Gordon is particularly critical of expensive new
construction on rail transit lines: "Urban rail transit is an 1890s idea, not
suited to societies with income levels high enough to sustain widespread
auto ownership . . . [and] increasingly irrelevant in the dispersed and decentralized modern American city."[63]

Why then are so many planners and politicians pushing hard for federal, state, and regional funds for new rail systems? Gordon blames the
planners for being too attached to the old monocentric model of the city
and for misunderstanding contemporary decentralizing trends. As for the
big city politicians, their role is "boosterism." They must attract big ticket
public projects to revive their downtowns. "Transit proposals are associated with the drive to put an empty convention center into every major
American downtown and to overinvest in downtown renewal," he observes. But with few exceptions, new rail projects are "expensive and
wasteful" because "most Americans have chosen to live and work any-
where but downtown."[64] Gordon is apparently too polite to mention the
"money train" aspects of rail revival that are its strongest appeal to urban
politicians and interest groups.

Thus the overall picture of transit performance under the public service
benefits regime is one of roughly stabilized outputs measured in terms of
annual passenger trips, but an ever-shrinking share of the total amount of
passenger miles traveled in all U.S. metropolitan communities. This has
been achieved at the cost of substantially increased inputs in terms of employees, compensation, total vehicle miles operated, and, of course, public
spending.

Surprisingly, transit's critics and its supporters agree that under existing conditions transit will be unable to achieve the ambitious goals of getting more people out of their cars and reversing metropolitan sprawl. Transit's detractors accept this and call for cutting back on federal transit
subsidies. Transit's supporters believe that more people must somehow be
induced to ride transit. They want to *change* existing political and administrative rules to enable transit to compete more effectively with the auto.
Public policy, they argue, must recreate a more centralized metropolitan

area so that rail transit can flourish and society can benefit from a truly rejuvenated transit system.[65] Chapter 6 examines the prospects for such recentralization. At this juncture, however, we have clearly seen the limits of what subsidies alone can do to restore transit.

Transit as Policy Monopoly and as Symbol

Since 1964, when Congress passed the Urban Mass Transportation Act, the transit lobby has established its own policy monopoly—smaller and less imposing than the highway coalition's perhaps, but a policy monopoly nonetheless. Some readers, accustomed to transit's poor-mouthing pleas for more federal aid and its constant calls for a level playing field, might have difficulty seeing transit policy in these terms. But consider the evidence developed earlier in the chapter. As federal transit aid grew in the 1970s, the transit lobby grew apace. It shrewdly institutionalized federal transit aid programs by embedding them deeply in the intergovernmental political, financial, and administrative systems. Transit funds are now considered by Congress as part and parcel of the overall surface transportation funding act. They are often handled by the same committees that handle highways. They flow out through the intergovernmental aid pipeline to cities and states largely according to hard-bargained formulas that have become quasi-entitlements.

No U.S. senator or representative, regardless of party affiliation, wants to see federal transit aid to his or her constituency cut back. No state or local politician wants to be accused of "losing" federal transit dollars because he or she failed to support funds for the local matching requirement. Transit even has its own mass transit account within the holy of holies, the highway trust fund. The Reagan administration of the 1980s and the Republican-dominated Congresses of the 1990s could not prevail against transit's solidly entrenched congressional support. In 1995 another lobby, Amtrak and the intercity passenger rail interests, sought to "poach" a half cent per gallon of gas tax revenue to which urban transit was entitled. The American Public Transit Association and its congressional allies reacted exactly like a policy monopoly: they slapped Amtrak down hard and squelched any thought that it could take transit funds.[66]

How strong is transit's policy monopoly, especially when compared with that of its arch-rival, the highway coalition? Such a question can hardly be answered with absolute scientific precision, of course. Transit,

Table 4-4. *Expenditures for Highways and Transit by All Levels of Government, Selected Years, 1982–92*

Millions of current dollars

	Expenditures		Transit spending as a percentage of total spending
Year	Highway	Transit	
1982	35,731	11,401	24.2
1984	40,481	13,588	25.1
1986	50,285	15,078	23.1
1988	56,521	16,777	22.3
1990	61,730	19,195	23.6
1992	67,417	22,350	24.9

Source: Department of Transportation, Bureau of Transportation Statistics, *Federal, State and Local Transportation Statistics, Fiscal Years 1982–1992* (1995), table 7, p. 22.

naturally, prefers to cultivate the image of an underdog beset by the powerful "road gang" of highway interests. But a key indicator of the relative political standing of the two lobbies is the amount of government spending for each mode. By this measure, transit's position looks remarkably strong and stable (see table 4-4). Remember that transit produces only 1 percent of the total surface transportation passenger miles, and that over half of this travel is concentrated in just ten metropolitan areas. Despite its limited base, transit received 24.2 percent of the combined government expenditures on highways and transit in 1982 and 24.9 percent in 1992. Thus transit survived quite handily the ideological challenge of the Reagan years and the budget-balancing challenge of the Bush years.

The main reason transit weathered these storms so well is shown in table 4-5. Although federal expenditures for transit stagnated in current dollars (and, of course, declined in inflation-adjusted dollars), transit supporters were able to persuade state and local governments to dramatically increase their spending. In 1982 state and local spending on transit ($7.4 billion) represented 188 percent of the $3.9 billion worth of federal transit spending. By 1992 state and local transit expenditures on transit ($18.7 billion) stood at 508 percent of the federal government's level of transit spending ($3.7 billion).

This is the genius of the American intergovernmental system. Federal politicians' efforts in the mid-1960s to rejuvenate transit helped create and

Table 4-5. *Expenditures from Own Funds for Highways and Transit, by Level of Government, Selected Years, 1982–92*
Millions of current dollars

| Year | Federal government | | State and local government | |
	Highways	Transit	Highways	Transit
1982	10,740	3,954	24,991	7,447
1984	13,036	3,811	27,445	9,776
1986	15,312	3,399	34,973	11,679
1988	15,252	3,316	41,270	13,461
1990	15,156	3,832	46,574	15,364
1992	16,772	3,675	50,645	18.675
Average growth rate 1982–92	4.56	–0.73	7.32	9.63

Source: Department of Transportation, Bureau of Transportation Statistics, *Federal, State and Local Transportation Statistics, Fiscal Years 1982–1992* (1995), table 10A, p. 32.

strengthen hundreds of publicly owned transit systems at the local and state levels. These transit enterprises quickly became an integral part of the cast of local public agencies providing services and jobs to the community. When political conditions turned against transit funding increases at the federal level, they were able to "change venues," in Baumgartner and Jones's terms, and persuade local and state authorities to offset the decline in funds.[67] As a result, transit kept its share of total surface transportation spending at roughly the level it had reached by 1982.

Household spending is another indicator of the transit lobby's ability to shift spending in its direction. In 1993 American households spent an average of $5,453 on transportation of all kinds: $5,139 (94.2 percent) for automobile transportation (including vehicle purchase, fuel, maintenance, insurance, registration fees, and parking) and $60 (1.1 percent) for "transit and school bus" services.[68] Transit's 1.1 percent share of *private spending* was roughly in line with its total national surface transportation passenger miles. Transit's 24.9 percent share of *public spending* (see table 4-4) was disproportionately greater than its total passenger miles. This is perhaps the bottom line in measurement of the influence of the transit policy monopoly established under the post-1964 benefits regime.

Has transit rejuvenation reached its limits? Will transit's intergovernmental policy monopoly ever be powerful enough to turn around its declining market share and capture 5 percent, or even 10 percent, of the urban transportation passenger miles? How much more public funding would that require? The American Public Transit Association published two scenarios for the future of transit funding in the period 1995 to 2004. According to APTA, transit will need $87.6 billion in capital investment and $209 billion in operating revenue to *maintain* current levels of service, including improvements mandated by the Clean Air Act and the Americans with Disabilities Act. The second scenario, to *expand* service, is estimated to require $138.8 billion in capital investment and $231 billion in operating revenue.[69] Unfortunately, APTA offered no estimates of how the increased funding would affect ridership or market share.

In the near to medium-term future, to reach total funding levels for transit in the range of $45 to $50 billion annually would require a federal policy departure as dramatic as the policy breakthrough in the 1964–70 period. It would mean putting federal transit aid on a footing of dollar-for-dollar equality with highway aid. In the context of the antitax, budget-balancing politics of Washington, D.C. (and many states and cities, too), this would seem to be an overly ambitious goal, to put it mildly.

If transit is to reclaim a significant share of ridership from the automobile, what it needs more urgently than public money is a changed assessment of its practical utility by potential customers and beneficiaries. It needs more than political support from mayors, city councils, and transit unions. It needs the economic support of real estate developers, businesses, home buyers, zoning boards, and commuters across the country. They must make millions of individual and collective decisions about the locations of their homes, jobs, and leisure activities and how they will get to them. Only their decisions can make America's communities transit friendly.

Transit rejuvenation, despite limited ridership, is an important symbol to the groups working for change in the auto-dominated transportation system. The ability to point to dramatically improved transit in the future (especially the high-tech rail depicted in glossy brochures from equipment manufacturers) is indispensable to the feat of political legerdemain that the anti-auto vanguard hopes to pull off. The mere possibility of building an impressive new transit system enables them to offer something in return for the personal sacrifices their auto-restrictive policies would require. After all, would voters even consider the higher gas taxes, parking surcharges, peak-hour road pricing, and land-use controls if there were not some shining goal at the end of it all, a veritable Camelot of sleek monorails, gleaming subways, and sporty light rail vehicles? The current performance of public transportation systems is not as important as transit's "once and future" possibilities.[70] New rail transit systems are like the cathedrals of the Middle Ages. They rose not because they were absolutely necessary to everyday life here and now (although they did provide jobs and profits), but because they were the physical embodiment of the high aspirations of the cities' "moral" leaders. So the anti-auto vanguard keeps alive the sacred promise of a purer community and a more "sustainable" way of life.

5

INTERCITY PASSENGER RAIL

Subsidies, Speed, and Suspense

In the second half of the nineteenth century, railroads became the dominant mode of surface transportation in America. The accessibility of any location was determined by its relation to rail lines and rail stations, and by the frequency, quality, and cost of the service provided. But rail did more than spread the U.S. population "from sea to shining sea." It also made possible the concentration of many people in great cities. Chicago, Kansas City, Omaha, and other large cities were made up of compact neighborhoods where people could easily find goods produced nationwide within walking distance of their homes. In rail's golden age, roughly from 1880 to 1920, the difference between urban and rural locations in terms of their access to the whole spectrum of human transactions was enormous, and was largely the product of proximity to intercity and intracity rail lines.

During this period the railroads faced little competition from other modes of transportation, especially for passenger service, and their operating practices and marketing philosophy reflected this modal monopoly. The benefits regime under which rail flourished was that of a private, for-profit business corporation well suited to take advantage of promotion policy incentives such as government charters, loans, and land grants. The for-profit corporation also adapted well to the era of regulation that began with the creation of the Interstate Commerce Commission in 1887. After 1920, rail's biggest challenge was competition from the automobile, the truck, and then the airplane, modes that fostered even more extensive mobility. Over the years rail's market share was inexorably reduced by this competition into fewer and fewer niches, and this was doubly true for intercity rail passenger service.

The Disappearing Railroad Blues

There are many divergent analyses of why the rail sector proved so slow and ineffective in responding to this challenge from competing modes. Albro Martin suggests that politicians and shippers allied to impose a stifling regulatory burden that prevented rail management from responding creatively to technological and socioeconomic changes.[1] In the view of Gabriel Kolko, however, the rail companies wanted federal regulation to stabilize the industry and prevent rate wars.[2] Stephen Salsbury argues that the arcane accounting methods forced on the rail companies by the Interstate Commerce Commission hindered the modernization of their management.[3] Stephen B. Goddard blames public policy for making a triple error: first, "in allowing railroads to exploit the people they served, then in breaking the railroads' spirit, and finally in overbuilding America's superhighways."[4]

This chapter does not pursue the intricacies of the debate over who bears the historical "blame" for rail's decline and near demise as a passenger mode. I will simply note an incisive point made by historian Gregory Lee Thompson. Based on his extensive research on road-rail competition in California, he offers a conclusion that encompasses the competing analyses of the early years and yet is relevant to the present and future dilemma of passenger rail. Thompson argues that rail's problems reflect an important "paradox of laissez-faire America":

> privately owned railroads were incompatible with a society that highly valued the unconstrained exploitation of land. Private railroad operation required profits. Unconstrained land exploitation demanded more transportation than railroads could provide at a profit. Railroad[s] . . . tried to resolve the conflict by subsidizing the strongest development interests . . . but those who were left out

turned bitter and eventually formed a coalition powerful enough to topple railroad dominance.[5]

The policy instrument used by dissident interests in California after 1910 was not stricter regulatory control of the railroads, but promotion of a rival mode—automobiles. Highways opened up land to feed the "growth machine" of real estate development interests, which quickly moved ahead of railroads as a political force. By the late 1930s California had built highways across all of the mountain passes separating its major cities and rendered the "trunk rail lines virtually obsolete."[6] Public promotion of highways was seen as a "progressive" tool of good government against the vested interests and for the common man.

After World War II America's private rail companies gradually realized their business was stuck in land-use and customer service patterns belonging to the old era of coal and steel industrialism. The country had barreled headlong into a postindustrial service economy. In the rail passenger business, competition from autos and airplanes, as well as the shifting of jobs and residences to more dispersed geographical locations, steadily undercut profitability, despite the efforts of some railroads to introduce new, modern equipment.

The Transportation Act of 1958 gave the ICC broad powers to approve discontinuance of money-losing passenger trains. By this time rail management wanted nothing more than to get out of the passenger business as quickly as possible without stirring up a hornet's nest of angry local politicians and rail passenger groups. Ironically, the more rail passenger service had shrunk, the more vociferous its ardent defenders had become (see table 5-1). They challenged many proposed abandonments before the ICC. They questioned the railroads' accounting and sought to prove that passenger service did not lose as much money as management claimed, or that it did not lose money at all. Even if passenger rail were unprofitable, they argued, it could be profitable if only it were managed more imaginatively with better equipment, better marketing, and better personal service.

Rail advocates then took a different tack: even if passenger rail was not profitable, it should be protected through public subsidies because of the benefits it provided to people without cars, to those with a fear of flying, to small towns with no airports, and to large congested cities. Passenger rail offered people a choice, they said. It was part of a balanced transportation system. Keeping passengers on the train kept them out of cars and thus reduced congestion and traffic accidents.[7] These arguments had more than a

Table 5-1. *Rail Passenger Service, Selected Years, 1920–70*

Year	Passengers (millions)	Passenger miles (billions)
1920	126.9	47.3
1925	90.1	37.7
1930	70.7	26.9
1935	44.8	18.5
1940	45.6	23.8
1945	89.7	91.8
1950	48.8	31.7
1955	43.3	28.5
1960	32.7	21.3
1965	30.5	17.2
1970	28.9	10.8

Source: George W. Hilton, *Amtrak: The National Railroad Passenger Corporation* (Washington, D.C.: American Enterprise Institute, 1980), table 1, pp. 3–4.

little in common with ones being made by pro-transit and anti-auto groups, and they can be heard to this very day in the debates swirling around passenger rail policy.

As the private railroads' financial picture steadily worsened, policymakers transformed the traditional benefits regime in the rail sector. The creation in 1970 of the National Railroad Passenger Corporation, Amtrak, relieved private rail companies of their obligation to operate passenger service. This shifted the financial losses caused by passenger service onto the public treasury. A publicly funded reorganization of the Northeast's bankrupt lines into Conrail took place in 1977. The Rail Freight Assistance Act of 1978 added subsidies for branch freight lines. This was followed by the Staggers rail deregulation act of 1980 and the abolition of the Interstate Commerce Commission, the nation's oldest federal regulatory agency, in 1994. The new deregulated framework left the private freight rail sector free to consolidate through mergers and takeovers. It spun off light-density lines to short-haul railroads and concentrated on its core business of long-distance haulage of a few bulk commodities and container traffic. Freight rail emerged from deregulation "leaner and meaner."

Passenger rail service in America, however, was left with a jury-rigged system that was barely able to protect it from complete oblivion. The institutional framework and benefits regime under which passenger rail has operated since 1971 came complete with many of the defects found in the public transit benefits regime, but with fewer of its intergovernmental advantages. Under this flawed regime, rail advocates experienced the frustration of seeing other nations forge ahead in developing modern high-speed trains. Can intercity passenger rail service in America make a comeback in the twenty-first century? The answer depends on the discovery of economically efficient and politically feasible ways of applying similar high-speed rail technology in America's multimodal transportation system and hypermobile society. Improved technology and improved business practices will be needed for success. Even more important, however, will be innovations in passenger rail's benefits regime.

This chapter analyzes the protectionist thrust of passenger rail policy and the still fruitless efforts to promote American variants of high-speed ground transportation (HSGT) technologies from Europe and Japan. Protecting Amtrak and promoting HSGT have led to one crisis after another. Rail interests and the general public are in a continual state of suspense as rail policy oscillates between promises of "supertrains" and threats of the financial collapse of existing train service. Unless a passenger rail regime that is more stable and successful than Amtrak can be developed, trains will make little contribution to a new politics of mobility in the twenty-first century.

The Amtrak Regime: Design Deficit

In 1970 the railroads had their lowest net earnings since 1932. That same year the largest rail company, Penn Central, which operated 75 percent of the remaining long-distance passenger trains, filed for bankruptcy.[8] Congress created Amtrak in 1970 in response to the financial crisis of the country's private rail industry. The Nixon administration wanted to help the railroads by relieving them of their obligation to continue money-losing passenger service. It also wanted to head off a Senate Commerce Committee bill that authorized $435 million over four years to subsidize passenger service. With these goals in mind, the administration developed a plan for a "quasi-public, for-profit" corporation to be called "Railpax" (later renamed Amtrak for public relations purposes). The plan recommended canceling more than half of the passenger trains then in operation and funding the remainder by a grant of $40 million and $100 million in loan guarantees to the new National Railroad Passenger Corporation.

Nixon's passenger rail proposal did not enjoy undivided support within the executive branch. The Office of Management and Budget questioned its financial feasibility, arguing that the amount of aid was insufficient to fund even the scaled down system.[9] The Department of Transportation pushed dubiously optimistic financial assumptions in order to support the creation of Amtrak, and it prevailed in the dispute with OMB.

Congress accepted the DOT's underfunded plan, fearing a White House veto of any proposal that required more public spending. The plan would allow passenger train advocates to "get a foot in the door" and come back for more money later. As R. Kent Weaver points out, a basic compromise brought Amtrak into existence: "for one side it represented the best method of cutting service, for the other the most effective way of preserving and improving service."[10] Amtrak's political architects thus designed an entity that was neither fish nor fowl. Its ostensible goal was to preserve as much intercity passenger rail service as possible. But its initial capitalization was sufficient only for a fairly rapid phaseout of all passenger trains. The Nixon administration felt compelled to claim the new corporation would be "for profit" and the government's involvement just temporary. All knowledgeable observers knew that it would take more than a $40 million appropriation and some loan guarantees to preserve passenger rail service. Amtrak's future deficits were designed into its finances from the beginning.

As it turned out, Amtrak did manage to preserve intercity rail service in America, although at a significantly lower level than expected. Between 1970, the last full year of private railroad passenger service, and 1972, Amtrak's first full year of operation, ridership plummeted from 28.9 million passengers to 16.6 million passengers, and passenger miles fell from 10.8 billion to 3.0 billion. As table 5-2 shows, Amtrak managed to produce gradual ridership increases over the next decade. After a period of cutbacks and consolidation in the mid-1980s, ridership increases resumed until the sharp fall in the mid-1990s.

As designed, the new rail passenger corporation uncomfortably straddled the ambiguous frontiers between the public and private sectors. Not only did Amtrak's creators saddle it with an ill-defined mission. They also promised the public that it would make a profit. It has been Amtrak's inability to achieve this "bottom-line" result that has created the most political difficulty for the corporation over the years. The remainder of this section explains particular design flaws in the passenger rail benefits regime.[11]

Isolation of Passenger Service from Freight Railroads

As noted earlier, the private railroads off-loaded passenger service onto the public budget and concentrated their operations exclusively on

Table 5-2. *Amtrak Ridership, Selected Years, 1972–95*

Year	Passengers (millions)	Passenger miles (billions)[a]
1972	16.6	3.0
1975	17.4	3.9
1978	18.9	4.0
1981	20.6	4.8
1984	19.9	4.6
1987	20.4	5.2
1990	22.2	6.1
1993	22.1	6.2
1995	20.7	5.5

Source: Frank N. Wilner, *The Amtrak Story* (Omaha, Neb.: Simmons-Boardman, 1994), table VI, p. 90; and Amtrak, *1995 Annual Report* (Washington, D.C.: 1996), statistical appendix, p. 3.

a. Includes only intercity rail passengers, not commuter rail passengers.

freight service.[12] This separation made passenger rail a bastard child of the U.S. rail industry, bereft of assets and denied legitimacy. When Amtrak was incorporated, the new entity owned no tracks, no locomotives, coaches, or Pullman cars, no railroad stations or repair yards. It did not even have any of its own employees operating the trains. For several years the private railroads operated passenger trains on a cost-plus arrangement.[13] It took years and billions of federal dollars before Amtrak could become a real railroad.

Even today privately owned freight railroads overshadow Amtrak economically (in assets, cash flow, employees, length of track) and politically (in number of lobbyists and campaign contributions). Freight needs dominate the rail equipment manufacturing sector as well. GM builds diesel engines, but no American company builds fast electric passenger locomotives. Since their deregulation in the early 1980s, private freight railroads stand as a potent symbol of an industry that "pays its own way" and does not require constant infusion of government subsidies.

To make matters worse, Amtrak must run its passenger trains on tracks designed for freight. In 1994, 97 percent of the route miles of track over which Amtrak's trains operated were owned by private freight railroads.[14] They have the muscle to see that freight retains "the right of way" when their needs conflict with Amtrak's.

Isolation of Passenger Service from a Stable Funding Mechanism

Since the creation of the federal highway trust fund in 1956, other modes have followed suit. There is an airport trust fund, a waterways trust fund, and an urban mass transit account within the highway trust fund. Indeed, trust funding has become the standard means of providing capital for infrastructure investment in all other U.S. transportation modes.[15]

Initially, no one proposed a trust fund for Amtrak because the corporation was intended to receive public subsidies for only a short time before becoming profitable. Planning for a more permanent public funding mechanism would have destroyed the fragile illusion that Amtrak was going to be a cheap and easy solution. It was only after Amtrak had been in existence for a decade that the corporation realized it needed to have a "stable funding mechanism."[16] During that period its annual appropriation from Congress soared from $40 million in 1971 to $907.3 million in 1981.

A related design flaw was passenger rail's isolation from the intergovernmental policy network of such benefit to highways and urban transit. Although Amtrak trains run through many states, the corporation is not organically connected to state or local authorities. It operates on their territory, but it does not operate under their authority. State and local bureaucracies apply for no matching grants from Amtrak. State and local politicians appoint no commissioners to Amtrak's board. The trains that Amtrak operates at 100 percent federal expense are nice to have. But Amtrak's money is not local money in the same way that federal highway or transit grants are.

To the extent the states deal with Amtrak at all, it is as (sometimes dissatisfied) paying customers. (Some states contract with Amtrak for short-distance trains and pay half of the costs.) Even paying part of the costs, states lack a sense of ownership in Amtrak. "Formula federalism" programs, which guarantee states and cities a "fair share" of the funds to be distributed, always have a broader and more secure base of political support than programs dependent upon federal appropriations that go to relatively few jurisdictions.

Dependence of Passenger Service on Congressional Allies

Because Amtrak depended on discretionary public funding for its survival, it needed to cultivate as much political support in Congress as possible. Its authorizing statute directed Amtrak to operate a national passenger rail system that included many lightly traveled routes. Not only do these stretches lose a lot of money, they also do not provide many social benefits (congestion reduction, pollution abatement) for the very reason that they are lightly traveled. Instead of being able to concentrate its capital, its human resources, and its entrepreneurial energy on routes that would carry the most passengers, Amtrak had to spread its resources dangerously thin across an entire continent.

Indeed, Amtrak's allies made things even worse by extracting "pork barrel" concessions. For example, in the 1970s Amtrak had to run trains to Montana for Senate Majority Leader Mike Mansfield and to West Virginia for Representative Harley Staggers, chairman of the House Commerce Committee; in the early 1980s, to Atlantic City for Representative Jim Florio of New Jersey, chair of the House Transportation Subcommittee.[17] Amtrak also had to agree to labor protection and "featherbedding" work rules as the price of union political support. For example, workers who lost their jobs as a result of the closure of a line were entitled to up to six years of salary as severance payments. In any given year, then, it was easier to continue to operate a money-losing, lightly traveled line than to shut it down and incur large financial closing costs—not to mention the wrath of the senators and representatives whose districts were affected.

Political Vulnerability for Commercial Deficits

The "for-profit" label attached to Amtrak at its inception left it increasingly vulnerable to criticism of its managerial performance and even of its very existence. To ideological conservatives, "for profit" meant that its goal should be to wean itself from direct federal subsidies. Amtrak's operating deficits and its need for federal capital spending to overcome years of disinvestment by private railroads rose substantially in the 1970s. And conservatives grew more vocal in their criticism. Amtrak's defenders pointed out that in most other modes of transportation, "for profit" is given a broader definition. In the highway and air modes, for example, government supplies the capital for infrastructure, and private operators cover the variable cost of moving goods and people over the road or through the airport.

The Amtrak Improvement Act of 1978 took a step in the direction of broadening the definition of a "for-profit corporation." The bill said Amtrak was to be "operated and managed" as a for-profit corporation, which seemed to indicate that an actual bottom-line profit might not be required as long as the corporation was well managed.[18] But in the 1980s, the Reagan administration returned to an insistence on the bottom-line definition and recommended on several occasions that all federal payments to Amtrak cease. Congress refused to zero out Amtrak's budget, but total budget-

Table 5-3. *Federal Operating Assistance and Capital Grants to Amtrak, Selected Years, 1971–95*

Millions of dollars

Fiscal year	Operating assistance	Capital grants[a]
1971/72	40.0	0
1975	276.5	0
1978	536.0	130.0
1981	686.8	220.5
1984	614.9	93.3
1987	579.0	26.5
1990	520.1	83.6
1993	350.0	190.0
1995	392.0	230.0

Source: Wilner, *The Amtrak Story*, p. 115; and Amtrak, *1995 Annual Report*, statistical appendix, p. 1.

a. Excludes appropriations for Northeast Corridor and labor protection costs associated with route termination and certain federally mandated pension benefits incurred by Amtrak's predecessors.

ary support for the corporation gradually declined. Then, in the mid-1990s, Amtrak's revenues dropped sharply (see table 5-3). Its deficit widened once again, just as it needed more capital funds for its new high-speed trains and other investments.[19] The Republicans' victory in the 1994 congressional elections precipitated the most serious round of calls for Amtrak to live up to the contested "for-profit" standard.

Reinventing Amtrak: Partnership, Privatization, or Liquidation?

Thomas M. Downs, a savvy transportation professional, was appointed president of Amtrak by Bill Clinton in 1993. Even before the 1994 elections Downs had begun a reorganization of Amtrak's internal structure to bring the corporation "closer to the customer." Strategic business units were created with more authority to make decisions about rail service in their areas.[20] Then, in response to the voices in the Republican majority who were calling for Amtrak's privatization or even its abolition, Downs announced a much more Draconian series of service cutbacks, layoffs, and cost reduction measures than had originally been planned.[21] His action was necessary in the first place to close a nearly $200 million budget shortfall in fiscal 1995. More importantly, it was necessary to show the new congressional majority that Amtrak management was deadly serious in its desire to reinvent the corporation and wean it from dependence on federal operating subsidies. Only by accepting the goal of zero federal operating subsidies by the year 2002 could Downs prove Amtrak was taking its "for-profit" mandate seriously.[22]

Legislative attempts to radically redesign Amtrak proved to be more complicated than the Republican critics had believed. During 1995 to 1997 congressional action encompassed two different policy thrusts. The first was embodied in the Amtrak Reform and Privatization Act of 1995. The goal of this House bill (H.R. 1788) was to repeal many of the anticompetitive mandates imposed on the corporation by previous (Democratic) Congresses (for example, the ban on contracting out work, the six years of severance pay given workers laid off because of route closure, and the legal mandate to operate a national system). Removing these burdens would not only reduce the need for federal subsidies but would also make it easier to privatize the corporation when the time came. The House approved H.R. 1788 by a vote of 406 to 5 in November 1995. But the Senate did not pass its version of the bill that year, and the 104th Congress expired without being able to restructure Amtrak.[23]

The Senate was split between the reform-to-privatize approach of the House bill and a more pro-Amtrak policy favored by Republican senator William Roth of Delaware, whose largest city, Wilmington, is well served by Amtrak's Northeast Corridor. He wanted to shore up Amtrak's finances by giving it access to the trust fund fiscal transfer mechanism that supported highways and transit. As chairman of the Senate Finance Committee, Roth sought to create an intercity passenger rail trust fund by channeling a half-cent per gallon of the existing gas tax to the proposed fund. (The half-cent was part of a tax of two and one-half cents that had been enacted in 1990 for deficit reduction purposes and was scheduled to revert to the mass transit account of the highway trust fund.)

Transit and highway interests squelched Roth's plan.[24] However, Roth persisted and finally found a different way to get funds to Amtrak. He successfully inserted into the budget reconciliation bill, the Taxpayer Relief Act of 1997 (TRA), a scheme to give Amtrak a "refund" of $2.2 billion from taxes that had been paid decades earlier by the privately owned railroads when they were carrying passengers. Roth accepted other Republicans' requirement that the money be used only for capital expenses and that Amtrak not get access to it until after the stalled Amtrak reform bill had been passed.

That bill, renamed the Amtrak Reform and Accountability Act of 1997 (P.L. 105-34), was finally voted into law at the end of the year. It restricted severance pay for laid-off workers to six months of wages, allowed contracting out of work, and removed the mandate to operate a national system. It also capped liability for lawsuits against the railroad at $200 million and required that nominations to the Amtrak board be confirmed by the Senate. Perhaps most significant for the future, the law established an Amtrak Reform Council to monitor the corporation's progress toward the goal of becoming financially self-supporting.[25] If the reform council determines that Amtrak is not meeting this goal and will need federal operating subsidies after December 2002, the council is required to develop and submit to Congress an action plan to liquidate the railroad.

In addition to its legislative struggles, Amtrak in December 1997 faced the threat of a strike by the Brotherhood of Maintenance of Way Employees. The strike was avoided at the eleventh hour when the Amtrak Board of Directors agreed to give the union the pay raise it sought.[26] But the settlement was seen as an expensive precedent for the other eleven unions with which Amtrak still had to reach agreement. Another bit of fallout from the labor settlement was the ouster of Thomas Downs from his post as president and CEO of Amtrak. The Amtrak board named as acting president George Warrington, who had been head of Amtrak's Northeast Corridor operations.

Serious political disagreements remain over how to implement Amtrak's $2.2 billion "refund." The amount is substantially below what Amtrak believes it will need for capital expenses over the next several years.[27] Some Republican leaders were determined that none of the money be used for operating expenses, and they have warned that they will not agree to appropriate any more operating funds for Amtrak.[28] The Clinton administration's position is that in fiscal 1999 Congress should appropriate $621 million more for Amtrak capital in addition to the $2.2 billion in TRA funds. It also believes that Amtrak should be allowed to pay for certain maintenance expenses formerly paid out of operating subsidies, a practice it thinks is similar to that governing federal capital aid to transit.[29]

Despite the expectations of Congress that Amtrak be financially independent of federal subsidies by the end of 2002, the corporation's financial condition remained "very precarious," according to a report issued by the General Accounting Office in May 1998. Amtrak borrowed $75 million in short-term money to meet its payroll in 1997, and it expected to have to borrow $200 million in fiscal 1998. Amtrak's revised strategic business plan issued in March 1998 projected higher net losses in 1998 and 1999 than had its previous plan. The GAO report reached this conclusion: "As currently structured, Amtrak will continue to require federal capital and operating support in 2002 and well into the future."[30]

Thus the suspense over Amtrak's future continues. What will happen? There are at least three possible scenarios: the modified status quo scenario, the regional partnership scenario, and the privatization scenario (see table 5-4).

Modified Status Quo Scenario

If Amtrak's new management and board of directors can show dramatic cost-control progress and increase ridership significantly, Congress might give the corporation the extra capital Amtrak claims it will need to be subsidy free by the year 2002. Clearly demonstrated progress toward eliminating the federal operating subsidy is the key performance goal for this outcome. But Amtrak still needs capital funding. Roth's $2.2 billion refund was a one time only operation. For a modified status quo scenario to succeed in the long run, Amtrak needs a guaranteed source of capital in the form of a capital trust fund—something it has sought unsuccessfully for over a decade. Unless Amtrak can wean itself from operating subsidies and achieve a capital fund, this scenario leaves the corporation vulnerable to the "trigger" that tells the Amtrak Reform Council to start planning for liquidation.

Regional Partnership Scenario

If Amtrak is unable to eliminate the need for federal subsidies, another scenario is possible: Congress could "devolve" to the states the responsibility for intercity passenger rail service. Large states like California, New York, and Illinois could add intercity rail routes to their existing repertoire of commuter lines. The Northeast Corridor and other important routes that cross state boundaries could operate under an authority created by interstate compact.

In this scenario states would develop their own mechanisms to provide capital and operating funds. They might be able to persuade Congress to allow them to "flex" a portion of their federal transportation assistance dol-

Table 5-4. *Three Possible Scenarios for Passenger Rail*

Scenario	Scope of service	Source of capital	Key clientele
Modified status quo	National system	Federal appropriations	Members of Congress and interest groups
Partnership	Regional segments	Public funds from states and federal "flex" funds	State and local governments and regional authorities
Privatization	Profitable segments	Financial markets and business income	Paying customers

lars to intercity rail capital investments on their territories. Such a regional framework would not be able to operate a national system of transcontinental routes and would concentrate train travel along the most heavily traveled corridors. But, historically, regional railroading is exactly the way that train travel developed and thrived in America.

Privatization

Like Conrail, Amtrak could be sold to the private sector and operate as a true for-profit common carrier. Relieved of the burden of operating a national system or any segment that does not yield an adequate return, it could fund its operations and investments out of revenue from fares and other business income (selling surplus electricity, leasing space in its rail stations, selling off real estate holdings). Its orientation would be to its cash customers, not to fuzzy notions of the public good. Of course, nothing would prevent state and local transportation officials from contracting directly with the privatized corporation to provide rail service. Ultimately, if a privatized Amtrak did not meet the market test, it would be liquidated, with its assets sold to private railroads or state and local rail authorities.

The privatization option, simple and straightforward as it seems, may actually be the most difficult to implement in political and organizational terms. From proponents of privatization there has been plenty of ideological and neoclassical economic criticism of Amtrak, but little development of a specific plan to get from the current regime to a privatized one.[31] Such a plan should include a political strategy to overcome the inevitable resistance from those interests that feel seriously threatened by privatization (for example, states and communities that would lose service, and rail unions that would lose jobs). It also should include a strategy for restructuring Amtrak's finances and reorganizing its operation as a private entity.

Once real investors are brought into a privatization process, they are likely to be much less enthusiastic about ending government subsidies and producing a "pure" private enterprise. In rail privatization projects in particular, there is a "tendency for the more complex privatization proposals to evolve into public-private partnerships or joint ventures." Private entrepreneurs often find that direct or indirect public subsidies and ancillary revenues are needed to make their involvement a profitable business strategy.[32]

Some of the complexities of moving beyond the Amtrak regime for passenger trains are noted by Joseph Vranich, a former Amtrak public relations official who now believes the corporation is a barrier to rejuvenating the rail mode in this country. For Vranich, the important thing is to get rid of Amtrak "through privatization of the parts that can be operated profitably; regionalization of unprofitable yet socially desirable services . . . and discontinuance of trains so useless that they offer neither profit nor social purpose."[33] He proposes creation of an independent agency, the Amtrak Transition Board, to liquidate Amtrak's assets and sell off or devolve the Northeast Corridor. The Railway Labor Act, the Federal Employers' Liability Act (FELA), the Railroad Retirement Act, and the Railroad Unemployment Insurance Act need reform, in his view, because of their inhibiting effect on new ventures in the rail sector, particularly proposals for high-speed rail projects. Amending this legislation will be much more controversial than passing the Amtrak reform bill was. Liquidation of Amtrak's assets, in particular, is certain to end up in court proceedings that could take years.

Despite his belief that "there is no useful role for Amtrak" in the future of trains in America, Vranich acknowledges its "staying power under assaults from the Carter, Reagan, and Bush administrations."[34] For the near future the Amtrak regime for intercity passenger trains is likely to survive but remain in constant political peril and financial crisis. Most of its flaws and failings are a heritage of its past. Its best hope is the successful outcome of the one project it is counting on to become the key to its future: high-speed rail on the Northeast Corridor.

A Bridge to the Future?
The Northeast High-Speed Rail Project

The Northeast Corridor high-speed project, if it is a success, could play a role as a bridge to the future, linking the Amtrak protectionist regime to a more decentralized, promotion-oriented regime for intercity passenger rail. If the project can succeed in attracting significant numbers of new riders and in generating enough new cash to substantially exceed operating expenses, it could turn Amtrak around financially and generate a wave of interest in high-speed rail in other parts of the country. If it flops, it will likely be the death knell for Amtrak and a crippling blow to the prospects of post-Amtrak rail rejuvenation.

The project has been in gestation for over thirty years. Its origins date back to the pre-Amtrak days of 1965, when Senator Claiborne Pell of Rhode Island prodded Congress into passing the High-Speed Ground Transportation Act that authorized $90 million for a high-speed demonstration project in the Northeast Corridor between Washington, D.C., and Boston.[35] The first fruit of this funding was a new high-speed passenger train, dubbed the Metroliner, and a contract with the private Pennsylvania Railroad to operate this service.[36] The Metroliner project went from the drawing boards to service in less than four years with the predictable shortcomings. Equipment was rushed into production with many bugs still unresolved, and the train arrived before enough track work had been done to permit extensive running of the trains at 120 miles per hour. Despite technical flaws, the Metroliner proved to be a success with the traveling public. It was fast enough to attract a clientele willing to pay a premium fare for speedy train service. In 1969, the first year of Metroliner operation, the number of passengers between New York and the nation's capital jumped from 509,000 to 731,000.[37]

But soon after the Metroliner's introduction, Penn Central plunged into bankruptcy. Washington's rail policymaking refocused on reorganizing the Penn Central and the six other bankrupt railroads into a new Consolidated Rail Corporation, Conrail. For a period Conrail was a "quasi-public" corporation before being sold to the private sector.[38] The intense congressional involvement with rail reorganization in the mid-1970s opened a policy window for another step in the direction of high-speed rail. Amtrak, backed by legislators from the New England and Mid-Atlantic states, persuaded Congress to let it purchase the rail corridor from Washington to Boston from the estates of the bankrupt railroads for $120 million. This sale in 1976 was followed by an authorization that amounted to $2.5 billion for the Northeast Corridor Improvement Project (NECIP) to improve track, signals, bridges, tunnels, and grade crossings.[39] In 1991 Congress authorized funding for the current Northeast High-Speed Rail Improvement Program (NHRIP). It continued incremental upgrading to the original Metroliner route and provided for electrification of the line between New Haven and Boston.

Amtrak then began to look for ways of buying European-designed, high-speed train sets to operate on the Northeast Corridor. The increasing stringency of the federal budgetary process required it to delay the purchase of new equipment in favor of putting money into the track and infrastructure. Eventually, Amtrak leveraged the NHRIP investment to forge a new relationship with two leading railway equipment manufacturers, Bombardier of Canada and GEC-Alsthom of France. In a deal that resembled a joint venture more than a simple purchase, the equipment manufacturers participated in financing the first set of fourteen new high-speed trains. Amtrak was expected to pay them off with the profits it is convinced that the new high-speed service will earn.[40]

Amtrak and its partners have a lot riding on the Northeast high-speed project, scheduled to begin limited service in October 1999 and full service before the end of 2000. The corporation projects 3.6 million annual passengers on the New York–Boston segment (compared with 1 million in 1995).[41] It is counting on the increased passenger revenues both to amortize the new equipment and to provide a bit of financial breathing space as federal operating subsidies are phased out. It projects profits on high-speed service of $93 million in fiscal 2000 and $219 million in fiscal 2003.[42] Bombardier and GEC-Alsthom want to showcase their high-speed rail train's advantages to public policymakers in other congested regional corridors across America. And passenger rail's political supporters in Congress and in state capitols around the nation need a technical and financial success in this most promising of corridors in order to justify ongoing public investments in passenger rail infrastructure.

Beyond Amtrak: The Allure of High-Speed Rail

The "action" in passenger rail policy development has not been limited to Amtrak. Since the early 1980s states have shown periodic spurts of interest in using high-speed technology to promote what some enthusiasts call a brand new mode of transportation: high-speed passenger rail. Perhaps the most important factor spurring this interest was the spectacular success of the French National Railways' *train à grande vitesse* (TGV).

The TGV, a new train using conventional steel wheel on rail technology, went into regular service on a newly constructed rail line dedicated exclusively to high-speed passenger service in September 1981. The new line ran between Paris and Lyon. It took a more direct route between the two cities, 427 kilometers compared with 512 kilometers for the old route. The electrified TGV train sets cruised the line at a top speed of 168 miles per hour. Combining the shorter route with higher speed enabled the TGV to cut the travel time from above three hours to two hours flat. The route served by the TGV was already the most heavily traveled axis in France, but even more passengers flocked to the new trains, helping decongest the parallel highways and the airport. The French National Railways had kept tight control of the cost of building the new line and the new train sets.[43] Therefore, management was able to trumpet the fact that TGV passenger revenues not only covered all operating costs, but also were sufficient to repay the capital costs of construction and leave a net profit for the railroad. The annual rate of return on investment was said to be 15 percent. By 1991 the initial capital investment had been recouped.[44]

Here was something to hearten the rail advocates of the world—a modernistic new train that attracted riders from other modes and paid for itself! It meant no more need to justify subsidies by preaching about external social benefits. Speedy, sexy new technology with a Euro-flair became the holy grail. Officials from all over North America and many other parts of the world flocked to France to ride the TGV and hear the export-oriented sales pitch that the French rail industry quickly developed. Other European railroads and equipment manufacturers speeded up their fast-train development efforts, both to cash in on export sales and to deploy the equipment on their own rail systems. Representatives selling Germany's Intercity Express (ICE) train, which began service in Germany in 1991, began to compete with the French in responding to requests for proposals in Florida, California, and Texas. Swedish and Italian manufacturers of high-speed rail technology joined in the competition as well. The Germans even had a second technology under development that they were trying to sell abroad, the super fast magnetic levitation system they called Transrapid. The late 1980s and early 1990s were heady times for both the international rail equipment manufacturers and the officials from numerous American states and localities who were considering how to bring the benefits of the new "super trains" home to their communities.[45]

Potential High-Speed Rail Corridors in America

Where are the most likely locations for deploying high-speed rail systems in the United States? The Federal Railroad Administration (FRA), working with analysts from the Department of Transportation's National Transportation Systems Center and several prominent consulting firms, addressed this question in a 1996 report. Its authors acknowledge that the high-speed projects they analyzed "do not meet the traditional private sector criterion for 'commercial feasibility.'"[46] They go on to argue that such criteria may be too narrow. Each of the major modes—air, highway, and rail—now share responsibilities for investing in infrastructure, equipment, and operations in the public and private sectors. They evaluate new high-speed systems, not for bottom-line profitability, but for "partnership potential"—the "capacity to draw the private and public sectors together in planning, negotiations, and, conceivably, project implementation."[47]

To have partnership potential, a project in a particular corridor must satisfy two conditions. First, private enterprise must be able to operate the corridor, once it has been built and paid for, as a completely self-sustaining enterprise. Second, the total benefits of a high-speed corridor must exceed its total costs. They include the full range of benefits and costs, including environmental effects and other nonmarket impacts on the general public.

The report considers three technological options for high-speed ground transport: magnetic levitation (maglev) systems, new HSR systems, and Accelerail systems. Maglev systems (such as Germany's Transrapid) are the fastest of the three technologies (attaining speeds of 300 miles per hour) and the most expensive. "New high-speed rail" represents the state of the art in steel wheel on rail trains. The French TGV is an example. Speeds of 200 miles per hour in commercial service can be reached. It is not quite as expensive as maglev, but it is usually at least twice as costly to build as the next option. Accelerail systems are upgraded intercity passenger trains on existing railroad rights of way. These systems can attain speeds from 90 to 150 miles per hour, and they can be powered by electric motors or fossil-fueled diesel or turbine motors. The faster the Accelerail option chosen, the more expensive. Electrified systems are more expensive than those that use fossil fuel.

The Federal Railroad Administration selected eight of the most promising corridors and "ran the numbers" in detail for six of them: California North-South (San Francisco/Oakland to San Diego by way of Los Angeles); Chicago Hub (lines branching South from Chicago to St. Louis, North to Milwaukee, and East to Detroit); Florida (Miami to Orlando to Tampa); Northeast Corridor (Washington, D.C., to New York and on to Boston); Pacific Northwest (Eugene, Oregon, to Portland, Seattle, and on to Vancouver, British Columbia); Texas Triangle (Dallas at the apex and San Antonio and Houston at the triangle's base).

The two corridors that did not receive full analysis were treated as extensions of the Northeast Corridor. New York's Empire Corridor runs from New York city to Albany and West to Syracuse, Rochester, and Buffalo. The Southeast Corridor runs South from the nation's capital to Richmond, Raleigh, and Charlotte, North Carolina.

Table 5-5 gives the predicted passenger miles and cost for each option in each corridor in the year 2020. The first column provides a benchmark by giving Amtrak data for 1993, where available. The predicted passenger miles for the other three options must be seen as based on plausible—certainly not pessimistic—assumptions about the cost and attractiveness of the trains, the competitive response of air carriers, and improvements made to intermodal connections. The bottom-line comparisons of total passenger miles produced by the high-speed systems in 2020 with Amtrak's performance in 1993 show the extent of rail rejuvenation that might take place in these corridors. The Accelerail 125F option triples the total annual rail passenger miles in these corridors. New HSR increases rail passenger miles nearly eight times; and maglev boosts the 1993 figures nine times. The only corridor in which maglev has a substantial lead over new HSR is in California North-South, where it is estimated to produce 1.1 billion more passenger miles per year.

Are the Federal Railroad Administration's figures on costs and ridership any more reliable than the notoriously overoptimistic estimates for new urban transit rail lines? This is the real question. It is unlikely that the FRA analysts erred on the side of caution, but there is no way of knowing how much they erred in the direction of optimism. The report cautions readers that detailed state-level studies are needed before proceeding with projects, and that its assessment of the partnership potential of a given technology in a specific corridor "does not constitute an express or implied criterion for Federal approval or funding." It concludes that Accelerail's potential for HSGT at a modest initial investment validates the Transportation Department's next-generation high-speed rail development program—which supports use of existing railroads—and confirms several states' decisions to implement Accelerail options.[48] The report sees partnership potential in the more expensive options of new HSR and maglev in several corridors. Presumably, if private sector investors have substantial sums of their own money at stake, they will want to participate in the cost and ridership studies and, in a sense, keep them honest.

Table 5-5. *Estimated Passenger Miles and Costs of*
Six High-Speed Rail Corridors, Selected Technologies, 2020
Billions of passenger miles

Corridor	Amtrak 1993 benchmark	Magnetic levitation (maglev) trains	New high-speed rail trains	Accelerail 125F[b]
California North-South	0.1	5.9	4.8	1.8
Chicago Hub	0.2	1.9	1.6	1.3
Florida	a	1.0	0.9	0.9
Northeast Corridor	1.5	5.1	4.8	c
Pacific Northwest	0.04	0.6	0.5	0.5
Texas Triangle	a	1.8	1.6	1.1
Total	1.8	16.3	14.2	5.6
Estimated total cost (billions of dollars)	n.a.	108.7	79.0	22.1

Source: Compiled by the author from corridor-by-corridor projections in Department of Transportation, Federal Railroad Administration, *High Speed Ground Transportation for America: Overview Report* (1996).
n.a. Not available.
a. Amtrak has no comparable rail service.
b. Accelerail 125F would be upgraded service powered by fossil-fuel diesel or turbine locomotives operating at speeds up to 125 miles per hour.
c. Present service already exceeds Accelerail 125F.

State Attempts to Promote High-Speed Rail

As U.S. state governments turned their attention to the high-speed rail issue, they could see three possible ways to bring HSR to their territories. First, they could try to promote a federal-aid HSR program like the "intergovernmental fiscal transfer" transportation aid programs for highways and mass transit. This would require state matching funds, of course, but the federal treasury would carry a large share of the costs. Second, states could fund the costs of an HSR program themselves, through annual appropriations, a dedicated tax, or a bond issue. Third, states could persuade private entrepreneurs to build and operate an HSR system, in return for an exclusive franchise, tax abatements, and other "innovative" economic development incentives. Since the early 1980s, the politics of state HSR policy development has revolved around numerous (and so far unsuccessful) attempts to find the right option or mixture of options from among these three possibilities.

The Intergovernmental Fiscal Transfer Option

What prevented states from developing the kind of federal aid partnership for HSR that had long been established for highways and had been created for public transit by the mid-1970s? Timing is important in launching new intergovernmental initiatives. Just as the success of the TGV began to attract interest in HSR programs in North America, the Reagan administration, with its hostile attitude toward new federal aid programs, dampened enthusiasm. Having slashed federal funds for Amtrak, it was not about to launch an expensive new program for HSR. Potential corridors for HSR are even more geographically restricted than Amtrak's service and much narrower than the political base for public transit, a serious flaw in the distributive politics of federal aid programs. Even in states where there was a real HSR possibility, there was only a potential constituency, not an actual, ongoing operation with thousands of riders and employees, as was the case with transit.

The Clinton administration took office favorably disposed to federal aid for HSR, proposing at one point a five-year program of $1.3 billion. This created high hopes among HSR advocates. But the White House was not able to get even a Democratic Congress to increase HSR funding to that level. Competing priorities, budget-balancing politics, and changes in congressional budgetary procedures have made it far more difficult to launch new spending initiatives than it was in the era when federal transit aid and Amtrak were created.[49]

The 103d Congress passed the Swift Rail Development Act of 1994, authorizing $184 million from 1995 to 1997 on HSR corridor planning and technology improvements. But it made it clear that lower levels of government would have to pay most of the bills:

New high speed rail service should not receive Federal subsidies for operating and maintenance expenses; . . . [s]tate and local governments should take the prime responsibility for the development and implementation of high-speed rail systems; . . . the private sector should participate in funding the development of high-speed rail systems.[50]

The State Funding Option

The second option, state funding of HSR projects, has had no success winning approval from voters or state legislatures. Ohio, a Rust Belt industrial state that once had a thriving rail sector, was the first state to attempt a mainly state-funded project. It was attracted to HSR as much for its promise of industrial and construction jobs as for its transportation benefits. By being the first to get rolling with a real project, it hoped to capture an "early bird" fiscal dividend by acquiring the high-tech design, engineering, and manufacturing jobs that would come with being the center of a new North American HSR industry.[51] Plans developed by the Ohio Rail Transportation Authority called for a 600 mile high-speed system connecting thirteen Ohio cities and including links to two out-of-state destinations, Detroit and Pittsburgh. The projected cost of the system was $8 billion. But Ohio's plans were dealt a devastating setback when, in a statewide referendum in 1982, the voters rejected a 1 percent sales tax earmarked for HSR.[52] Since then no other HSR project based purely on state-level public funds has been able to move beyond the preliminary planning stages.

The Private Sector Option

The most notable attempt to use the third option, funding only from the private sector, took place in Texas. In 1989 the state legislature passed the Texas High-Speed Rail Act. A new high-speed rail authority was authorized to solicit proposals from private enterprises to build and operate an HSR system. The act prohibited any state funds from being spent on the project. In 1991, after spirited competition between two consortiums representing the builders of the German ICE and the French TGV trains and their local partners, the Texas authority awarded a fifty-year franchise to the group that came to be known as Texas TGV. Service was to connect Dallas/Fort Worth to Houston, San Antonio, and Austin. A ridership study by Charles River Associates predicted that the high-speed rail system would carry 14 million riders and generate revenues of $618 million annually by the year 2010.

As the TGV company moved through the preliminary planning stages, it had to meet requirements for public hearings and for an environmental impact statement; it was also required to raise $170 million in equity financing by the end of 1992. While this was going on, public criticism and opposition mounted across the state. Southwest Airlines sought to stop the project in the courts. Farmers and small-town land owners opposed the project in public hearings. A group calling itself DERAIL (Demanding Ethics, Responsibility and Accountability in Legislation) lobbied the legislature. The authority's executive director was forced to resign under a cloud for having falsified her résumé. Raising the required installment of $170 million in private capital proved difficult, and the deadline had to be extended for another year. Finally, Morrison-Knudsen Corporation, a major local partner in the TGV consortium, admitted publicly that private funding could not carry 100 percent of the cost of building the system. Eventually, it withdrew from the project. In August 1994 the high-speed rail authority formally canceled Texas TGV's franchise, and the project came to an end, with the loss of some $40 million to various stockholders.[53]

The Florida Formula: Public-Private Partnership

Florida's high-speed rail development effort also began amid the HSR euphoria of the mid-1980s. And it also failed. But Florida has been one of the most persistent states in pursuing HSR, and it seems to have learned from earlier failures, both in other states and in Florida itself. The first Florida HSR push led to the Florida High-Speed Rail Act of 1984, creating a High-Speed Rail Commission to take the lead on the project. The commission sought to fund construction through the "value capture" method. It assumed that real estate development projects would flourish around HSR stations and that the state's claim on a portion of the future value created by HSR could finance the system. But a sharp decline in the Florida real estate market and skepticism in the real estate development and financial community doomed this strategy.[54]

In 1991 the legislature abolished the independent commission and transferred its responsibilities to the Florida Department of Transportation (FDOT). A legislative revision in 1992 of the High-Speed Rail Act further streamlined the implementation process. The state's secretary of transportation, Ben H. Watts, enthusiastically supported HSR. He relaunched development efforts and made them a central component of Florida's intermodal transportation planning and investment decisions. In early 1995 Florida's Transportation Department issued a new request for high-speed rail proposals. This time, however, the state promised to spend an average of $70 million of its own money annually for up to thirty years to attract private investors to the project. State funds would be especially helpful in the early stages of the project when expensive environmental, engineering, and permitting costs must be incurred before the final green light for construction can be given. Having received five formal responses to its RFP (two based on maglev technology, one based on the Swedish X2000 train, and another from a subsidiary of the Italian State Railways), FDOT selected Florida Overland eXpress (FOX). This consortium includes the contracting firm of Fluor, Daniel, Odebrecht; the Canadian rail car manufacturer Bombardier; and the French company that produces the TGV, GEC-Alsthom.[55]

The Florida Overland eXpress proposal calls for TGV-type trains to operate between Miami and Orlando beginning in 2004, with service extended across to Tampa two years later. All-new, dedicated, high-speed track will be built, but the route will use existing corridors for 65 percent of its 320 mile proposed length. The state will own all the infrastructure, while the private company will purchase the rolling stock. FOX will operate the trains as a private, unsubsidized business, drawing its income from passenger fares, and it will pay the state a fee for the use of its infrastructure. Projections are for as many as 6.3 million riders to use the system by the year 2010.[56]

FOX promised nearly $350 million in private sector equity and guarantees to the project. With the state's proposed expenditure of $70 million annually for up to thirty years, there is an obvious financial gap still to be filled to reach the project's estimated $4.8 billion total price tag. Secretary Watts has emphasized that federal participation is "critical to the success of the project," and the financial plan calls for some $300 million in federal funds over a six-year period beginning in 1998, and federal loan guarantees to support issuance of construction bonds.[57] At the end of 1996, Secretary Watts announced that FDOT and FOX had reached a fifteen-month agreement to share the costs of further ridership, engineering, and environmental studies. FDOT will pay 75 percent of the costs, while the private firm will contribute 25 percent. Watts again emphasized that a federal contribution is essential.[58]

The Prospects for Fast Trains:
Stakeholders in a New Promotion Regime

The Florida formula is being hailed in the rail industry press as the breakthrough that will result in successful implementation of high-speed rail in America. This may be premature. There are many hurdles still to be overcome, with financing remaining foremost among them. Drawing on the still incomplete Florida experience, as well as the earlier failures in other states, what can we say about the possibility of constructing a new benefits regime for promoting high-speed passenger rail? Who are its likely participants, and what kinds of financial incentives will it have to embody to attract them? The following analysis of potential stakeholders suggests answers to these questions.[59]

Elected Officials

State governors and legislative leaders will have to approve the expenditure of many taxpayer dollars to launch HSR. The time between when an elected official publicly endorses an HSR project and when the trains begin to carry passengers will certainly be longer than his or her term of office. Therefore, a politician's prime concern will be to minimize the short-term political risks of sponsoring such a project. Most elected officials can be expected to take a relatively low profile role until a broad coalition is formed, and public opinion has been persuaded to support the effort.

State Transportation Departments

Special high-speed rail commissions, composed of a few politically appointed commissioners with limited professional staff, have shown themselves ill suited for the "long march" of building a successful HSR coalition. Consequently, state DOTs, as permanent operational departments, will have to provide the bulk of the bureaucratic leadership and technical expertise in the early phases of project evaluation and selection. Later on they will have a continuing oversight role. State departments of transportation evolved out of and are still heavily influenced by their highway department past. Often they developed their nonhighway planning, administrative, and operational capabilities in response to federal grant programs rather than strong needs or spontaneous pressures. True to form, most state-level HSR planning in the past decade has been financed with federal grants. It seems likely that some federal HSR planning money will continue to flow to state departments of transportation. But to move HSR beyond the study stage, they must become intermodal agencies, not just a collection of single mode agencies under one bureaucratic roof.[60] When intermodalism is accompanied by new resources, as in Florida where 14.7 percent of the state's gas tax receipts are earmarked for nonhighway projects, state DOTs will have incentives to take a more active role. In many cases, however, new resources will not be forthcoming. In these states a zero-sum shift of funds will surely provoke instant opposition from other modes, and lead state DOTs to take a more neutral stance until the political dust has settled.

Equipment Manufacturers

While competing for contracts, foreign equipment manufacturers have been willing to invest seed money in planning, public relations, and lobbying. They were a key force behind the creation of the High-Speed Ground Transportation Association, the leading trade and lobbying group promoting awareness of new HSR options. Equipment manufacturers know they will have to provide as many good North American jobs as possible, and they have sought American partners to add "local content" to their presence and efforts.

They also realize they will be called to make an even more important contribution: up-front financing of ridership, engineering, and environmental studies as well as the legal costs of getting a project to the certification stage. In addition, substantial equity investment will be needed in the public-private enterprise that will operate the new high-speed rail line. Foreign manufacturers are becoming familiar with the equity requirement. For example, in order to win cabinet approval for the construction of the new maglev line from Hamburg to Berlin, the German government insisted that Siemens, Thyssen-Henschel, and other manufacturers invest in the company that will operate their equipment in commercial service on the line.[61] Politically, assuming this kind of commercial risk is necessary to win approval for a subnational project in North America.

Private Freight Railroads

The cooperation of private freight railroads will be essential for HSR trains running on existing right-of-way at speeds lower than the TGV but higher than seventy-nine miles per hour, the limit for Amtrak intercity trains outside the Northeast Corridor. Having shed financial responsibility for the passenger rail business when Amtrak was created in 1971, the freight railroads are not going to do anything that would leave them with any financial exposure. They might cooperate on passenger projects, but they will have to be well paid for it. Their requirements are already emerging. First, they want limitation of liability for accidents that occur on their lines. Then they will insist that the improvements in track and signals required for HSR be provided at no cost to them, and that passenger train scheduling not seriously interfere with freight shipments. They will also ask for other incentives ranging from special tax write-offs to a favorable regulatory climate for mergers and acquisitions.[62]

Real Estate Interests

Some advocates still see a "value capture" strategy as a likely way of raising money for HSR projects. This raises two types of questions. First, how much would an HSR system change the shape and density of land use in the areas it serves? In a built environment dominated by the automobile for more than fifty years, is it possible to create new high-density central destinations along convenient feeder corridors?

The second question concerns the political feasibility of value capture. Can enough of the value of high-speed rail be captured without driving investors away from the project? From the point of view of real estate developers, is an HSR-related, possibly controversial, and highly politicized project more attractive than a suburban office park, a golf-course community, or an in-fill housing development off an existing expressway?

The Anti-Auto Vanguard

One might assume that the environment-conscious vanguard would strongly support rejuvenating railroads as a mode of passenger transport and high-speed rail as the most likely means to attract riders away from automobiles and airplanes. Indeed, the vanguard often does support more funding for trains, but usually for existing slower trains.[63] It is uneasy about trains that would take primarily business passengers very far, very fast. Even the dynamics of environmental politics do not inevitably play out in favor of new HSR projects. While the potential energy savings and pollution reduction benefits of a successful HSR line are attractive to environmental advocates in principle, these benefits may not be sufficient to overcome their concerns about the negative local effects of specific HSR projects. For example, Green groups in Germany made common cause with local residents and raised many objections to the routing and new construction required for the high-speed Intercity Express trains. They are still resisting specific aspects of the Hamburg-Berlin Transrapid line.[64] And U.S. transit advocates clashed with train supporters over their efforts to tap into the mass transit account of the highway trust fund. The vanguard pushes much harder for bike paths than for high-speed rail.

NIMBYs

A major infrastructure project tends to focus antigrowth, NIMBY (not in my back yard) sentiments and to catalyze citizens' resistance. Like limited access expressways, HSR lines might be perceived as an inconvenience to many people along the route, while providing direct land-use profits and transportation benefits to only a few clustered around the stations. Their broader benefits (congestion reduction of roads and airports, energy savings, air quality improvement, safer travel) are hard to capture privately. The benefits are also contingent on financing and ridership. If communities across America have been able to reject interstate highways largely paid for by federal dollars, how much more easily will they be able to derail HSR projects that require significant amounts of state, local, and private funds?

Airlines and Airport Authorities

Some high-speed rail supporters believe that airlines and airport authorities could be recruited into a pro-HSR political coalition and perhaps even induced to invest in high-speed rail. By enabling many more passengers to travel by rail between Boston and New York, Chicago and St. Louis, and Los Angeles and San Francisco, HSR could be a solution to the "winglock" of airport and airway overcrowding, and the tremendous difficulty of constructing new airport capacity.[65] But after the bitter political battle Southwest Airlines waged against the Texas TGV, it is clear that regionally based airlines will oppose HSR as a direct competitor.

Highway Interests

Highways paralleling a successful high-speed rail route should benefit from not having to increase capacity. Highway departments should be, at worst, neutral toward HSR projects. But some of the interests in the highway coalition, particularly the low-tax, antidiversion forces, could be turned into enemies if HSR advocates propose using gasoline tax revenue from federal or state highway trust funds to pay for high-speed rail construction. Nothing is more likely to raise their hackles than such a proposed "diversion." HSR supporters will probably try to avoid a head-on confrontation with the highway coalition by supporting the general trend toward flexibility and intermodalism in transportation funding. Because of the political flak, they are likely to tap those intermodal funds, rather go after a specific HSR-project-related diversion.

Orchestrating the Benefits Regime

A safe and successful high-speed rail system involves three extremely complex tasks: planning (routes, stations, environmental impact mitigation); construction (new track, bridges, tunnels, signals, catenary lines, and power stations as well as new engines, and rolling stock); and operation (trains, repair facilities, tickets and reservations, payrolls, and personnel). Although these tasks are analytically distinct and separable, they are usually performed by a single, well-established rail enterprise (like the French National Railways, which developed the TGV). That advantage is not present in the American environment. HSR implementation on this continent will require a *lead agency*, but it will not be accomplished by a *single agency*.

The lead organization will need access to the borrowing capacity of the government. It also will require firm support from the political executive (the U.S. president or a state governor) and substantial autonomy from political interference and legislative micromanagement. Finally, it must be able to stay the course for an expensive, decade-long process. No matter how careful the ridership projections and financial plans are, HSR requires a willingness to gamble the first time around.

For the foreseeable future, state HSR projects will not receive much assistance from budget-conscious Washington. The federal government will continue to fund exploratory corridor studies, high-speed safety research, and other planning activities. But a large program of federal grants for HSR project construction will not be forthcoming. Thus state leaders in HSR policy development will need to find state funding—a huge political and budgetary challenge. They also will have to create enough fiscal and financial incentives to attract private capital and private expertise to high-speed rail projects. This means the creation of the right mix of instruments (dedicated tax expenditures, earmarked public revenue streams, exclusive franchise arrangements, guaranteed loans, regulatory exemptions) and the right timing of each stage of the process to win public support.

A new benefits regime for HSR promotion will be even harder to create than for highway promotion or for transit protection. A single national framework linked federal motor fuel taxes to 90 percent funding of interstate highway construction projects in all fifty states. It appears, however, that an HSR formula will need many site-specific elements. In other words, high-speed rail development requires "custom tailoring" compared with the "off the rack" arrangements for highways.

The Amtrak protectionist regime is crumbling. If intercity passenger rail transportation is to be rejuvenated, a new benefits regime must be created—one that is more centralized, more commercially justifiable, and more closely linked with state governments and private corporations. Whether the stakeholders in America's rail policy community can develop such a regime remains to be seen. Orchestrating the political and economic coalition that could produce competitive high-speed train service is like the task of a symphony conductor who, before he can lead the concert, must write the music, found the philharmonic, build a hall, hire the musicians, and sell the tickets! Can the country find modern rail policy maestros capable of such prodigious feats?

6

"RATIONALIZING" SPRAWL

Can Access Be Improved by Restricting Mobility?

Mobility and access are related but analytically distinct concepts. They have different implications for organizing the transportation system. Mobility can be defined as "the potential for movement." It is not easy to measure potential movement, however. Empirical studies usually use the concept of "revealed mobility" as an indicator of a person's potential for movement. Revealed mobility is simply "the number of miles traveled or trips taken, over some unit of time such as a day, week, or year."[1] The assumption is that, other things being equal, people with a high potential for movement will travel more than people with a low potential, and that they "reveal" this potential when they travel. For example, if Jane drives 20,000 miles per year, while Jim drives only 10,000, then Jane may be said to have twice as much revealed mobility as Jim. But such a statement can be misleading. Does it mean that Jane has twice the mobility (the potential for movement) that Jim has? Not necessarily.

This is where the concept of access can help. Access is the ability to reach one place from another. It expresses the relationship between locations and is usually measured by the amount of time it takes to move from one point to another. For example, it might take Jane one hour to drive from her home to her job. If Jim has to drive only a half hour to his job, and if they both drive at the same speed, that would account for Jane's greater revealed mobility. But it would not mean that Jane is deriving twice the benefits from the transportation system as Jim. It means Jim has better (closer, more convenient) access to his job from his home.

Or let us assume that Jane has been making a fifty-mile trip to work each day. She decides to buy a new house closer to her job, and now she has to make only a five-mile trip. Her revealed mobility has declined by 90 percent. But have the benefits she derives from the transportation system also declined by 90 percent? Most people would say just the opposite: she is saving time and money on the daily grind. Paradoxically, her quality of life has improved by consuming less transportation!

By relocating, Jane improved her access to her workplace. If her new home is also closer to shopping, friends, and medical facilities, she has improved her access in general and reduced her total need for travel. In addition to the individual benefits that Jane derives from this decision to reduce travel and improve access, the community derives benefits. The roads are slightly less busy because she is not on them as long. Because she drives fewer miles, she and other drivers are somewhat less exposed to the risk of accidents. There is less air pollution because she burns less fuel. By reducing her travel and improving her access, Jane is better off and so is the community.

Rationalization as an Alternative to Sprawl

If what Jane has done is such a good idea, why not arrange things so that everyone does the same? Would it not be more "rational" to plan the geographic layout of our communities so that everyone lives closer to their jobs and can spend less time commuting and more time enjoying life? This proposition is at the bottom of a political effort to formulate a new philosophy of transportation policy in America. Some of its proponents call it "holistic" transportation policy; others call it a more "rational" approach to transportation. I put the terms "rational" and "rationalization" in quotes here to indicate that such a policy is not better than other policies in some absolute sense (although its proponents certainly claim it is). A value judgment is involved. The terms mean that the new type of policy would require more coordinated or comprehensive planning of transportation infrastructure investments, land-use controls, and traffic restrictions than would the current system.

Rationalization also indicates that this type of policy shares the aspirations, the appeal, and the problems of the "synoptic" (or God's eye) viewpoint that Charles E. Lindblom has examined so well.[2] The synoptic point of view is irresistible to the anti-auto vanguard, which has long decried the unplanned system of auto-dominated sprawl as irrational and wasteful—almost sinful. The vanguard has made a more rational approach to transportation policy and the automobile one of its favorite shibboleths.

The aim of rationalization policy is not to expand the transportation system and increase mobility. It assumes that we already have all the transportation we need. Indeed, in the case of the automobile, we have too much. Rationalization focuses on reducing the need for so much mobility in order to reduce its external or social costs. In passenger transportation policy, rationalization's proponents are primarily urban and regional planners, environmental activists, transportation analysts, and others attracted by the vanguard's vision of the evils of automobility. They are convinced that the unplanned, auto-dominated sprawl of our metropolitan areas cannot be changed by existing market forces and political mechanisms. They want to lead a rational redesign of the links between transportation and land use that will increase access for all, while minimizing the need for socially and environmentally damaging automobility.[3]

But in moving from the level of individual decisionmaking exemplified by Jane's choices to the collective level of decisionmaking exemplified by a strong regional land-use and transportation planning agency, the proponents of rationalization are confronted by thorny paradoxes and political problems. For example, suppose Jane's case involved moving from her old home in an inner city neighborhood to a brand new housing development close to her job at a small-town health clinic on the fringe of the metropolitan area. Such a move could be seen as contributing to the undesirable pattern of sprawl development, even though Jane did what was best for her as an individual. If the regional planning organization in Jane's area had established a strong urban growth boundary that restricted new housing developments on the edge of the built-up area, Jane might not have been able to find or afford the kind of housing that enabled her to improve her access and reduce her need for mobility.

The target of rationalization policy is sprawl: that characteristic American style of low-density suburban development that is "poorly planned, land-consumptive, automobile dependent, designed without regard to its surroundings."[4] Two of sprawl's worst features are the "sellscape" of fast food franchises, shopping strips, malls, discount outlets, and car dealerships that line major highways, and the "leapfrog" development of single-family homes into previously undeveloped areas. The automobile and the highway are universally cited as the major culprits in making sprawl possible on such a massive scale. Contributing factors range from the practical (federal mortgage insurance and the tax deduction for home mortgages) to the romantic (Americans' pioneering desire to push back the frontier and settle new land).

Another factor contributing to sprawl, the one cited almost as often as the automobile, is the fragmentation of political jurisdictions in metropolitan areas. The New York metropolitan region has more than 700 local governments with zoning authority, not to mention three separate state governments, more than thirty county governments, and hundreds of special purpose districts, independent authorities, and boards with the power to levy some kind of property tax or travel toll. None of these jurisdictions has much incentive to prevent tax-paying individuals or businesses from acquiring and developing land within their boundaries. Consequently, the urbanized land area surrounding New York expanded by 65 percent between 1960 and 1985, even though the total population of the area grew only by 8 percent. The same thing happens everywhere, even in places where the population is declining. For example, Cleveland's regional population dropped by 11 percent between 1970 and 1990, but the region's urbanized land area increased by 33 percent.[5]

Rationalizers maintain that the sprawl pattern of land development is more costly in almost every respect than a rationally planned pattern of development would be.[6] They start from their perception that sprawl "consumes" more land (that is, removes it from agricultural production or its natural state) than a more compact planned community would. Sprawl leads to more consumption of energy, for single-home heating and especially for auto travel, and hence more region-wide air pollution. They assert that sprawl is more costly to the public treasury because it requires more public infrastructure investments for roads and sewers, for suburban schools, and the like. In addition to increasing consumption and expenditure costs, sprawl has deepened our society's class and racial divisions by attracting a region's affluent residents and its newest and best jobs to the "edge cities" and the suburban periphery, while concentrating poverty, crime, and unemployment in the inner cities.

These assertions about the costs of sprawl are contested. In fact, planners and policy analysts have long had a running battle comparing sprawl's public and private costs with those of more rational models. Alan Altshuler and his colleagues argue that sprawl is not nearly as costly as its opponents have claimed. They develop evidence that fears of a cropland shortage are unwarranted. They also argue that the energy savings claimed for high-density development disappear upon close examination. Data from actual communities showed that per capita public spending was higher in denser communities than in less dense ones, they note. Finally, Altshuler and his colleagues cite evidence that the rate of population dispersion from central cities has been nearly constant for a hundred years. Even without federal highway and housing policies favorable to the auto and single-family houses, the pace of suburbanization would have been about the same, in their view, though it might have been somewhat more compact. "Absolute physical distances between the classes and races would probably be less . . . but there is little reason to believe that psychological, economic, and political distances would be any less."[7]

The opponents of sprawl are not less opposed because its "true costs" are arguable, however. They would oppose it on esthetic, almost moral, grounds. For them, sprawl is such a blight on the landscape and such a threat to their vision of community that we should create policies and institutions to tilt the balance away from the "forced" automobility of sprawl development. Any policy that could reduce the need for more auto travel finds favor with them.

Intermodalism is the mildest form of rationalization policy. It stresses the efficiencies to be had by improved transportation planning and better coordination of investments among different means of transportation (for example, more park-and-ride locations for commuters, more rail links to airports). Intermodalism has had a certain amount of success in freight transportation, especially where a single private company can integrate road and rail shipments.[8] In passenger transportation, intermodalism readily finds allies among supporters of urban transit and intercity trains, since many intermodal projects try to facilitate the transfer of passengers to those modes. Bills and programs with "intermodal" in the title usually signify modes and activities (for example, bike paths, pedestrian planning, historic preservation) not previously included in federal surface transportation funding and federal transportation planning mandates. The auto's adversaries assume that in an era of budget caps, if other activities get more money and attention, the automobile will get less.

A stronger rationalization strategy seeks to use incentives and regulations in the area of land-use controls (suburban growth boundaries, in-fill development regulations, mixed-use development permitting and zoning, innovative community designs) to influence more than an individual's choice of transport mode. At issue are other concerns: where to live and work, what type of housing to buy or rent, and lifestyle decisions about shopping and leisure activities. The goal is broader than marginally improved efficiency in the use of transportation resources. It is a reduction in the total amount of mobility required to operate the system. These rationalizers want to change the spatial organization of Americans' lives into more pleasing, more "sustainable" forms, thus transforming the social meaning of mobility in modern life.

Rationalization versus Restriction

Policies to *reduce* mobility and policies to *restrict* mobility are different. The former encourage a more efficient location of activities, and they allow people to make their own choices about how they want to travel. The latter have the direct intent of discouraging travel by a particular mode, the automobile; the location of jobs, housing, and recreation is affected because people will have to make more of their trips by nonautomotive modes. Viewed as available instruments in the planner's toolbox, the two types of policies may seem indistinguishable. Their political ramifications, however, are distinct.

Auto-restrictive policies include congestion pricing on freeways, employer parking surcharges, and federally mandated rush-hour ride-sharing programs. They aim directly at making auto travel more expensive and less convenient. These policies cross an important political line. They require politicians to impose significant costs on many individuals. The costs must be imposed in the present, although the presumed benefits (less congestion, cleaner air, more compact communities) cannot be felt until some time in the future. Moreover, these benefits are collective (such as a slowdown in global warming) rather than individual (such as a faster trip to the office). Policies that impose significant costs on a wide range of individuals in the present in order to obtain collective benefits in the future go beyond the "entrepreneurial politics" discussed in chapter 1. This is "vanguard politics" par excellence.

Making any changes in the template governing future growth in America's metropolitan landscapes will be very difficult. At present, American political institutions have trouble swallowing even the milder forms of rationalization. Despite its incrementalist approach, intermodalism is still more of a buzz word than an actual policy achievement.[9] Policymakers at all levels find themselves hemmed in by the institutional and infrastructural achievements of the past, from the federal highway trust fund to the malls and office parks that put once sleepy farming communities on the map as edge cities. State and local officials have strong incentives to take a narrow view and work to benefit a single mode or a single town. Changing these incentives and operating practices will inevitably be a protracted and uneven process.

Moderate rationalizers know that the step-by-step small changes they propose will take decades to have an impact on a large scale. There is a danger, however, that the vanguard, impatient to roll back automobility, will "hijack" moderate rationalization efforts by pushing policies to directly restrict the auto. This risks undercutting the political support for the moderate, incremental efforts that might make a modest but positive contribution to improving access without restricting mobility.

Access and Holistic Transportation

The holistic approach to transportation starts from the premise that what is really important is for people to have access to the things they need to live their lives. Access in the auto-based transportation and land-use system demanded ever-increasing mobility, but many of the consequences of this system were undesirable. The new approach maintains that it is possible to design new urban communities that improve access to employment, education, services, and recreation, while decreasing mobility, hence reducing many of automobility's undesirable consequences.

The foundation of the new approach is to "redefine access in terms of community":

> The accessibility paradigm . . . places the overall needs of community residents at the pinnacle of the hierarchy of values. . . . As opposed to the mobility paradigm, which enshrines individual mobility at the expense of other goals, the access paradigm re-enacts the social contract on which democracies are based . . . in that the ability to go anywhere, anytime, at any speed is not a fundamental right, nor even an ideal for individuals to aspire to.[10]

Rather than moving residences, jobs, and services farther and farther out on the metropolitan frontier, empowering some individuals and leaving others behind, the access paradigm suggests that "opportunities must be placed where people already are, so that they can tap into the power that resides within their cities, towns, neighborhoods, and ultimately within themselves."[11]

A holistic approach to transportation would use a "few simple tests" to evaluate a transportation proposal: "Does it serve the community? Are my neighbors' and my quality of life improved. . . ? Do we have safer neighborhoods, better access to daycare, more open spaces, more affordable housing?" The object of holistic transportation is "making each community more self-sustaining and coherent, rather than simply connecting places to one another like so many dots on a map."[12]

The holistic paradigm promotes a "compact community" form of living. With smaller scale communities, more trips can be made on foot and on bicycles. The new communities will support more small neighborhood stores and businesses. In the auto-dominated cityscape, large shopping malls, discount stores, and supermarkets "receive a hidden subsidy." By driving their own cars to the mall, shoppers pay part of the freight cost for their goods. By paying slightly higher prices for their purchases, they also indirectly pay for the large number of parking places malls provide. A person who walks to the mall indirectly subsidizes those who drive there. In compact communities, public policies can be designed to "give local community-based stores a more level playing field." For example, their taxes could be reduced because "their location reduces the need to provide infrastructure."[13]

Daniel Carlson, Lisa Wormser, and Cy Ulberg describe life in compact communities "at road's end," the title of their book. Trip substitution and telecommuting enable residents to spend more time at home and with their neighbors. Work at home or at "neighborhood telework centers" replaces peak-hour trips to work. Electronic shopping and information exchange reduce trips to the mall. United Parcel Service and Federal Express bring goods directly to one's door. "Each delivery replaces another cold start, protecting air quality and removing another vehicle from the roadway." Lest people become isolated in their homes, connected to others only by phone, fax, and the Internet, neighborhoods have "general stores as focal points." Goods ordered by phone or computer can be delivered there, thus combining "the efficiency of delivery service with a meeting place such as a general store and post office." Such centers, accessible on foot or bike, attract other service businesses (such as restaurants, dry cleaners, and ATM machines) that increase local social interaction and community spirit.[14]

These self-sufficient communities resist new freeways and additional road capacity. They view with suspicion "smart highways" and improvements in communicating traffic congestion and alternative routing information to motorists. Highway-oriented communication advances, they fear, would divert cars from congested arterial roads and dump them onto local streets. The goal of holistic transportation planning is to protect the integrity of the neighborhood community as a place safe for pedestrians, bicyclists, and children. Boundaries and barriers are used to repulse potential auto invaders. "Traffic-calming" techniques borrowed from Europe, such as speed bumps, widened sidewalks, pedestrian zones, bollards, and liberally distributed stop signs and stop lights, prevent neighborhoods from being overrun by outside drivers seeking a quick short cut around a traffic jam.

The compact neighborhood also has transportation links to the larger city with its broader choice of amenities. Light rail systems would be the preferred technology, but subways, commuter rail, even electric trolley buses on designated busway lanes could be deployed where circumstances warranted. Another important feature would be community-based car sharing. Car sharing would lessen residents' psychological dependence on the auto, and their proclivity to make the auto their first and often only mode of travel. Residents would have access to cars for trips where cars made sense, such as exploring winding country roads on weekends, vacation travel, and special business travel. But they would not use cars for virtually all their daily trips, as they often do now.

In the end the new holistic paradigm comes down to changing people's beliefs and feelings about their communities. As Carlson, Wormser, and Ulberg note, "elected officials respond to public opinion; and if that opinion is based on shallow understanding or misinformation, it can lead to very bad policy indeed." A campaign of education should be pursued at all levels. A university transportation curriculum is a vital place to start. But the new approach to transportation and community "should be part of the educational curriculum starting in elementary school," so young citizens can gain a more complete understanding of the implications of the new paradigm. Access will be fostered by redesigning and rebuilding communities, not by individuals' continued reliance on automobiles. The right of communities to ensure their residents' "access to equal opportunities is a protected right, against which each individual must negotiate his or her personal choices of residence, job, and lifestyle."[15]

The New Urbanism: Back to the Future?

New philosophies of transportation do not build communities. They remain theoretical unless they can be marketed as profit-making ideas. As it happens, many of the ideas from the holistic approach form the basis of the "New Urbanism" movement within the city planning and architecture professions. New Urbanism "has captured the imagination of the American public like no urban planning movement in decades."[16] This is somewhat ironic since its basic premise is to return to traditional town designs from the era before the automobile became dominant.

Andres Duany and Elizabeth Plater-Zyberk, a husband and wife team of architects, and developer Robert Davies launched the "neotraditional" design movement (renamed New Urbanism) in the town of Seaside, Florida. This recreational community on Florida's panhandle coast was conceived in the early 1980s and built under strict design codes that ensured Seaside would resemble a small town from the 1920s. The codes required each house to have a front porch that extends at least halfway across the house's front and is at least eight feet deep. The porch must be sixteen feet from the street, and the front yard must be surrounded by a white picket fence. Seaside's streets are narrow to discourage parking and made of cobblestones to discourage speeding. They are laid out in a connected grid pattern, instead of the winding cul-de-sacs typical of suburbia. Seaside was a success with the public. The value of its lots tripled in a few years, and architects and planners began to flock there. Duany and Plater-Zyberk proved adept at publicizing their new concepts for town design. They developed a model of town planning codes to replace the postwar zoning laws that fostered sprawl.[17]

Another leading proponent of the New Urbanism is Peter Calthorpe. In *The Next American Metropolis* he describes a reconstructed landscape of "pedestrian pockets" and "transit-oriented developments" (TODs). Calthorpe calls for "a new paradigm of development, a new vision of the American Metropolis, and a new image of the American Dream." At the core of his vision is the pedestrian. Calthorpe believes that we must plan "as if there were pedestrians" and that this will become a "self-fulfilling act"—turning "suburbs into towns, projects into neighborhoods, and networks into communities." His goal is to put housing, shops, schools, parks, jobs, and transit stations within walking distance of each other.[18]

Like Duany and Plater-Zyberk, Calthorpe extols the model of the traditional American town, whose design principles "can be adapted to the contemporary situation." To get back to those principles, planners and developers should "take the standard 65' by 100' lot and cut it in half, and add an alley and an in-law unit over the garage in the rear" for a relative, a home office, or to generate income.[19] The economics of combining small lots, rental unit income, and reduced auto costs are very favorable, in Calthorpe's view. Pedestrian pockets enable a two-car family to become a one-car family. People who were shut out of one-house-per-acre suburban developments can become landlords in these six-units-per-acre neighborhoods. In this way the New Urbanism eases the crisis of affordable housing.

Calthorpe recognizes that this transformation cannot be realized by localized measures to control growth. Progressive policies at the federal and state levels are needed. Regional control of land use is the key to achieving the right balance of urban redevelopment, suburban infill densification, and peripheral growth management. Once a progressive coalition of environmentalists, developers, and urban advocates agrees on a working alternative to sprawl, "the task of creating a regional framework for growth is possible."[20] The core element of that framework will be the regional "corridor plan" for transit investments and the location of the sites for new TODs. On the edge of the region new growth will be permitted, but it should be shaped into pedestrian-friendly, transit-oriented patterns from the beginning, even if the transit lines have not reached the location. Until new rail transit arrives, car pools and bus service can fill the gap.

What are the chances that the New Urbanism will dramatically reshape American communities? A realist might look at past fashions in city planning and foresee a few model communities largely swamped in the general sprawl. Neotraditional town planning has many legal and institutional hurdles to overcome before it can become a practical template for commercial home builders and town planners. Changing zoning laws on a neighborhood-by-neighborhood or town-by-town basis will be daunting. The public and private benefits that are claimed for New Urbanism designs can be realized only when the full community package is available. "New Urbanists have . . . learned the hard way that the promise of a diversified community, with many types and prices of homes, retail stores within walking distance, and other community amenities, requires a highly sophisticated effort to bring all the components 'on line' in the right sequence."[21] This will raise the developer's initial costs, perhaps offsetting the savings in land and infrastructure expenses and making neotraditional developments more expensive than conventional suburbs. Retrofitting neighborhoods with granny flats over garages, converting single-family homes to duplexes, and bringing in community general stores and telework stations also will be an expensive, politically delicate, and time-consuming process.

Two noteworthy communities in the New Urbanist pattern are the Laguna West development in California and the Kentlands development in Maryland. Laguna West, twelve miles South of downtown Sacramento, is a pedestrian-pocket-type development designed by Peter Calthorpe and Associates. The original plan called for about 3,000 dwellings and a population of around 9,000, but sales have been slow, and financial difficulties have arisen. Building began in 1990. By 1997 only 550 units had been completed.

Kentlands is a smaller neotraditional development designed by Duany and Plater-Zyberk. It is set on the historic Kent family farm on the edge of Gaithersburg, Maryland. Its total of 1,600 dwelling units was scheduled for completion in 1998. It is not an independent entity but is surrounded by other suburbs and dependent on the larger metropolitan region for most services and jobs.

Neotraditional design principles influenced the Disney Corporation's new town of Celebration, set on 5,000 acres outside of Orlando, next to Disney World. Its aim is 8,000 new homes.[22]

Despite the original success of Seaside, the construction of New Urbanist communities has been slow. Although New Urbanist writings and town designs have been around for well over a decade, only a few thousand people are living in projects inspired by their vision. By contrast, a decade after Levitt pioneered his now-scorned ready-made suburb, millions of families lived in developments inspired by his methods. Stimulating as the ideas of the New Urbanists have been for planners and their profession, they "have had little influence" on what has been built to date. After comparing the promise and the performance of the new designs, one observer concluded that "there is little urbanity in the New Urbanism." The neotraditional models "are essentially anti-urban, sanitized versions of the small town, and they exclude much of what it takes to make a metropolitan region work. Real towns must do more than house middle-income people."[23]

What about the transportation benefits of the New Urbanist communities? Empirical evidence suggests that "a change in land use increasing 'access' . . . invariably leads to shorter trips." But in terms of the frequency of trips made, their modal split, or the total of miles traveled, the evidence is not nearly as conclusive. "Whatever the merits of neotraditional and transit-oriented designs, and there are many, their transportation benefits have been oversold,"[24] writes Randall Crane in his article on cars and drivers in the new suburbs. A journalist who visited Disney's Celebration was even less sanguine: "one only has to climb the tower at the visitor's center to see that the new town is really just one more in a series of residential pods hanging off the classic suburban strip . . . by a single asphalt thread." Although residents may be able to walk to Celebration's "downtown" on weekends, "on Monday morning most of them will have no choice but to climb back into their cars for the half-hour commute to Orlando."[25]

Indeed, even when it comes to the ideal situation for designing transit-oriented developments—high-density residential housing around new rail stations—it is hard to link housing and transportation benefits. Marlon Boarnet and Randall Crane have examined zoning data for all 232 existing or proposed rail transit stations in southern California. They found that "local planners and politicians . . . have shown little willingness to cede land use authority to regional bodies." They prefer to use the land near rail stations for economic development rather than transit-oriented housing. From the local perspective, commercial development yields a higher ratio of tax revenues to new services required. Locating high-density, transit-based housing within easy walking distance of new rail stations "would seem to face an uphill battle in most communities."[26]

The probability is that the New Urbanism will remain little more than an intriguing fad. Neotraditional design might become a perk or a plus (like a golf course or a man-made lake) that can be added to an upscale community to enhance its charm and help in the marketing campaign. But if examples of New Urbanist communities remain literally few and far between, they will not significantly affect suburban sprawl.

The "retail" mode of spreading New Urbanist communities as if they were a commercial enhancement, like split-level houses or two-car garages, is unlikely to be effective. The alternative is to try the "wholesale" approach—changing zoning laws, land-use planning, and community design requirements for large swaths of territory and numerous towns simultaneously. This would mean "tilting" the legal, regulatory, and financial playing field to favor the kind of compact, transit-oriented designs preached by the New Urbanists.[27] Land development, transportation investment, and zoning would have to be done on a broader geographical basis than in the past. The success or failure of the New Urbanism, and of other manifestations of rationalization, is closely linked to the possibilities for creating strong regional institutions in the United States.

Portland as the Promised Land

One place that does have strong regional institutions is Oregon, particularly its largest metropolitan area, Portland. The coordination of transportation planning and land-use regulation in the Portland area is indeed impressive. New light-rail lines focusing on the downtown business district
have reduced the need for parking, and a transit mall encourages pedestrian
circulation and transit usage. The Portland area canceled or postponed several new freeways that could have led to edge-city developments. Oregon
and Portland have become models of regional transportation and land use.[28]

In the late 1980s nonauto modes of travel (rail, bus, bike, and walking)
accounted for 40 percent of commuter trips to Portland's central business
district. From 1960 to 1980, decades when most metro areas experienced
rampant suburban sprawl and severe declines in the percentage of jobs located downtown, Portland increased its share of metropolitan employment.
In 1989 Portland had the lowest amount of non-central-business-district office space per capita of any major metropolitan area in the country.
Working to meet a state mandate, Portland planners intend to use their
great strength in land-use and transit planning coordination to achieve a 20
percent reduction in per capita automobile vehicle miles traveled over the
next thirty years.[29]

Portland planners' exceptional powers to coordinate transportation investments with land development and permitting are the result of actions
taken more than twenty years ago. In 1973 the Oregon state legislature enacted a law to preserve the state's forests and farms. A state agency, the
Land Conservation and Development Commission (LCDC), was created to
oversee, coordinate, and approve county and local area plans. It was given
the power to withhold the revenues from state excise taxes due to local
governments if they were willfully noncompliant with its rules.[30] The law
required each of the state's metro areas and freestanding cities to establish
an "urban growth boundary" sufficient to serve twenty years of growth.
Land-use planning authority in the Portland metro area was given to the
Columbia Region Association of Governments, now merged with the Metropolitan Service District (Metro). Transportation planning is guided by
the Tri-County Metropolitan Transportation District (Tri-Met). These formal institutions were politically supported by informal planning and environmental groups such as 1,000 Friends of Oregon.

The Portland area has had talented policy entrepreneurs among its
elected officials. Foremost among them is Neil Goldschmidt—elected

mayor of Portland in 1972, appointed U.S. secretary of transportation by President Carter (1979–81), and elected governor of Oregon in 1986. As mayor, Goldschmidt was instrumental in focusing growth around transport corridors served by light rail. Returning home in 1981, Goldschmidt went on to win office as Governor of Oregon. He has had the rare opportunity to further Portland's transportation and land-use planning goals at the local, national, and state levels.

Paul G. Lewis argues that Portland's success in shaping suburbia is not because its people or its politicians are smarter than the rest of us, or because it has a unique "Oregon political culture" receptive to planning initiatives. He puts the reason for its success squarely in the realm of institutions. The "dominance of large, relatively technocratic government units—the city of Portland, Metro, Tri-Met, and the state"—enabled politicians and planners to preserve the viability of the central city and its downtown, restrain growth at the metropolitan fringe, and inhibit job and housing imbalances. "A centralized, insulated policy-making system is more susceptible to 'issue networks' and expertise," writes Lewis, than is a system "closer to local public opinion." It enables decisionmakers to take a broad and long-range view of things unlike the typical narrow vision of politicians in fragmented suburbs. The traditions of suburban "home rule" and "city bashing" were not able to find much institutional support in the Portland area. "Despite pretensions of citizen participation, the land-use and transportation planning system has by and large been an elite process." Lewis even quotes a planning director of a suburb near Portland as saying, "Every day, I'm working for things that most of our residents would vote against if they had the opportunity."[31]

From this description it might seem that the Portland area's institutional structure would be the perfect operating environment for the anti-auto vanguard. But there is an additional dimension that is important. The urban growth boundary and the metropolitan institutions were seen by most area residents as home-grown products, not as something that was imposed on them from the outside. Indeed, Portland area residents helped provide the votes to overcome a series of referendum challenges to the state land-use planning law in 1976, 1978, and 1982. They also approved the 1992 referendum that established the charter of the metropolitan service district.[32]

Can the "lessons" from Portland be easily learned by other cities and their suburbs? Or did its success depend on a combination of circumstances that are relatively rare and difficult to replicate elsewhere? Paul G. Lewis is certainly no apologist for sprawl, but even he acknowledges that Portland's success will not be easy to transfer to other regions. "The Oregon urban growth boundary rule . . . is unlikely to be adopted in such a strong form elsewhere," he notes.[33]

Timing, history, and local geography played a key role in permitting the formation of strong regional planning institutions in Portland. In the early years of the great wave of U.S. suburbanization, the city of Portland was still quite dominant in its region. As late as 1970, the largest suburban municipality in the metro area had a population of only 18,500. Portland also carried great weight within the state. In 1997, 41 percent of the population of Oregon lived within the boundary of the Portland metro area.[34] The weight of numbers and the political skills of the city's leaders kept metropolitan institution building and policy development focused on the central city to an unusual degree. Conservation activists, "riding the first wave of environmentalism" in the early 1970s, were able to push through their program of land-use controls. They were aided by the high value of farmland in the Willamette Valley.[35] African-Americans made up only 7.7 percent of the city of Portland's population in 1990, and its schools, unlike Denver's, never had to undergo court-ordered desegregation. Race has been less influential in driving suburban development in Portland than in most large U.S. metro areas.[36] For these reasons Portland is not as useful a model for building metropolitan institutions and containing sprawl as many people would like to think.

The Automobile and the Prospects for Metropolitan Governance

A full discussion of the politics of metropolitan-wide institutions is far beyond the scope of this book.[37] It is possible to examine the relationship between building regional governance and policies to rationalize land development and automobile use. The literature on holistic transportation, reducing auto use, and the New Urbanism assumes that region-wide institutions will be available to implement these innovative approaches.[38] The rationalizers believe that the urgent need to stop sprawl is so self-evident that leaders and citizens around the region will soon climb aboard regionalism's bandwagon. The new institutions can then be turned to the task of rolling back automobility. I submit that this relationship is more complicated than the rationalizers assume. An agenda aimed at "getting people out of their cars" and into buses and vanpools is likely to be so unpopular that it will hinder the prospects for regionalism, not enhance them. In most U.S. metropolitan areas, progress toward regional governance will not be associated with anti-automobile measures. It will add to residents' mobility choices rather than restrict them.

Consider, for example, the recent success of regionalism in Minneapolis–St. Paul as recounted by one of the architects of the process, Myron Orfield. An attorney and state legislator from Minneapolis with a talent for coalition building and computer mapping, Orfield wrote a book on the political strategy that brought about the resurgence of regional institutions in the Twin Cities. The key to success was forming a political coalition of state legislators representing the central city and legislators representing the blue-collar and middle-income inner suburbs. In 1994 this "metro majority" in the legislature was able to pass the Metropolitan Reorganization Act that transformed the Twin Cities Metropolitan Council "from a $40-million-per-year planning agency to a $600-million-a-year regional government operating regional sewers and transit." In addition, the Council was given supervisory authority over the major decisions of another $300-million-a-year agency that runs the regional airport.[39]

Orfield is optimistic that the Minnesota experience can be repeated in other metro areas, including Chicago and Philadelphia, which on the surface appear rather unpromising. A pivotal role is played by the close-in suburbs. "These middle-income (often working class) suburbs, which have been a loose cannon politically since 1968, hold the balance of power on these regional issues and arguably on most political issues in the United States." Although Orfield is a severe critic of sprawl, he does not offer any evidence that auto-restrictive issues helped cement the metropolitics coalition in Minnesota.[40]

To coordinate transportation and land use, regional institutions and policies are indispensable. Like Orfield, the well-known political and urban analyst Anthony Downs sounds this theme. His book *Stuck in Traffic* specifically addresses the problem of peak-hour traffic congestion. After reviewing a wide variety of possible solutions, Downs found, not surprisingly, that the most effective remedies for congestion must be planned and implemented across the entire metropolitan area. Few U.S. metro areas, however, have strong governmental institutions at the regional level. Indeed, "resistance to effective regional administration of anticongestion tactics—or any other policies—is extremely strong in most metropolitan areas."[41]

Downs suggests that regional auto-restrictive tactics will be politically feasible only in limited circumstances. Congestion throughout the metro area must be so bad that most of the citizens as well as most local and state officials, especially the governor, regard it as a crisis. In addition, they must believe that regional remedies are essential and unavoidable. The entire metro area must lie within a single state; coordination across state lines poses too many political and administrative problems. And finally, it would be very helpful to have the proper regional institutions legally established in advance, so that action can be taken immediately before public attention shifts elsewhere. Very few metro areas meet these conditions.[42]

In *New Visions for Metropolitan America* Downs describes the "dominant vision" of unlimited sprawl based on automobiles and single-family homes, and he acknowledges its organic link to many problems confronting our society. He then identifies three alternative visions of the future spatial organization of American communities. The vision of "bounded high-density growth" is the opposite of sprawl. Jobs are concentrated in designated areas surrounded by multifamily housing, mobility is heavily dependent on public transit, and the powers of local government are largely shifted to elected regional institutions. "New communities and greenbelts" is a vision of concentrated growth in planned communities separated from each other and the older center by green swaths and linked by mass transit. In the third scenario, "limited-spread mixed-density growth," the more permeable boundary is enforced by decisions not to provide public infrastructure beyond it. Transit is supplemented by subsidized ride sharing, and both housing and jobs continue to be rather widely dispersed.[43]

What kind of effort would be required to channel growth into these nonsprawl forms? To get an approximate idea, Downs attempts to gauge whether Peter Calthorpe's transit-oriented development approach could have accommodated the suburban growth in the 1980s in the standard metropolitan statistical areas with a 1990 population of over 1 million. Downs assumes that all growth was contained in transit-oriented developments extending in a circle with a radius of 2,000 feet from a rail station (the greatest distance most people say they are willing to walk to a station). He also assumes an average net residential density of fifteen dwelling units per acre, with the units containing an average of 2.5 persons. Given these assumptions, each U.S. metro area with more than 1 million people would have had to build sixty-three new TODs to contain their 1980–90 population growth. If each new TOD were to be connected by a rail line with stations 1.5 miles apart, the total length of the new rail line would be ninety-six miles. Thus each of the U.S. metro areas with over 1 million residents would have had to build a new rail system longer than the Washington Metro just to accommodate one decade's worth of suburban growth.[44] Clearly, such an ambitious program of transit spending is beyond the realm of possibility.

All three of Downs's alternative visions will require strengthening regional policymaking institutions. Can sufficiently strong regional institutions be created? Downs frankly admits the "the odds are against it." There are too many vested interests still reasonably happy with the status quo, and the sense of an impending social crisis has not arisen. But if regional institutions could be created, the vision with the best chance of being adopted would be the limited-spread mixed-density plan. It "is likely to arouse less political resistance, so it is more likely to occur."[45] Downs warns against the allure of the high-density vision of future growth. "Recognizing the serious failings of unlimited low-density growth," many planners and public officials "leap to the conclusion that adopting nearly opposite policies would be the best way to remedy those failings. That conclusion is false."[46]

What then are the prospects for metropolitan governance? In the transportation realm, residents of central cities and "streetcar suburbs" may well favor improved public transit facilities and service. They may even support regional policies to plan more efficient (and less costly in terms of tax dollars) land-use and infrastructure investment on the suburban periphery. But it is doubtful they will line up behind regional measures to restrict their ability to use or park their cars, or to increase taxes and fees on their vehicles.

The Vanguard's Venue: Federal Planning Mandates and Mobility Restrictions

In most U.S. metropolitan areas (Portland and the Twin Cities are notable exceptions), federal planning mandates are the greatest impetus for regional programs. The pressure is effective: areas that fail to conform to the requirements risk losing federal funds. By stressing area-wide planning, Congress and various federal agencies have created a new and congenial "venue" for the vanguard—an environment in which they can operate comfortably, shielded from public opinion, and in a position to enhance the impact of their ideas beyond the weight of their numbers.

The basic process by which federal mandates have created a new institutional locus for the vanguard started from relatively noncontroversial premises, moved on to more complex realms, and then plunged into surprisingly controversial areas. The three-decade-long process began with the simple desire to help states and metropolitan areas put federal transportation assistance funds to effective use. The Federal Aid Highway Act of 1962 mandated regional transportation planning as a condition for receiving federal highway funds. Of the total federal aid funds to each state, it earmarked 1.5 percent for "continuing, comprehensive, and cooperative" planning and research. In many metropolitan areas the so-called 3C planning process was the stimulus that led to the creation of the first region-wide planning agency.[47]

Over the years transportation planning became more complicated. Urban public transit, handicapped access, environmental impact statements, ambient air quality standards, alternatives analysis, public and private partnerships, and mandates for increased public participation were among the many issues on the table. To keep the flow of federal aid coming through the pipeline, planners had to comply with increasingly complex federal planning requirements. Less effort was spent on planning transportation projects "on the ground" and more on complying with federal mandates.

The Clean Air Act amendments of 1990 required that metropolitan area transportation improvement plans (TIPs) conform to state implementation plans (SIPs) for improving air quality in "nonattainment areas" (that is, regions where air quality does not meet EPA standards). The Intermodal Surface Transportation Efficiency Act of 1991 prohibited the expenditure of federal funds for any TIP project not in conformity with the clean air goals embodied in the SIP. As a result, the "tail of air quality began to wag the dog of transportation." To reduce mobile source emissions in nonattainment areas, states and metropolitan areas began to implement increasingly intrusive auto-restrictive schemes.

The Employer Trip Reduction Program

The Employer Trip Reduction program, also known as the Employee Commute Option (ECO), arose from a provision of the Clean Air Act amendments of 1990 affecting states in severe or extreme nonattainment areas. The implementation plans for improving air quality in these states had to require employers with more than 100 employees to increase the average passenger vehicle occupancy rate among their commuting employees by 25 percent. In late 1992 the Environmental Protection Agency issued a "guidance" document to state and metro-area planners that specified actions that employers had to take (registration with the planning agency, notification of employees, establishment of an employee transportation coordinator in charge of compliance). States also had to include in their SIPs a range of penalties for an employer who did not submit or implement a compliance plan. The EPA reserved the right to approve the penalties as part of its review of the states' SIPs. At the time the EPA issued its guidance, there were severe and extreme nonattainment metro areas in California, Connecticut, Delaware, Illinois, Indiana, Maryland, New Jersey, New York, Pennsylvania, Texas, and Wisconsin.[48] The precise compliance deadlines varied from state to state, but most employers would have had to submit their plans by 1995 and achieve their goals by 1997.

The planners at EPA were eager to pass on tips to their colleagues at the state and metropolitan levels on the kinds of commute options firms could offer their employees. The choices were many: monetary incentives, time off for willingness to participate, a guaranteed ride home program in case of emergency or unscheduled overtime, a noontime shuttle so workers could run errands during lunch hour. For workers switching to public transit, they could get a subsidy for part of their fares and flexible hours to coincide with transit schedules. Employees unwilling to participate in the trip reduction program could expect a parking fee.

A trip reduction regulation very similar to the federal one had already been put into effect in southern California—the Southern California Air Quality Management District's Regulation XV. Enacted in 1987, it set average vehicle occupancy rates for commuting employees working in firms with 100 or more employees. As the process got under way for nationwide implementation of the ETR/ECO program, southern California's regulatory experience was closely scrutinized for its impact on commuting, congestion, and air quality.

In 1993 well-known transportation consultant C. Kenneth Orski reported on two evaluations of southern California's trip reduction experience by the Institute of Transportation Engineers and the Business Transportation Council, a group sponsored by the U.S. Department of Transportation to foster closer government-industry partnerships.[49] Modest increases (2 to 5 percent) in average vehicle occupancy were obtained in the first year of the program in southern California, but these increases were difficult to sustain in subsequent years. The studies found that "the statutory goal of a 25 percent increase in average vehicle occupancy (AVO) . . . appears arbitrary . . . [and] this one-size-fits-all approach penalizes areas that have already made good faith efforts to reduce traffic."[50] Commuters employed at work sites with 100 or more employees constitute only about 10 to 15 percent of the total motoring public in major metro areas, and both fairness and effectiveness require all travelers to play a role in reducing vehicle emissions. Orski concluded that the evidence "tends to cast doubt on the feasibility and cost-effectiveness of regulatory, employer-based trip reduction programs as a tool of regional air pollution and traffic congestion mitigation."[51]

The California Air Resources Board examined the improvements in vehicle occupancy rates in the state between 1989 and 1992–93 and concluded that they had decreased hydrocarbon emissions by six tons per year at a high cost of $35,000 per ton. This is substantially more than the board's $20,000 per ton cost-effectiveness standard for air quality programs and far above the EPA's $10,000 per ton standard.[52] Another review of southern California's transportation-related efforts to fight air pollution also was critical. "It may be tempting to justify investments in mass transit and efforts to promote ridesharing programs as air quality measures," the authors wrote. But "the automobile emissions problem is much more amenable to technological solutions . . . than to remedies that rely on transportation planning and policies based on radical changes in travel behavior."[53]

As firms and workers nationwide began to realize what was in store for them under the ECO program—an unfunded mandate—they began to complain loudly. Local and state elected officials joined the angry chorus. Following the Republican victory in the 1994 congressional elections, EPA concluded that it had to relent on the employee commute option, or a congressional backlash might lead to major revisions of the Clean Air Act itself. In January 1995 EPA renounced enforcement of the ECO sanctions, and the ECO program faded away in most areas.[54]

Road Pricing

Lack of regional institutions poses a major hurdle to another idea that has long been floating around in auto policy discussions: road pricing. The idea did not originate among anti-auto activists; it came from economists who applied their analytical tools to the problem of overcrowded highways.[55] Electric utilities, phone companies, and airlines successfully use peak-load pricing to shift demand to off-peak hours. Applied to highways, the same principle is called "congestion pricing." Fees are charged for road use during peak hours in order to reduce demand for rush-hour road space. The aim is to flatten demand at the peak, reduce highway congestion, and eliminate the economic losses of drivers' time that congestion entails. Supporters of road pricing say it could save billions in infrastructure costs by reducing the need to build new highway capacity.

Road pricing can be based on new electronic toll technology. Technological developments in automatic vehicle identification and electronic funds transfer make it feasible to impose road user charges without expensive (and traffic-slowing) toll booths to collect the fees.

The vanguard has picked up on road-use pricing as one way to make the auto pay more of its "true social costs." The last thing it wants, however, is a new system that merely makes traffic flow more smoothly. Its idea is to add pollution ("smog") charges to a base fee charged for all road use and then put time-of-day congestion charges on top of the pollution charge.[56] The smog charges might be assessed as part of a vehicle's annual state inspection on the basis of odometer readings of total vehicle miles traveled. In addition, the anti-auto vanguard wants the revenues from all congestion and pollution fees to be invested in alternate means of mobility such as public transit, bike paths and pedestrian facilities.[57]

Road pricing raises numerous practical problems, however. There are equity issues (the fees would impose a heavy burden on low-income motorists who must commute during rush hour) and privacy issues (the system might create and store data on where and when people drive their cars).[58] Should the revenues generated from the fees go to the general treasury, or to the states to pay for new roads and public transit, or to homeowners for property tax relief? The answers vary, but all observers agree on one thing: the key problem with road pricing is how to sell it to the voters. It is no coincidence that the pioneering experiences with road pricing took place in Singapore and Hong Kong—small, crowded Asian city-states with governments that did not have much of a need to cater to voters' concerns. And even in Hong Kong the government had to back off from an ambitious road pricing plan because of public opposition.[59]

Highway tolls per se are not the political problem. Motorists from New York to Chicago have been paying turnpike tolls for decades. Evidence shows that motorists will accept the new electronic toll technology rather readily. In 1993 the New York State Thruway introduced the "E-Z Pass" system based on electronic tags purchased by motorists. It has been adopted by the Triborough Bridge and Tunnel Authority and the Port Authority of New York and New Jersey, which also operates bridges and tunnels. The George Washington Bridge had 54 percent of its crossings paid for by E-Z Pass in 1997. The Holland and Lincoln tunnels had about 40 percent of trips paid electronically. At the end of 1997 there were some 1.8 million E-Z Pass electronic tags in use in the greater New York area. Soon the E-Z Pass system will be used on the New Jersey Turnpike and the Garden State Parkway, and it is expected to spread South to the Atlantic City Expressway and to Delaware.

Preliminary traffic analysis suggests that electronic toll collection has helped prevent a worsening of congestion on the New York region's bridges and tunnels.[60] But so far electronic toll collection has simply been a substitute for the old-fashioned, roll-down-the-window-and-hand-over-the-money method. It has not been used to support higher rush-hour pricing.

The political crunch will come when toll road, bridge, or tunnel authorities attempt to charge regular commuters higher fares during their morning and evening trips. Many bridge authorities around the country still offer commuters price discounts—exactly the wrong incentive from the point of view of congestion pricing. This has created an interest group that will loudly resist even the slightest move in the direction of rationing scarce road space by price. An even worse crunch will come when tolls are imposed on roads that have always been free. Who will impose the fares? A new regional traffic management authority with the power to levy tolls on "free" roads is bound to be so controversial that few regions will embark on it voluntarily. Could heavily congested and polluted regions be required to adopt regional congestion pricing by the federal government under threat of loss of federal highway funds? The employer trip reduction program suggests that EPA might be willing to consider such a possibility. But the response from most regions put under that kind of mandate is sure to be negative.

Despite economists' promises that road pricing is *the* solution to highway congestion, widespread adoption is unlikely. To succeed, any congestion pricing program must create more winners than losers.[61] Discrediting the whole notion of regional governance by ill-conceived and ineffective auto-restrictive measures serves no one's interest. If road pricing can improve the flow of traffic for most motorists without creating large losses for those who are "pushed off" the road, it might become a useful tool of traffic management in limited circumstances. But if road pricing is aimed at forcing people out of their cars, it will never achieve such a goal, because it will never be adopted.

The vanguard will continue to use its issue networks in Washington, D.C., to turn metro-area planning organizations into proponents of auto-restrictive policies. These efforts are certain to be politically controversial and administratively awkward. The road to regional governance does not run through restricting citizens' rights to use their automobiles.

The Search for "Home Town, U.S.A."

Urban planners are on a perennial search for a better balance between access and mobility, between the power of place and the freedom of movement. As for the New Urbanists, even their ardent supporters would not claim that they have produced the last word. It is clear, however, that their neotraditional design ideas have touched a chord, a postmodern yearning for the roots and reassurance of smaller, simpler communities like Bedford Falls in Frank Capra's *It's A Wonderful Life*. It is easy to see why planners as well as ordinary people would be attracted to this type of self-contained community.

The pull of small towns is more than just cinematic nostalgia, however. Two million more Americans moved from metropolitan areas to rural areas in the 1990s than migrated the other way! This appears to be predominantly a white, middle-class migration from "crowded" suburbs to small towns and rural areas.[62] If 2 million metropolitan citizens, most of them suburbanites, have moved to the "exurbs," and around 10,000 people have moved into New Urbanist developments, what does that tell us about who is winning the war on sprawl? How many exurbanites live in pedestrian pockets? How many drive a new pickup truck or sport utility vehicle? Will small-town sprawl be the next target for the rationalizers?

The ideas of the New Urbanists remind us that there are many modest ways to improve the spatial layout and transport connections of the new settlements built every year in America. Access can be improved without restricting mobility. Designing bike paths and pedestrian zones and creatively clustering homes and shops are useful ideas that deserve to be given a chance. These improvements will cost money, however, and they will not revolutionize land-use planning or lead most people to scrap their automobiles. The means available for people who want to enjoy the benefits of neotraditional picket fences and pedestrian pockets are the classic American ones: the opportunity to purchase them in the market, and the freedom to encourage their friends, neighbors, and fellow citizens to support their adoption by means of democratic political argument and local choice. The American metropolitan landscape has always been too lively and changeable for public planners and grand ideas to dominate for long. The decentralized nature of American communities and institutions will give individuals and groups with a better idea of how to solve people's transportation needs a chance to be heard.

— 7 —
TOWARD A POLITICS OF MOBILITY
"The Auto, Plus"

On the verge of the twenty-first century, disagreement about transportation policy abounds. Should auto travel be discouraged in order to reduce its negative environmental and social consequences? Or can Americans continue to rely on the automobile while working to improve its performance? How can transportation policymakers, opinion leaders, and the general public make sense of the differing values, interests, and policy recommendations? It is all quite confusing unless one has an organizing viewpoint that can relate the divergent opinions to a few central principles. Such a viewpoint is called a paradigm—an intellectual organizing stance that gives coherence to the complex choices in transportation policymaking. Paradigms function as destinations, road maps, and yardsticks. That is, they provide a goal to strive for, identify promising policies, and set standards for evaluating whether a given decision will lead to the goal.

Competing Paradigms in Transportation Policy

There are, broadly speaking, three paradigms of automobility in U.S. society: the anti-auto vanguard's paradigm, the intellectually fuzzy but widespread "status quo" paradigm, and what I call the "Auto, Plus" paradigm. In this concluding chapter I compare their values, strengths, and weaknesses. By sharpening the policy recommendations from the preceding chapters, I try to show the superior ability of the Auto, Plus viewpoint to analyze auto-related transportation policy issues. Only this paradigm can point the way toward effective policy responses, rather than toward deadlock or policy failure.

The Vanguard and the End of Automobility

The vanguard explicitly calls for a paradigm shift toward the values and policies it has sought for decades. Its goal is not the abolition of all cars, just a dramatic decline in their importance in the transportation system. It wants to end the "forced dependence" on the automobile that is necessary for full mobility and access in our society. But it goes far beyond seeking "balanced transportation" by improving public transit. Its remedy for every auto-related problem is less automobility. It relies heavily on making auto travel more expensive and less convenient and on moral exhortations about Americans' duty to carpool, walk, and eschew the suburbs. Its strengths are its proponents' commitment and its allure as something new and innovative. Its weakness is that its goal is defined by an elite and runs counter to deeply entrenched mass preferences and existing market forces.

Political Realism and the Auto, Plus

The Auto, Plus viewpoint stresses personal mobility and social access—the immense benefits that the auto provides to most Americans. It is committed to preserving these benefits, and it judges that the automobile is the best way of doing this. It also recognizes that, like any technology, automobiles can cause collective problems that require public action. It maintains that these specific problems should be addressed in ways that are cost effective, complement the strengths and achievements of the auto system, and enhance individuals' mobility choices.

The "plus" indicates many potential innovations in regulatory policy, in energy-efficient auto technology, in community design, and in alternate modes of transport. These innovations could reduce the social costs associated with the automobile without undermining its basic achievements. The Auto, Plus outlook recognizes the necessity of broad and durable public support for problem-solving actions. This means avoiding policies that are in direct confrontation with mass preferences on individual mobility choices, that are unnecessarily complex, and that are costly and difficult to administer in our decentralized federal system. It is "conservative" in the best sense of the term. That is, it seeks to conserve the benefits of automobility while addressing its problems and permitting as much room for alternative choices as is genuinely desired by individuals and communities.

Entrenched Interests and the Status Quo

The contrast between "the end of automobility" and the "status quo" paradigms is clear. But how does the Auto, Plus outlook differ from that of the status quo? In the first place, the status quo is not really a paradigm, at least not one that is as self-conscious as the other two. It is more narrow, concerned with the short-term view. It is articulated and defended mainly by entrenched interests. It is not much concerned with problems in the future, and it defines the future as that period of time beyond the next election or the next business cycle.

U.S. auto manufacturers are a classic bastion of the status quo. In the nineties their reliance on increasing sales of gas-guzzling sport utility vehicles took the fuel efficiency of the fleet backwards by exploiting a loophole in corporate average fuel economy (CAFE) standards. The status quo also finds much support among suburban politicians (home rule resistance to regional initiatives), big city mayors (support for pork barrel rail transit projects), and the driving public. But it is ineffective at formulating coherent policy responses to perennial problems (for example, traffic congestion), let alone newer "threats" such as global warming.

The Automobile, Plus: Pragmatic Analysis, Effective Policy Choices

Approaching discussions of the politics of mobility from the Auto, Plus perspective will help point the way to effective policy responses rather than political deadlock or policy failure. I start from the proposition that the

American people overwhelmingly want to retain the practical convenience and individual empowerment they get from their automobiles. The auto will therefore remain the dominant mode of surface transportation until something even better comes along to replace it. The Auto, Plus perspective recognizes that the transportation system in general and the auto system in particular have problems that need to be addressed by public policy. Identifying practical and politically effective remedies should be the goal of a new politics of mobility.

Of course, there will be disagreements over which problems are the most serious and over the distribution of the costs and benefits of the policies developed to address the problems. Whereas the vanguard emphasizes long-term, collective costs and proposes controversial auto-restrictive measures, Auto, Plus proponents acknowledge the vast benefits of automobility and try to influence the policy agenda accordingly. The average motorist wants politicians to reduce the current costs of his or her car, not create intrusive programs that raise those costs and restrict enjoyment of its benefits. By focusing debate on policy proposals that acknowledge the benefits the auto provides, the Auto, Plus approach will do a far better job of cost-benefit analysis than the other two paradigms.

This section presents problem assessments and policy recommendations in a variety of areas. I begin by considering from the Auto, Plus perspective two broad issues: sustainable transportation and global warming. I then address issue areas considered in chapters 2 to 6: fuel efficiency and emissions, gas taxes, the trust fund regime, road-use charges, public transportation and regional planning, fast trains and maglev technology, and finally the topic of biking, walking, and community design.

Sustainable Transportation

"Sustainable transportation" is a term that is much in vogue, the latest buzzword in the policy debate. It is an idea that is being pushed hard by the vanguard. It implies that the United States needs to reduce the amount of inputs (resources) that the automobile-dominated transportation system consumes so that it also can reduce the outputs (pollution, accidents, forced mobility). This presumably will bring the system into a better balance with nature and foster a sustainable community with a sustainable economy. Couched in such generalities, sustainable transportation hardly seems objectionable as a goal of automobile policy.

The concept of sustainable transportation, however, glosses over problems with the vanguard's agenda. In the first place it is too vague to be a useful goal of transportation policy. Even its advocates admit that they have difficulty defining what they mean by it. In her paper entitled "Sustainable Transportation: What Do We Mean and How Do We Get There?" Deborah Gordon of the Union of Concerned Scientists writes: "Sustainable transportation, it seems to me, is one of those slippery concepts like a 'sound economy' or a 'good school system.' All of us are for it, but no one is certain exactly what anyone else means by it."[1]

The best that she could do to define sustainable transportation was to say it involved changing people, changing technology, and changing prices. More than half of the paper is addressed to the question "how do we get there?" It turns out that the definition of sustainable transportation is largely a description of the vanguard's policy agenda. There is no "hard" scientific definition of sustainable transportation. As a specification of a system distinct from the existing one, sustainable transportation is scarcely more precise than this—less automobility than we have now and more of the alternative means of transport that the vanguard thinks we should have. Gordon writes that "environmental quality, energy efficiency, and aesthetics deserve as much attention in transportation policy debate as personal freedom, convenience, and safety. . . . [T]here must be options other than driving alone if the transportation system is to be ecologically sustainable."[2]

Nor are the proponents of sustainability able to offer credible predictions of when the present system will become unsustainable or what that would mean in precise terms. The closest they come to specifying what is unsustainable about the system now is their litany of its problems and costs. For example, Gordon sees a "host of societal problems" brought on by excessive automobility. They range from the indisputable (air pollution, traffic accidents, and congestion), to the dubious ("military costs to secure oil imports"), to the devilishly difficult to deal with (global warming). But the vanguard of the nineties is no closer than the prophets of the sixties to explaining the time frame for the collapse of the "unsustainable" car culture.

The automobile system has been nothing if not sustainable for about a century now. In America it has survived depressions, wars, energy and pollution crises, foreign industrial competition, and a thirty-year campaign of intellectual vilification and political attacks by a group of determined enemies. In every country that permits its citizens to own cars, the automobile soon becomes the most popular form of transportation, with people scrambling to own a car in spite of high taxes and bad roads. In light of this intense popularity and durability, and in light of the premature predictions of the auto's demise, calling an as yet nonexistent future system with fewer automobiles more sustainable than the present one would be laughable if it were not so successful a ploy in shaping the policy debate.

Sustainability is not science. It is not even a very useful policy goal since the concrete costs (and benefits) of moving toward this nebulous notion are poorly (and it must be said, tendentiously) presented by proponents. Sustainability is rhetoric designed to portray the vanguard's anti-auto preferences as the wave of the future, thus enhancing the acceptability of its elitist agenda among policymakers and opinion molders.

Global Warming

Many respected scientists take the greenhouse effect and the possibility of global warming seriously.[3] There have been high-profile international conferences attempting to determine how the nations of the world should respond to the potential danger it represents. Scenarios of what could happen if the Earth's temperature rises significantly have appeared prominently in the media and range from hurricanes and floods submerging Bangladesh to a new ice age descending on Europe and threatening mass starvation.[4] These dramatic possibilities have mobilized a sustained campaign by segments of the elites in North America and Europe to change the lifestyles of their fellow citizens.

I respectfully suggest, however, that one reason global warming excites so much interest is not the cold calculus of risk assessment, but the social values, reformist hopes, and aesthetic sensibilities of these elites. As global warming becomes fashionable in the issue-attention cycle, the vanguard uses it to push its anti-auto agenda. Global warming offers the chance for social reform, for doing something about the exploitative and materialistic lifestyle of the West, perhaps even for redistributing economic growth to the developing nations.

For the vanguard, global warming is the latest in a long list of problems it has skillfully used to press its case. Global warming even has some political advantages that those earlier problems (like smog and the energy crisis) did not possess. For example, it is not susceptible to a relatively easy technical solution. (Smog was sharply reduced by catalytic converters and other antipollution devices.) As long as cars have internal combustion engines that burn carbon-based fuels (or even motors powered by electricity generated from coal- or oil-fired plants), they will be associated with the production of carbon dioxide, the premier greenhouse gas culprit. In addition, global warming is not likely to be solved by short-term market adjustments. (The energy crises of the 1970s stimulated higher oil production in non-OPEC countries.)

Global warming is a long-term, collective problem involving the ultimate global commons. Constructing a regime to stabilize greenhouse gases in the atmosphere will require unprecedented international cooperation, which will take decades to have any effect at all. Until then, the problem permits the vanguard to remain in its prophetic mode—calling for repentance and for regulations intended to change our evil ways without offering realistic, affordable, and competitive alternatives to the automobile.

Into its policy equation the vanguard factors enormous collective benefits to be obtained in the future from avoiding global warming. At the same time it minimizes the very real present costs, disruptions, and dislocations of moving to its "sustainable" system with greatly reduced automobility. In 1990 the Intergovernmental Panel on Climate Change set a goal of reducing carbon dioxide emissions worldwide to 40 percent of the 1990 level. To achieve this goal, "the people of the OECD countries would have to reduce their CO_2 emissions by 86 percent, Americans by 91 percent," according to Marvin S. Soroos, an "environmental security" analyst sympathetic to international efforts to prevent climate change. Soroos is very concerned about global warming, but even he recognizes that "such Draconian reductions are clearly not feasible even over several decades."[5]

More attention needs to be given to the costs and benefits of proposed changes in policy. Certainly, environmental concerns should not be disregarded. Global warming is a serious matter warranting serious scientific scrutiny. But it is desirable to protect the benefits of automobility while protecting the environment. The Auto, Plus paradigm favors a "no regrets" approach to the greenhouse gas problem. Reasonable and cost-effective measures aimed at energy efficiency and carbon dioxide reductions should be our aim.[6] But hasty, ill-conceived, and unilateral responses to the still poorly understood threat of global warming could result in far greater economic costs than the floods and hurricanes they are supposed to prevent. The outcome of any U.S. actions designed to stabilize the global climate "depends upon the uncertain prospect that most other nations responsible for the rise in [greenhouse gas] concentrations would take similar steps."[7]

The worst outcome would be for the United States to make wrenching changes in its lifestyle, only to see China, India, Brazil, and other developing nations succumb to pressures for carbon-intensive industrial growth. Thus Americans could lose their automobiles and their suburbs and still get the hurricanes, floods, and droughts of global warming!

Policies should be evaluated on their own terms rather than on the terms of their contribution to achieving nebulous long-term collective benefits. The best yardstick for making such a practical evaluation is political. How will the policies be received by motorists (that is to say, voters)? Is the policy adoptable only in an atmosphere of crisis? Does its passage require major exceptions and loopholes that will undercut its effectiveness after the urgency has ebbed? Many of the measures passed during the energy crises of the 1970s were no longer in effect in the 1980s. For transportation policies to be effective, they must last long enough to shape people's lives and habits. Self-interest is the great American motivator, and policies that overlook that fact usually fail.

Fuel Efficiency and Emissions

If the goals are substantial reductions in automotive energy consumption and emissions levels, policies aimed at inducing auto manufacturers to design and market cleaner, more fuel efficient vehicles promise the biggest bang for the buck. The environmental payoffs for improving auto propulsion technology will be larger and more politically sustainable than virtually any policy that is politically feasible in other areas, such as fuel taxation, provision of alternative modes of transportation, or direct restrictions on auto use. As Daniel Sperling, a transportation energy use analyst, has noted:

> Technical fixes preserve the fundamental attractions of [auto] travel—mobility, convenience, and privacy—while requiring few behavioral changes. They support rather than subvert travelers' wishes and needs. Given . . . the huge promise of new technologies, the focus of any effort to create a more environmentally benign transportation system should be technical innovation.[8]

In fact, the United States has been the world leader in "technology-forcing" automobile regulations. The federal government adopted exhaust emissions standards nearly twenty years before most European countries, and American standards are still stricter than in any European country. The same is true for fuel efficiency standards.

Predictably, the auto industry will be the biggest hurdle to public policies aimed at making automobiles cleaner and more efficient. Detroit has always believed it can make the most profit by selling large, heavy, and expensive vehicles. From tail fins and muscle cars to minivans, pickups, and sport utility vehicles, bigger cars have meant bigger profits. Left to its own devices, Detroit will prefer to tap into the lucrative lode of consumer preferences for large, powerful cars than to undertake the risk and expense of introducing fuel efficient new vehicles. Thus Detroit cannot be simply left alone.

Does this mean that enhanced fuel efficiency and lower emissions will depend on a renewal of adversarialism between the government and the industry? Perhaps not, assuming that politicians and executives have learned something from the past thirty years. Detroit does not want to experience a second coming of Ralph Nader. And despite the ever-present temptation of media celebrity for individual members of Congress, the institution as a whole is not the fertile ground for political entrepreneurialism on automobile issues that it was in the 1960s, when those issues were still a novelty.

The automakers strongly oppose further increases in the corporate average fuel economy standards, believing that a hike would raise production costs, increase the price of their cars to consumers, and lower total sales, especially sales of their expensive and profitable sport utility vehicles and large luxury vehicles.[9] Indeed, they would prefer abolition of CAFE standards altogether. But since they were unable to accomplish this during the Detroit-friendly Reagan administration, they have judged abolition politically unlikely and have not pressed very hard for it. In addition, the automakers strongly oppose state-level requirements to manufacture and sell significant numbers of electric vehicles. Needless to say, California's zero emission vehicle (ZEV) mandate discussed in chapter 3 was not very popular. Their basic position is this: "If electric vehicles are desirable and can be marketed and sold at a fair price . . . mandates are not needed. . . . If electric vehicles are not marketable, mandates could create distorted markets with severe adverse unintended consequences."[10] They fear having to sell subsidized electrics far below their cost, driving up the cost of gasoline-powered cars and lowering sales. They claim mandates might even lead to "gray markets" with cheap, used internal combustion engine cars flowing into California and subsidized electric cars flowing out of the state to be resold at a higher price elsewhere.

The auto companies would prefer to continue the kind of research collaboration represented by the Partnership for a New Generation of Vehicles (see chapter 3), especially when there is little pressure to actually produce the vehicles and propulsion systems. But the leaders of the auto industry today are much more politically astute than the leaders thirty years ago. They realize that, in the face of an upsurge of public concern over greenhouse gases and global warming, they cannot stand pat and refuse to cooperate. The technology for improving fuel efficiency and reducing emissions is available, and Detroit's executives are aware that the government knows it.[11] They see the advantages of compromise more readily than did the old bulls that Nader faced in his 1960s *corrida*.[12] They would be willing to offer some cooperation in return for less punitive and more flexible regulations. Indeed, in 1998 the automakers publicly promised to produce "superclean" cars (low emission vehicles, or LEVs) in return for assurances that other states would not follow California's lead and demand zero emission vehicles.[13]

In a crunch Congress has no stomach for levying massive fines and insisting on compliance deadlines that could cost thousands of autoworkers their jobs. Members know that in dealing with Detroit they must have both carrots and sticks. If the stick is higher federal fuel-economy standards, the carrot must be flexibility in meeting the standards and perhaps a chance to participate in designing the new regulations.

How high could the new negotiated standards be? Increases in CAFE standards up to 36 miles per gallon for passenger cars and 27.5 miles per gallon for light trucks would be cost effective under most fuel price assumptions.[14] Detroit would be reluctant to go that far with the kind of CAFE rules in force today. The key to getting an effective increase in federal fuel-economy standards will be flexibility. Manufacturers must be permitted to continue marketing their profitable lines of sport utility vehicles and minivans while making steady progress toward improved overall fuel efficiency.

One simple way to do this would be to give auto manufacturers "carryover" credits: if they exceeded the standards in their automobile fleet, they could use the credits on their light truck fleet. A more complex possibility might be "carryover" between the emissions standards area and the fuel economy area. Perhaps companies that received credits for meeting a ZEV quota could use them to offset fuel economy shortfalls in their conventional car or light truck fleets. For example, for every ZEV unit sold, an automaker could count the sale of a 17.5 miles per gallon sport utility vehicle as if it were a 27.5 miles per gallon vehicle. Or a trading system could be instituted whereby a small new company that specialized in manufacturing electric ZEVs would receive a transferable credit that it could then sell to a full-line manufacturer to be counted toward the large company's ZEV quota. GM might find it initially cheaper to buy such quota credits than to actually incur the cost of building electric cars. And small electric vehicle makers would be encouraged by the extra source of income the scheme offered them. Later General Motors could simply buy a successful electric vehicle manufacturing company and use its established sales to meet its own quota.

Other creative ways of making fuel economy standards more flexible could certainly be found. For example, manufacturers and car dealers could market special packages promoting "green" sales: a customer buys a fuel efficient vehicle but is guaranteed the use (for a certain number of free or reduced cost days) of a sport utility vehicle or pickup truck when he needs to take the boat up to the lake or move cousin Joe across town. There has been a lot of talk, especially by the vanguard, about "community-based" ways of enabling people to have access to cars without having to own one individually. But so far there has been little action. The best way to get moving along these lines would be to take the effort out of the hands of energy activists and environmentalists and put it into the hands of people who know how to market cars.

There are far more possibilities for innovative combinations of incentives and regulations than can be mentioned here. But the incentives and regulations that go into the mix must be in the form of broad performance criteria that can be met by a range of technologies. They cannot be tailored to one kind of propulsion system. For example, if the specifications were uniquely designed for battery-powered electric vehicles, they might inhibit the development of hybrid-electric or hydrogen-fueled vehicles. Broad criteria will allow as much room as possible for market forces and consumer preferences to operate, and avoid the pitfall of prematurely picking a technology that turns out to be less valuable than originally thought.

Gas Taxes

In a curious convergence of opinion, the vanguard and the major U.S. auto manufacturers both favor increasing gasoline taxes to reduce automotive energy consumption. Detroit's position is that higher gas taxes are preferable to higher federal CAFE standards. One industry-sponsored study concluded that higher gasoline taxes could achieve the same level of reductions in petroleum consumption as increased CAFE standards at 40 percent less cost.[15] Paul McCarthy, a research economist at Ford Motor Company in the mid-1990s, called higher fuel taxes "the great under-explored conservation policy in the United States."[16]

Is Detroit's support of gas tax hikes a cynical public relations gamble—taken because it knows that the political chances of major increases are exceedingly slim? Perhaps, but it is also completely logical in terms of J. Q. Wilson's typology of policies discussed in chapter 2. It comes down to a question of shifting the burden of costs and benefits. If policies to improve automotive fuel efficiency are adopted, the industry prefers that the costs of those policies be spread widely over motorists and taxpayers, rather than concentrated narrowly on itself.

If Detroit does not want higher CAFE standards, but says it does want higher gasoline taxes, why not give it an incentive to work for gas tax increases? Why not explicitly link progress up the ladder to higher CAFE standards to progress on increasing motor fuel taxes? There is a precedent for this kind of link. Transportation secretary Elizabeth Dole built a so-called "trapdoor" into the department's airbag regulations in the mid-1980s. If two-thirds of the states adopted mandatory seat belt laws, auto manufacturers would not have to install airbags. With that incentive, Detroit lobbied hard for seat belt laws in state legislatures across the country.[17] Similarly, a scheduled increase in CAFE standards could be postponed if gas taxes rose to a certain level. This would provide an incentive for Detroit to "put its money where its mouth is" and to lobby the U.S. Congress and the state legislatures in support of gas tax increases that have the equivalent effect of the scheduled hike in CAFE. If the gas taxes go up, the standards do not. This innovative linkage would help bypass the contentious and ultimately fruitless debate over whether regulations or taxes are more effective in bringing about energy efficiency. In either case, higher CAFE standards or higher gas taxes, Detroit would have an equal incentive to pursue improvements in the fuel efficiency of its vehicles.

The Trust Fund Regime: Time for a Change

There remains the question of what to do with the revenues from any hike in gasoline taxes. If there ever was an issue in need of a paradigm shift, it is the "ownership" of the gasoline taxes motorists pay. The trust fund regime, wonderfully useful in building highways in the interstate era, is increasingly problematic now that the great period of highway promotion policy is over. The problem is what to put in its place.

The vanguard recommends large ($1.00 per gallon) increases in the gas tax to discourage driving and to force the automobile to pay its social and environmental costs. At the same time the vanguard calls for large cuts in road spending, with the funds transferred to transit and other modes. These prescriptions will be fiercely resisted by supporters of the status quo; they want to keep all gas tax revenues dedicated to the trust fund and spend more on highways. The impasse leaves little room for innovative initiatives and tends to protect the pork that has crept into the highway program over the years.

The Auto, Plus paradigm recognizes that the institutional durability of the trust fund regime is now a drawback rather than an asset. Any serious effort to implement intermodal transportation policies will require the decoupling of gas taxes from the political and administrative straitjacket imposed by the trust fund regime. Historically, gas tax hikes have come in increments of pennies or nickels per gallon. There is little chance gasoline taxes will suddenly be raised by the vanguard's $1.00 per gallon. What needs to change are the rigid requirements of the trust fund regime that hold down gas tax levels and prevent other public programs from receiving gas tax revenues.

The best way to move beyond the trust fund regime is to establish a new principle: taxing motor fuels for revenue, not for roads. Only legislators' thirst for money to fund their favorite programs is potentially strong enough to defeat the principle of exclusive dedication.[18] Pressures for adequate general revenues succeeded, temporarily, in producing the modest 2.5 cents and 4.3 cents per gallon hikes in the Bush budget deal and the Clinton program of 1993. Those revenues were subsequently restored to the trust fund, but the precedent for "diversion" has been set.[19] Making gasoline taxes into an accepted source of general revenues will gradually result in the automobile paying more of its "true costs" as desired by its adversaries. Indeed, European gas taxes, so much admired by the vanguard, got to be as high as they are because national governments needed the money, not because they were trying to keep motorists off the roads and in public transit.[20]

Practical steps are needed to establish the principle of motor fuel taxation for general revenue. Most likely they will entail political compromises with the still powerful interests benefiting from the trust fund regime. It will probably be necessary to "grandfather" or guarantee the existing level of appropriations to highway and transit spending programs to reassure their stakeholders that they will not face abrupt declines in federal support.

It is time to end the sterile debates over whether to take the trust fund off budget and devote more energy to substantive issues of transportation policy and to making U.S. automotive design more energy efficient. Moving beyond the trust fund regime will oblige transportation officials and legislators to be more parsimonious in the planning and selection of highway and transit projects. Fewer pork barrel, overdesigned, and overbudget projects may be the good result.

In fact, the era of funding highway programs by dedicated taxation of motor fuels may eventually end for technical as well as political reasons. Internal combustion engine cars are becoming more efficient under pressure from new propulsion technologies such as the electric, hybrid-electric, and fuel-cell-powered vehicles. Consequently, gasoline consumption will level off and begin to decline and so will gas tax revenues. Either taxes on the shrinking base of petroleum fuels will have to escalate sharply, or new revenue streams will have to be brought on line. Perhaps this will open the door to road-use charges by means of electronic fare collection. It is conceivable, indeed likely, that before the middle of the new century the issue of dedicating gasoline taxes to highway trust funds will have been superseded by the issue of electronic road-use charges. What kinds of road-use fees should be imposed? Who should collect them? How should they be spent?

The custom of dedicating revenues from auto-user fees exclusively to highways will undoubtedly play a role in such debates. For the time being, tolls are collected by independent authorities in charge of bridges, tunnels, and turnpikes. Even with perfected toll collection technology, these decentralized and fragmented authorities will have every incentive to resist being submerged in a road-pricing authority that is national or region wide. They will surely oppose having such an authority dictate their policies on toll levels and toll spending. Their interest is to maximize their revenues and maintain their credit rating. At present few central cities and even fewer regions in the United States have toll authorities that could plan and execute a city-wide or region-wide system of integrated transportation management based on congestion pricing of key roads, bridges, and tunnels.

Public Transportation and Regional Planning

Railroads and electric rail transit once had the power to shape the growth of dense, centralized cities. That power is now gone. It began to fade as early as the 1920s, when the automobile and the motorbus became the key transport modes shaping development on the periphery of U.S. cities. By the 1950s the auto also had become the dominant mode of travel within U.S. central cities, except for a handful of the very largest. By then the automobile was the mode that merited the designation of "mass transit," while subways and buses were left with a shrinking number of riders and passenger miles. Despite more than $140 billion in federal, state, and local subsidies since 1964, public transit continues to lose market share to the automobile. Interestingly, the vanguard supporting the end of automobility and the big city politicians supporting the status quo both maintain that transit and the central cities could make a comeback together if only more public subsidies were provided.

But public policy cannot recreate the past. As long as people are free enough and wealthy enough to own automobiles, no amount of public investment in transit can stop sprawl and recentralize America's cities. The most that can be expected is that new-rail transit investments combined with land-use planning will modestly influence development in the immediate area of the rail stations and attract some additional riders to the transit system. The new riders will almost certainly not be enough to pay for the system's operating cost (not to mention the capital costs), and they will probably not even be enough to increase transit's modal split of passenger miles vis-à-vis the automobile.

In May 1997 transit industry leaders and transportation professionals met for three days under the auspices of the Transit Cooperative Research Program to "search for new paradigms" for public transportation. Their report, *Reinventing Public Transportation*, admitted that "the transit industry needs to be reinvigorated and transformed—to break out of its entrenched practices . . . to consider bold, new services and innovations." The industry's traditional customers, suburb-to-downtown commuters and people without cars, represent a declining share of the travel market. Transit agencies must redefine their role from operating fleets of vehicles to coordinating delivery of a portfolio of services. The report recommended that they become "mobility managers," overseeing customer-friendly delivery of transportation services, including jitneys and car pools, which could be operated by public organizations, private contractors, cooperatives, or voluntary organizations. Drawing on advanced information technologies, transit must become "at least as smart, if not smarter, than its chief competitor, the private car."[21]

Outsmarting (as well as out-accommodating and out-speeding) the car will be a tall order, probably an impossible one. Despite the report's brave rhetoric about bold new services and innovations, it acknowledged the need for more competition and more participation by the private sector—"language reminiscent of pronouncements . . . during the Reagan era."[22] The industry is not counting on significant increases in federal transit spending to be the agent of its rejuvenation. Traditional transit systems will continue to have a role supporting the central business districts of large cities. The role of transit in serving and shaping suburban development, despite the hopes of the new paradigm seekers, is weak and is not likely to become any stronger.

What about the possibility that in at least some U.S. cities the forces of regionalism could succeed and "force feed" new customers onto transit using a combination of strict land-use controls and restrictions on automobile use? I argued in chapter 6 that there are not many U.S. metropolitan areas where conditions are ripe for a regional authority with enough power to pull off such a dramatic modal shift. The "metropolitan paradox" is a great obstacle. To pursue effective policies, metro regions "must . . . command popular and elite consensus, yet regional bodies whose policies go beyond the bounds of consensus are apt to lose their viability."[23]

The problem is that the kind of planning, land-use, and auto-restrictive powers needed to stem the tide of automobility are, literally, un-American. For years many American transportation analysts, including myself, expressed admiration for the modern and well-patronized urban transit systems in Europe.[24] But most of the admirers did not fully grasp how difficult it would be to imitate Europe's successes. They did not understand that it was not just a question of more subsidies or better transit technology. As early as 1981 I pointed out that West Germany's greater success at protecting and rejuvenating its urban transit was attributable to a number of advantages that were difficult to replicate in the United States. These included greater population densities at the national and metropolitan levels, stronger land-use control laws and institutions, greater ease of constructing metro-area planning authorities, much higher gasoline taxes, and a lower level of car ownership. I noted that Germany, and most of the other West European nations, began to protect transit before people's travel habits, location decisions, and living patterns adjusted to doing without transit. Once that happens (the case in the United States), it is much more difficult to restore transit and the compact settlements that support it.[25]

Since then several other North American researchers, notably John Pucher and Anthony Perl, have developed in-depth studies detailing just how great the policy and institutional differences between Europe and the United States are in the area of transit, railroads, and the automobile.[26] But an interesting phenomenon has taken place in the past twenty years: while many Americans were wishing, vainly, that the United States could become more like Europe, Europe became more like us! Auto ownership has been growing at a faster rate in Europe than in the United States, and suburban development is proceeding apace.

Although the United States led the way in shifting from public transportation to the car, Western Europe has been "following the American example for the past two decades, and Eastern Europe is now following the example of Western Europe."[27] This was the conclusion reached by John Pucher and a French colleague, Christian Lefèvre, in a recent comparative study. Transit's modal split is declining everywhere in Europe, and people and jobs are rapidly moving out to the suburbs in what has been called "Eurosprawl."[28] As opponents of sprawl, Pucher and Lefèvre take some comfort in the fact that, so far, "suburbanization is occurring in Europe . . . at a much higher density than in the USA." But they are alarmed that "France and England are showing increasing signs of 'ex-urban' development (the rapid growth of distant towns and rural areas not contiguous to the built-up metropolitan area)."[29]

According to Pucher and Lefèvre, only a few European countries—the Netherlands, Germany, and Switzerland—can really be said to have adopted successful policies to protect transit. These are the countries that have gone the farthest down the road to placing heavy taxes and direct restrictions on autos. The Netherlands is the most densely populated country in Europe. With their famous dikes the Dutch have reclaimed much of their land from the North Sea. ("God made the world, but the Dutch made Holland," they say.) How different that is from America! Switzerland is a lovely country, with almost all of its population squeezed into the *Mittelland*, the plateau comprising less than one-third of the national territory between the Jura mountains and the Alps.[30] Would the citizens of Kansas City submit to the dictates of Swiss- or Dutch-style land-use controls, traffic-calming measures, and parking prohibitions? Even the burghers of Belgium, Holland's next-door neighbors, will not. So the Brussels agglomeration continues to sprawl out into the Brabant countryside. If many European cities and countries, with all their legal, historical, and geographical advantages for urban transit, have been steadily losing ground to the great democratic demand for automobility, there is not much chance that these policies are the answer to America's auto-related problems.

Fast Trains and Maglev Technology

Why has the United States lagged so far behind other nations in protecting its intercity passenger trains and in deploying the new fast trains like the TGV in France, the Shinkansen in Japan, and the ICE in Germany? After World War II, European and Japanese governments saw rebuilding and strengthening their nationalized rail systems as the key to their postwar reconstruction. They continued a steady stream of public investment in their rail sectors even after prosperity returned in the fifties and sixties. They did not institutionally separate freight service from passenger service, and the passenger side of railroading remained a large part of the total business of these publicly owned entities. In the seventies and eighties, although economists worried about the growing burden of rail subsidies, European and Japanese national railroads had sufficient political strength, operating acumen, and technological support from their rail equipment manufacturers to launch their rejuvenation of passenger service based on fast trains.[31]

In the United States, as chapter 5 explained, all of these advantages were absent. Intercity passenger rail service since 1971 has limped along under the flawed Amtrak regime. Even in the Northeast Corridor, one of the few places where Amtrak has retained a substantial level of service, its contribution is not really comparable to the European networks' performance. For example, Amtrak brings far fewer intercity passengers into New York, a city of 7 million, than the French National Railways brings into Paris, a city of 2 million inhabitants. Amtrak has rolled the dice and expended its last reserves of cash and credit on its Northeast Corridor improvement program and its purchase of new high-speed trains (although they will not go as fast as the European or Japanese fast trains). Unless this new service along the Northeast Corridor doubles the passengers and the revenues as Amtrak hopes, the corporation might well go bankrupt.

With the Amtrak passenger rail regime hanging on by a thread, the prospects are mediocre for creating a new regime of public-private partnerships to rejuvenate conventional steel wheel on rail service, even in the corridors that have been identified as the most promising. The vanguard has been tepid in its support of high-speed rail initiatives in the United States. It is concerned that newly built HSR lines might be nearly as intrusive as highways. Insofar as HSR proposes to spend a lot of money to enable people to go very far very fast, it conflicts with the vanguard's desire to substitute access for mobility.

In promising HSR corridors the Auto, Plus paradigm recommends well-planned investment where it could support existing high-density cities and help relieve highway and airport congestion. But there are fewer than half a dozen such corridors outside the Northeast. Given that limited geographical base, the political prospects for a major federal aid program for HSR are dim. States and private investors will have to take the lead in promoting high-speed rail. This will slow the speed of new fast train projects. But it will mean that those that do get built will be aimed at real transportation markets, not just at attracting federal subsidies.

The prospects are even dimmer for creating a benefits regime to promote magnetic levitation trains. Maglev, both its German and its Japanese versions, works. At least it can run trains on test tracks quite well. But it has yet to be tested in large-scale commercial service. The U.S. federal government has canceled its plans for a national maglev initiative to develop a home-grown American version of the technology. This has disappointed those who had been pushing maglev: consultants, equipment manufacturers, university researchers, and local politicians looking to sell their towns as a destination. But few other groups, including especially private investors, have expressed a willingness to expend much money or political effort promoting maglev. It is a solution looking for a problem, and no one has been able to find a transportation problem that could not be dealt with by simpler, less costly solutions. Maglev is a futuristic technology that may remain just over the horizon until it becomes obsolete.[32]

Bicycling, Walking, and Community Design

Walking and bicycling are low-tech, environmentally friendly, and relatively inexpensive technologies for which the vanguard has high hopes. Enthusiasts for these modes point out that in certain European countries pedestrians and cyclists account for 30 to 40 percent of daily trips, while in the United States the figure is below 10 percent.[33] Their goal is to increase the market share of walking and biking in the United States until it comes closer to the European range.

Actions to improve the lot of two-legged and two-wheeled transportation are commendable insofar as they add to the mobility choices available to individuals and improve access for all. In fact, they are part of the "Plus" in the Auto, Plus policy vision. The relatively small amounts of money that may become available through interstate surface transportation legislation can certainly be used to enhance the attractiveness of walking and biking in many neighborhoods, as can purely local funding. The Auto, Plus paradigm does not even object to the imposition of reasonable changes in auto traffic regulations to free up some of the street for cyclists and pedestrians. This is America, of course, and what is reasonable will be determined in "dialogues" (to put it gently) between streets departments, city councils, cyclist groups, and pedestrian forces across the country.[34]

Given the tremendous sunk costs represented by the highways, housing, shopping malls, and office parks in our decentralized metro areas, retrofitting existing communities will be a slow process. Designing bike paths and pedestrian facilities into new communities built on holistic, neotraditional principles is easier. But until now the New Urbanism has been overhyped and underbuilt. If its products become more attractive and economically competitive, perhaps the world will indeed build a (bike) path to its door. But political realism should temper excessive optimism. Biking and walking can reduce the total need for auto travel only slightly. People may be glad to bike a mile to the village center, but biking ten miles to work is an entirely different matter. At best, bike paths, pedestrian zones, and new community designs can improve access in local neighborhoods. For access to the wider metropolitan community, the auto will still be the means most people will use.

The Problem of the Carless

What about the critics who charge that sprawl has contributed mightily to the growth of a poverty-ridden underclass isolated in urban ghettos and cut off from middle-class society and suburban economic opportunities? Many of the urban poor cannot afford car ownership, and existing transit service connects them to the new jobs in the "edge cities" poorly or not at all. This has created a "spatial mismatch" between the people who need entry-level jobs and the employers who need workers to fill them. Research has shown, for example, that the proportion of regional jobs within ten miles of the center of Newark, New Jersey, dropped from 62 percent in 1960 to 40 percent in 1988.[35] Many in the vanguard see this as a strong argument to restore a centralized metropolis served by public transit. Physical proximity will help bring the whole community together to solve its social problems. The middle class will not be allowed the easy escape of automobility and will have to face up to its responsibilities. Social justice demands an end to auto-induced sprawl, the vanguard says.

A transportation technology should not be made a scapegoat for deep-rooted social pathologies, however. Automobiles are not responsible for the crime, drug abuse, fatherless families, and execrable schools that produce so much of the inner cities' misery. As a practical matter, the solution to the access problems of the carless should not be to reorganize society's land-use and transportation patterns to make access less convenient for the vast majority of citizens who do own cars. Nor should the response be to build expensive new-rail systems from the ghetto to the urban fringe to facilitate the transition from welfare to work. The most effective (and least expensive) solution to the problems of the carless poor is to make automobile-based mobility alternatives more widely available by means of user-side "mobility subsidies" for the truly needy. Reliance on producer-side subsidies for massive public transit monopolies that cannot compete with the automobile for most trips most of the time is a recipe for financial failure in transit and continued frustration among the carless.

The most automobile-like public transit mode, taxicabs, already carries more passengers than all of the other kinds of public transit in the nation put together. Taxis provide service that is superior to regular public transit for most destinations for the elderly, the handicapped, business persons, and tourists. The main drawback of taxis for poor people is cost—the fare averages about five times higher per mile than transit.[36] Transportation economists have argued that existing regulations limit competition in the taxi industry enough to peg fares at artificially high levels. Restrictions on entry into the taxi business have given rise to a black market in so-called "gypsy" cab service. Illegal taxis often flourish in low-income black neighborhoods that legal cab companies serve poorly or not at all.[37]

Deregulation of taxi service could promote competition, lower fares, and improve service in minority neighborhoods. The benefits would be greater if deregulation permitted more private jitney, paratransit vans, and express shuttle buses to compete in the market for urban transit services.[38] As noted earlier, even transit leaders are seeking a new paradigm for their industry. They have recognized that they need to start delivering services more like the automobile if they want to be players in the decentralized metropolis. Once a significant portion of transit services is provided in the form of paratransit, vanpools, and jitneys, there is little justification for retaining a centralized, monopolistic structure to deliver those services. Deregulation becomes harder to resist on public interest grounds.

Coupling deregulation of the urban transit market with user-side mobility vouchers provided by social service agencies would give the carless access to a level of urban mobility that is closer to automobile quality than to conventional transit.[39] Targeting public subsidies directly to those who need them most avoids the problem of public transit assistance funds subsidizing rail service for high-income commuters and wage increases for well-paid unionized bus drivers and mechanics. It would certainly cost the public treasury much less money than attempting to run conventional rail or bus transit to the myriad of dispersed destinations in today's metro areas. Trying to provide adequate mobility to the carless in the current metropolitan environment by means of 1910-style fixed-route public transit service is like trying to provide adequate communications capability by means of an Underwood manual typewriter: it can do a very basic job, but the quality and convenience of the product cannot compete in an environment that has become adapted to networked personal computers.

Preserving Automobility, Improving Automobiles

Americans should be decidedly skeptical about the vanguard's project of promoting a major shift away from automobility as the dominant form of surface transportation in this country. Past experience teaches that public policy can accelerate a shift that is already under way. For example, the interstate highway program in 1956 gave added impetus to the rising dominance of the auto. Public policy also can attempt to slow a modal shift. The Urban Mass Transportation Act of 1964, for example, sought to slow transit's decline. But public policy alone cannot produce a modal shift without a suitable new transportation technology to take the place of the old one. In past modal shifts the rising new technology had inherent technical advantages (higher speed, greater capacity, lower costs) and a benefits regime that attracted strong political support. The most notable effect of previous modal shifts was a major reorganization in settlement patterns as new territories were opened up. The railroads helped settle the western frontier, and the automobile shifted population to the "crabgrass frontier" of the suburbs.

At this point in American transportation and for the foreseeable future, no technology has enough advantages vis-à-vis the car to displace the automobile-highway system. Therefore, it does not make economic, environmental, or political sense to try to reduce problems associated with the automobile by trying to resuscitate alternate modes of travel that the car has long since vanquished for most trips. That is like trying to put out a fire by seeding the clouds instead of turning the fire hoses directly on the burning building. If automobiles have undesirable emissions and energy problems, it is far better to address those problems by improving the performance of automotive technology than by attempting to prop up the auto's defeated rivals.

Worse yet are the proposals to roll back the tide of automobility by systematically restricting the masses of individual motorists. An example is the employer trip reduction program. These regulations are reminiscent of a British law passed at the dawn of the automobile age that required a motorist bringing his car to town to be preceded by a man with a red flag to warn pedestrians and horse and buggy drivers.[40] It is one thing for local communities to try to enhance their attractiveness by promoting a pedestrian-friendly environment. That has always been their prerogative. Few American towns have been able to implement truly stringent anti-auto policies for very long because it generally does not pay. But it is quite another matter for lawmakers and bureaucrats in Washington, D.C., to threaten employers with fines or states with loss of their federal-aid highway funds if they fail to comply with auto-restrictive measures. The mandates are unpopular, and the transportation control measures are ineffective.

Federal efforts to promote innovations in the management of roads and highways, rail lines and buses, should rely less on new national spending programs and new regulations laid down in Washington. The money (what little there is) gets spread too thinly across this vast continent, and the regulations impede local innovation and experimentation. A more useful federal role would be to offer incentives for innovations in the context of a genuine policy experiment. Washington should provide matching funds and seed money for limited local initiatives in congestion pricing, ride-sharing arrangements, intermodal facilities, deregulation of transit and paratransit, and the like. The intent of the legislation would be true demonstration programs, not pork barrel projects. The federal government also should ensure that the results of these jointly funded experiments are care-

fully and independently evaluated. Then the information on notable successes can be widely disseminated to states and communities to be implemented, adapted, or rejected according to their own needs. It is cheaper to
experiment and evaluate than to fund nationwide programs or to mandate
that local governments and private businesses fund programs. Had California's Regulation XV employee ride-sharing program been treated as a
careful experiment, objectively evaluated on its ability to reduce air pollution and traffic congestion, and adjusted over a period of years, it could
have warned Washington that a federally mandated ride-sharing program
was headed for big trouble.

The Auto, Plus approach to transportation policy has one great advantage: it recognizes that the car is *the solution* to the mobility needs of the
vast majority of Americans. Although it acknowledges the problems created by the auto's massive success, it insists on remedies that preserve the
automobile's benefits. In this way the Auto, Plus paradigm avoids a number of common policy pitfalls.

First, the car should not be blamed for problems it did not cause. For
example, the automobile did not cause the poverty, crime, and welfare de-
pendency that plague our cities. In fact, access to a reliable car is one of the
best tools for getting out of poverty and staying out.

Second, policy "solutions" should be avoided that assume it is possible
to shift a significant share of travel to nonautomotive modes. A program to
reduce air pollution by increasing ridership on buses and subways will fail
to reduce air pollution. Most likely it will not even increase transit
ridership. But even if it did, car travel will increase more.

Third, the federal government should not give states and local communities an ever-widening number of regulatory mandates and threats to cut
off their federal highway dollars. Give them more flexibility in how to use
their federal assistance funds and more practical information about how to
implement innovative choices. We need not fear that they will abandon investment in their automotive infrastructure. But we can hope that they will
be able to implement their own modest initiatives for intermodal connections, bike paths, and perhaps even ride-sharing more effectively than they
would under inevitably resented national regulations from Washington.

The most effective policy response to the truly pressing auto-related
problems is not to discourage people from using their cars. Rather, it is to
encourage improvement in the technology of the auto itself. It is easier and
more politically sustainable to use Washington's arsenal of powers and incentives against Detroit than against tens of millions of citizen-motorists.

From the creation of the jeep in World War II to the airbag-equipped, CAFE-conforming fleet of passenger cars today, the U.S. auto industry has proved that it can adapt to the country's needs and demands. The American people want, not the end of automobility, but the kinds of new automobiles that will be able to meet their individual and collective needs as far into the twenty-first century as anyone can reasonably foresee.

NOTES

Chapter One

1. American Automobile Manufacturers Association, *Motor Vehicle Facts and Figures 1996* (Washington, D.C.: 1996), p. 32. Note that a change in the definitions of trucks and cars makes the data discontinuous in recent years.

2. See, for example, Peter Marsh and Peter Collet, *Driving Passion: The Psychology of the Car* (Boston and London: Faber and Faber, 1986).

3. See, for example, Deborah Gordon, *Steering a New Course: Transportation, Energy, and the Environment* (Washington, D.C.: Island Press, 1991); and Michael Renner, *Rethinking the Role of the Automobile* (Washington, D.C.: Worldwatch Institute, 1988).

4. Sudhir Chella Rajan, *The Enigma of Automobility: Democratic Politics and Pollution Control* (University of Pittsburgh Press, 1996).

5. Paul Froiland, Beverly Gerber, and Jack Gordon, "Baby, You Can't Drive Your Car," *Training* 31 (January 1994): 126–28; and "Carpooling: Convenient Today, Mandatory Tomorrow?" *Supervisory Management* 39 (July 1994): 10.

6. A number of commentators have noted that "the sixties," as a period of political and cultural upheaval, really run from November 22, 1963, the date of President John F. Kennedy's assassination, to the August 9, 1974, resignation of President Richard Nixon.

7. For two well-known accounts of the counterculture and the social changes of the era while they were happening, see Theodore Rozack, *The Making of a*

Counterculture (Doubleday, 1969); and Charles Reich, *The Greening of America* (Random House, 1970). For a more retrospective view, see Todd Gitlin, *The Sixties: Years of Hope, Days of Rage* (Bantam Books, 1987).

8. Sherman Paul, *Repossessing and Renewing: Essays in the Green American Tradition* (Louisiana State University Press, 1976).

9. See Jane Jacobs, *The Death and Life of American Cities* (Random House, 1961); and Lewis Mumford, *The Highway and the City* (Harcourt, Brace, 1963). See also Mark Luccarelli, *Lewis Mumford and the Ecological Region: The Politics of Planning* (New York: Guilford Press, 1995).

10. John Keats, *The Insolent Chariots* (Philadelphia: Lippincott, 1958); A. Q. Mowbray, *Road to Ruin* (Philadelphia: Lippincott, 1969); Helen Leavitt, *Super-highway-Superhoax* (Doubleday, 1970); Kenneth R. Schneider, *Autokind vs. Mankind* (Norton, 1971); and Tabor R. Stone, *Beyond the Automobile* (Prentice-Hall, 1971).

11. James J. Flink, "Three States of American Automobile Consciousness," *American Quarterly* 24 (October 1972): 451–73.

12. James J. Flink, *The Car Culture* (MIT Press, 1975), p. 233.

13. Emma Rothschild, *Paradise Lost: The Decline of the Auto-Industrial Age* (Random House, 1973), pp. 245–47, 250.

14. U.S. Congress, Senate, Committee on the Judiciary, Subcommittee on Antitrust and Monopoly, *Industrial Reorganization Act Hearings on S. 1167*, 93 Cong. 2 sess, appendix to pt. 4: Bradford C. Snell, "American Ground Transportation: A Proposal for Restructuring the Automobile, Truck, Bus and Rail Industries," pp. A1–A103.

15. Ibid., pp. A-55, A-56.

16. For a recent restatement of Snell's antitrolley conspiracy thesis, see Stephen B. Goddard, *Getting There: The Epic Struggle between Road and Rail in the American Century* (Basic Books, 1994), pp. 130–35.

17. "Statement of George W. Hilton, professor of economics, University of California at Los Angeles," *Industrial Reorganization Act Hearings*, pt. 4, p. 2204.

18. Scott Bottles, "Mass Politics and the Adoption of the Automobile in Los Angeles," in *The Car and the City*, ed. Martin Wachs and Margaret Crawford (University of Michigan Press, 1989), pp. 194, 195. The chapter was adapted from Scott Bottles, *Los Angeles and the Automobile* (University of California Press, 1987).

19. Sy Adler, "The Transformation of the Pacific Electric Railway: Bradford Snell, Roger Rabbit, and the Politics of Transportation in Los Angeles," *Urban Affairs Quarterly* 27 (September 1991): 51.

20. Cliff Slater, "General Motors and the Demise of Streetcars," *Transportation Quarterly* 51 (Summer 1997): 60.

21. Mark S. Foster, *From Streetcar to Superhighway: American City Planners and Urban Transportation, 1900–1940* (Temple University Press, 1981), pp. 7, 177.

22. James J. Flink, *The Automobile Age* (MIT Press, 1988), pp. 404, 406, 408, 409.

23. Emphasis in original. See Bill McKibben, "Not So Fast: The Environmental Optimists Are Wrong: There Is No Market-Oriented Technological Fix. Simply, and Radically, People Have to Change Their Lives," *New York Times Magazine,* July 23, 1995, pp. 24–25.

24. Ibid.

25. James Howard Kunstler, *The Geography of Nowhere: The Rise and Decline of America's Man-Made Landscape* (Simon and Shuster, 1993), pp. 105, 108, 114. See also James Howard Kunstler, *Home from Nowhere: Remaking Our Everyday World for the Twenty-First Century* (Simon and Shuster, 1996).

26. Kunstler, *Geography*, pp. 112, 124, 245–47.

27. Kunstler, *Home*, p. 56.

28. Kunstler, *Geography*, p. 248.

29. Kunstler, *Home*, pp. 60–61.

30. Ibid., pp. 78–79.

31. Jane Holtz Kay, *Asphalt Nation: How the Automobile Took over America and How We Can Take It Back* (Crown Publishers, 1997), pp. 2–7, 9, 357.

32. Steve Nadis and James J. MacKenzie, *Car Trouble* (Beacon Press, 1993), pp. 166–67. See also Michael Renner, "Rethinking the Role of the Automobile," paper 84 (Washington, D.C.: Worldwatch, 1988); and Deborah Gordon, *Steering a New Course: Transportation, Energy, and the Environment* (Washington, D.C.: Island Press, 1991). Gordon is a member of the Union of Concerned Scientists.

33. Elmer W. Johnson, *Avoiding the Collision of Cities and Cars: Urban Transportation Policy for the Twenty-First Century* (Chicago: American Academy of Arts and Sciences, 1993).

34. Ibid., pp. 44–45.

35. Paul A. Sabatier and Hank C. Jenkins-Smith, eds., *Policy Change and Learning: An Advocacy Coalition Approach* (Westview Press, 1993), p. 5.

36. Ibid., p. 13.

37. Ibid., p. 19.

38. James J. MacKenzie, Roger C. Dower, and Donald D. T. Chen, *The Going Rate: What It Really Costs to Drive* (Washington, D.C.: World Resources Institute, 1992).

39. These are just some of the groups listed as having representatives on the executive and steering committees of the STPP. See Surface Transportation Policy Project, *Bulletin* (December 1992), p. 10.

40. Policy Dialog Advisory Committee, *Majority Report to the President to Recommend Options for Reducing Greenhouse Gas Emissions from Personal Motor Vehicles,* http://essential.org/orgs/public_citizen/CMEP/transportation/cartalk.html.

41. A recent report by the Working Group on Public Health and Fossil-Fuel Combustion claimed that 701,000 premature deaths could be avoided if the more stringent European targets for greenhouse gas reduction were adopted. See Robert Barr, "Europe's Emissions Plan Could Save Many Lives, a Study Says," *Philadelphia Inquirer,* November 7, 1997, p. A30.

42. Anthony Downs, "Up and Down with Ecology: The Issue-Attention Cycle," *The Public Interest* 28 (Summer 1972): 38–50.

43. John W. Kingdon, *Agendas, Alternatives and Public Policies*, 2d ed. (Harper Collins, 1995), pp. 172–73.

Chapter Two

1. Joseph Vranich, *Supertrains: Solutions to America's Transportation Gridlock* (St. Martin's, 1991), pp. 348–49.

2. See among numerous others Ben Kelly, *The Pavers and the Paved* (New York: Donald W. Brown, 1971).

3. Alan Altshuler, with James P. Womack and John R. Pucher, *The Urban Transportation System: Politics and Policy Innovation* (MIT Press, 1979), pp. 28–31.

4. Frank Dobbin, *Forging Industrial Policy: The United States, Britain, and France in the Railway Age* (Cambridge University Press, 1994), p. 29; and George Rogers Taylor, *The Transportation Revolution, 1815–1860* (Rinehart & Co., 1951), p. 98.

5. John B. Rae, *The Road and the Car in American Life* (MIT Press, 1971).

6. Kenneth T. Jackson, *Crabgrass Frontier: The Suburbanization of the United States* (Oxford University Press, 1985).

7. For a superb study of the political shrewdness of these "nonpolitical" engineer-bureaucrats, see Bruce E. Seely, *Building the American Highway System: Engineers as Policy Makers* (Temple University Press, 1987).

8. Charles L. Dearing, *American Highway Policy* (Brookings, 1941), pp. 178–79.

9. Philip H. Burch Jr., *Highway Revenue and Expenditure Policy in the United States* (Rutgers University Press, 1962), p. 38.

10. The Road Information Program, *1996 Highway Funding Methods, Conditions and Use* (Washington, D.C.: TRIP, 1996), pp. 12–13.

11. See Frank R. Baumgartner and Bryan D. Jones, *Agendas and Instability in American Politics* (University of Chicago Press, 1993), pp. 6–9.

12. See James Q. Wilson, "The Politics of Regulation," in *The Politics of Regulation*, ed. James Q. Wilson (Basic Books, 1980), pp. 357–94.

13. Ibid., p. 370.

14. On the importance of "institutional durability" in transportation infrastructure finance, see Anthony Perl, "Financing Transport Infrastructure: The Effects of Institutional Durability in French and American Policymaking," *Governance* (October 1991): 365–402.

15. The bill did not dedicate federal gas tax revenues, however. It was never invoked to punish those states that did not dedicate every dime of their gas taxes to special highway funds.

16. The 1956 gasoline tax increase has been the most studied of all the increases because it promoted construction of the interstate highway system. Among the many books and articles that cover this ground, the most useful sources are Gary T. Schwartz, "Urban Freeways and the Interstate System," *Southern Califor-*

nia Law Review 49 (March 1976): 406–513; Mark H. Rose, *Interstate: Express Highway Politics, 1941–1956* (Regents Press of Kansas, 1979); Seely, *Building the American Highway System*; and American Association of State Highway and Transportation Officials, *The States and the Interstates*, 1991.

17. Seely, *Building the American Highway System*, pp. 214–15.

18. Rose, *Interstate*, p. 92.

19. U.S. Senate, Committee on Environment and Public Works, Subcommittee on Transportation, *Funding for the Federal Aid Highway Program, Hearings*, August 19 and September 9, 1980, 96 Cong. 2 sess., Government Printing Office, p. 210.

20. "Statement of William Bulley, President of the American Association of State Highway and Transportation Officials," in ibid., pp. 22–23.

21. "Statement of William B. Eline, Chairman of the American Road and Transportation Builders Association," in ibid., pp. 212–13.

22. "Written Statement of the American Automobile Association," in ibid., pp. 360–61.

23. "Statement of the Highway Users Federation," in ibid., pp. 208–09.

24. Richard D. Lyons, "Judge Rules Carter Cannot Impose Fee on Gasoline Sales," *New York Times,* May 14, 1980, p. A1; and Martin Tolchin, "House and Senate Vote Down Oil Fee by Large Margin," *New York Times*, June 5, 1980, p. A1.

25. U. S. Senate, Committee on Environment and Public Works, "Testimony of Andrew L. Lewis Jr.," *Hearings*, January 13, 1981, 97 Cong. 1 sess., Government Printing Office, p. 20.

26. "Transit Funding: Triumph . . . Then Tribulation," *Mass Transit*, April 10, 1983, pp. 14–18.

27. Pamela Fessler, "First Installment of 'Down Payment' Clears," *Congressional Quarterly Weekly Report*, June 30, 1984, p. 1541.

28. "Text of Presidential News Conference," *Congressional Quarterly Weekly Report*, October 2, 1982, p. 2454.

29. Judy Sarasohn, "Reagan Endorses Increase in Gasoline Tax," *Congressional Quarterly Weekly Report*, November 27, 1982, p. 2914.

30. "CQ House Votes," *Congressional Quarterly Weekly Report*, December, 11, 1982, p. 3018. On the House amendment to the Transportation Assistance Act that actually authorized the gas tax increase, eighty-seven Republicans voted nay and ninety-six Republicans voted yea.

31. Judy Sarasohn, "Filibuster Slows Action on Gas Tax Hike," *Congressional Quarterly Weekly Report*, December 18, 1982, p. 3047; and "Battle Weary Senate Clears Highway–Public Transit Bill Raising Fuel and Truck Taxes," *Congressional Quarterly Weekly Report*, December 25, 1982, p. 3088.

32. The average retail price for all types of gasoline peaked in March 1981 at $1.39 per gallon. Prices declined slowly and erratically for the next twenty-one months. When the gas tax increase was passed in December 1982, the average retail price of gasoline stood at $1.24 per gallon. By March 1983 the price per gallon had dropped to $1.13. In April, when the nickel per gallon increase took effect, the retail price popped back up to $1.20 and stayed up through the summer driving sea-

son. But the average price for gasoline for 1983 was still below the average for 1982, and the downward trend continued until hitting bottom at $0.83 per gallon in November 1986. U.S. Department of Energy, Energy Information Administration, *Monthly Energy Review* (December 1984): 92; and (October 1988): 96.

33. David Wessel, "Fed Chief Backs Gasoline Tax Rise, Cuts in Programs for Elderly to Lower Deficit," *Wall Street Journal*, March 3, 1988, p. 4; Jessica Mathews, "A $1 per Gallon Gasoline Tax without Tears," *New York Times*, June 28, 1988, p. A25; and Robert W. Crandall and others, *Regulating the Automobile* (Brookings, 1986), p. 158.

34. "Dan Rostenkowski's Courage," *New York Times*, December 12, 1988, p. A18; "Time to Raise Taxes," *Washington Post*, July 28, 1985, p. B6; and "Planet of the Year—Endangered Earth: What the U.S. Should Do," *Time*, January 2, 1989, p. 65.

35. Steven R. Weisman, "Japan, Weary of Barbs on Trade, Tells Americans Why They Trail," *New York Times*, November 20, 1989, p.1.

36. Diana T. Kurylko, "Gas Tax Could Peril Auto Sales: Chrysler, Ford Support Increase," *Automotive News*, December 19, 1988, p.1.

37. Tom Kenworthy and Ann Devroy, "Deficit Goal Linked to Tax Increase: Key House Chairman Say New Moneys Needed, Bush Must Call Tune," *Wall Street Journal*, December 7, 1988, p. A6.

38. "Gas Tax for Deficit Reduction Opposed," *AASHTO Journal*, vol. 88, December 23, 1988, p. 1.

39. David E. Rosenbaum, "Budget Passed by Congress, Ending a Three-Month Struggle; Bush Says He's Very Pleased," *New York Times*, October 28, 1990, p. 1; "No New Spending Likely from Fuel Tax," *The AASHTO Journal*, November 2, 1990, p. 1.

40. Mike Mills, "Roe Wins Job He's Waited for in Ascent on Public Works," *Congressional Quarterly Weekly Report*, December 8, 1990, p. 4062; Mike Mills, "Push for Second Gasoline Tax Hike Gears up in the House," *Congressional Quarterly Weekly Report*, April 20, 1991, p. 974; and Mike Mills, "Lawmakers Lard Highway Bill with $6.8 Billion in Projects," *Congressional Quarterly Weekly Report*, July 27, 1991, p. 2063.

41. Mike Mills with David S. Cloud, "House Dispute over Gas Tax Puts Highway Bill on Hold," *Congressional Quarterly Weekly Report*, August 3, 1991, pp. 2153–55.

42. Mike Mills, "Highway and Transit Overhaul Is Cleared for President," *Congressional Quarterly Weekly Report*, November 30, 1991, pp. 3518–22.

43. Moynihan was an early and articulate critic of Eisenhower's highway program and auto safety policy. See Daniel Patrick Moynihan, "New Roads and Urban Chaos," *Reporter*, vol. 20, April 14, 1959, pp. 13–20; and "Epidemic on the Highways," *Reporter*, vol. 20 April 30, 1959, pp. 16–23.

44. Mike Mills, "Senate Panel Passes Overhaul of Federal Highway Policy," *Congressional Quarterly Weekly Report*, May 25, 1991, pp. 1366–68.

45. A clear overview of the nearly 300-page bill is given in U.S. Department of Transportation, *Intermodal Surface Transportation Efficiency Act of 1991: A Summary*, FHWA 92-008, Government Printing Office, 1992.

46. Neal Denno, "ISTEA's Innovative Funding: Something Old, New and Borrowed," *Transportation Quarterly* 48 (Summer 1994): 283.

47. Robert W. Gage and Bruce D. McDowell, "ISTEA and the Role of MPOs in the New Transportation Environment: A Midterm Assessment," *Publius* 25 (Summer 1995): 133.

48. Richard Mudge, "ISTEA Legislation: The Promise versus the Reality," *Municipal Finance Journal* 64 (Winter 1994): 35.

49. Steven Greenhouse, "The White House Struggles to Save Energy Tax Plan," *New York Times*, May 10, 1993, p. 1.

50. However, under a provision added to the overall budget reconciliation bill, the 2.5 cents for the Bush budget deal that went to the general treasury would be returned to the highway trust fund after October 1, 1995. "Clinton Signs Reconciliation Bill," *AASHTO Journal Weekly Transportation Report*, vol. 93, August 13, 1993, p. 1.

51. The wheeling and dealing between the White House and Congress over the energy tax is conveyed in Bob Woodward, *The Agenda: Inside the Clinton White House* (Simon and Shuster, 1994). For the story of the final vote on the president's bill, which passed by votes of 218 to 216 in the House and 51 to 50 in the Senate, see George Hager and David S. Cloud, "Democrats Tie Their Fate to Clinton's Budget Bill," *Congressional Quarterly Weekly Report*, August 7, 1993, p. 2122.

52. Adam Nagourney, "Dole Calls for the Repeal of a 1993 Gas Tax Increase," *New York Times*, April 27, 1996, p. 1. President Clinton announced that he would sign a gas tax repeal bill if the Republicans would let him have a bill increasing the minimum wage. In the end the issue died as gas prices softened, and the campaign moved on to other issues.

53. Rich Henson, "Shuster's District is Paved with Gold," *Philadelphia Inquirer*, May 6, 1996, p. B7.

54. Shuster's version of what the bill's goals are is found in U.S. House of Representatives, Committee on Transportation and Infrastructure, *Truth in Budgeting Act; Report to Accompany H.R. 842*, Report 104-499, pt. 1, 104 Cong. 2 sess., Government Printing Office.

55. Kasich's committee provided the arguments against Shuster's point of view. See U.S. House of Representatives, Committee on the Budget, *Truth in Budgeting Act; Adverse Report*, Report 104-499, pt. 2, 104 Cong. 2 sess., Government Printing Office.

56. Mike Mills, "Trust Fund 'Sanctity' Crumbling under Pressure from Budget," *Congressional Quarterly Weekly Report*, October 20, 1990, pp. 3501–04.

57. Congressional Budget Office, "Statement of James L. Blum, Assistant Director, Budget Analysis Division, before the Committee on Environment and Public Works, U.S. Senate," March 5, 1991.

58. Alan K. Ota, "Shuster Prepares for Onslaught against Member's Projects," *Congressional Quarterly Weekly Report*, March 21, 1998, p. 737.

59. See National Academy of Public Administration, *Organizing the Administration of Surface Transportation Policies and Programs to Meet National Needs*, 1991.

60. Federico Pena, "Letter to the Honorable Newt Gingrich, Speaker of the House of Representatives, and Draft Bill 'To Amend Title 49, United States Code (Transportation) to Simplify and Improve the Organization of the Department of Transportation, and for Other Purposes,'" gopher://gopher.dot.gov/00/general/DOTTALK/bills/dotreorg.txt.

61. U.S. Department of Transportation, "Highlights of the FY 1996 Budget," gopher://gopher.dot.gov/00 general/96budget/bib96.txt.

62. Ken Silverman, "Proposed DOT Reorganization Proposal Draws Fire," *American City and County* 110 (April 1995): 20–23. See also David Barnes, "DOT Drops Plan to Realign, Consolidate," *Traffic World*, March 18, 1996, p. 12.

63. Judy Sarasohn, "Highway Plan Would Drop Aid to Some Major Programs: Shifts Costs to States, Localities," *Congressional Quarterly Weekly Report*, April 25, 1981, p. 699.

64. "Another Turnback Advocate," *Washington Letter on Transportation*, vol. 15, March 5, 1996, p. 5.

65. Ibid.

66. Alan K. Ota, "Senate's Solution to Road Wars: Deliver More Money," *Congressional Quarterly Weekly Report*, March 7, 1998, pp. 554–56.

67. Alan K. Ota, "Conferees Trim Bill, New Agreement, But Clinton Still Threatens Veto," *Congressional Quarterly Weekly Report*, May 16, 1998, p. 1269.

68. Alan K. Ota, "Congress Clears Huge Transportation Bill, Restoring Cut-Off Funding to States," *Congressional Quarterly Weekly Report*, May 23, 1998, pp. 1385–87.

69. "Budget Breakthrough on Reauthorization Conference," *AASHTO Journal* 98, no. 20, May 15, 1998, p. 1.

70. "Actual Spending Levels Uncertain," *AASHTO Journal* 98, no. 23, June 5, 1998, p. 4.

Chapter Three

1. Local auto dealers' complaints against the big companies, especially General Motors, never took off as a political issue because "the dealers were not a coherent, unified body. . . . More important, there was at least as much support for protecting the public from the automobile dealers as there was for protecting the dealers from their producers." See John B. Rae, *The American Automobile Industry* (Boston: Twayne Publishers, 1984), pp. 132–33.

2. Wilson was misquoted. When asked if he saw any conflicts between his life-long career in the auto industry and his proposed public position as President Dwight Eisenhower's secretary of defense, Wilson told a Senate panel: "I have always thought what was good for the country was good for General Motors, and vice-versa." See Paul F. Boller Jr. and John George, *They Never Said It: A Book of Fake Quotes, Misquotes, and Misleading Attributions* (Oxford University Press, 1989), p. 131. But putting GM first in the quote was irresistible to feisty reporters, critical columnists, and satirical cartoonists.

3. Richard Harris and Sidney Milkis, *The Politics of Regulatory Change: A Tale of Two Agencies* (Oxford University Press, 1989), p. 55.

4. Ibid., p. 10.

5. James Q. Wilson, ed., *The Politics of Regulation* (Basic Books, 1980), p. 370.

6. Ralph Nader, *Unsafe at Any Speed* (Grossman, 1965).

7. Jerry L. Mashaw and David L. Harfst, *The Struggle for Auto Safety* (Harvard University Press, 1990), p. 55.

8. Ibid., pp. 51–52.

9. James R. Crate, "A Dangerous Device," in *America at the Wheel: 100 Years of the Automobile in America: Special Issue of Automotive News*, September 21, 1993, p. 158.

10. Mashaw and Harfst, *The Struggle for Auto Safety*, pp. 59–60.

11. For a list of the groups Nader had founded by 1974, see Hays Gorey, *Nader and the Power of Everyman* (Grosset and Dunlap, 1975), appendix A.

12. That is how John B. Rae, a historian very sympathetic to the auto industry, characterized the response of General Motors in particular. See Rae, *The American Automobile Industry*, p. 182. I believe that the description could be extended to the entire industry without much injustice to Ford and Chrysler, however.

13. Dan Cordz, "The Face in the Mirror at General Motors," *Fortune* 74 (August 1966): 116–19.

14. Hugh Heclo, "Issue Networks and the Executive Establishment," in *The New American Political System*, ed. Anthony King (Washington, D.C.: American Enterprise Institute, 1978).

15. Robert F. Buckhorn, *Nader: The People's Lawyer* (Prentice-Hall, 1972), pp. 197–200. In this popular biography Roche was given an entire chapter to rebut his nemesis.

16. Quoted in Harris and Milkis, *The Politics of Regulatory Change*, p. 80.

17. The penalties prescribed by the National Traffic and Motor Vehicle Safety Act of 1966 were set at $1,000 per vehicle or per infraction. The 1970 Clean Air Act raised the ante to $10,000 per infraction. The 1975 CAFE regulations set the penalty at $5 for every 0.1 mile per gallon that a company's fleet average fell below the standard, multiplied by the number of vehicles sold. Thus if a company with sales of 2 million vehicles per year fell one mile per hour below the standard, it would face a fine of $100 million.

18. For the clash of issues and methodologies in the cost debates of these years, compare Lawrence J. White, *The Regulation of Air Pollutants from Motor Vehicles* (Washington, D.C.: American Enterprise Institute, 1982); and U.S. Environmental Protection Agency, Office of Mobile Source Air Pollution Control, *The Cost of Controlling Emissions of 1981 Model Year Automobiles*, 1981.

19. For a thorough discussion of the Amtrak and Conrail initiatives and their significance for the debate over industrial policy, see R. Kent Weaver, *The Politics of Industrial Change: Railway Policy in North America* (Brookings, 1985).

20. Robert B. Reich and John D. Donahue, *New Deals: The Chrysler Revival and the American System* (Penguin Books, 1985), pp. 315–18.

21. Ibid., p. 159.

22. Ibid., p. 282.

23. In May 1980 UAW president Douglas Frazer was elected to a seat on Chrysler Corporation's board of directors. See ibid., p. 125.

24. Alan Altshuler and others, *The Future of the Automobile* (MIT Press, 1984), p. 201.

25. Motor Vehicle Manufacturers Association, *Automobile Facts & Figures, '91*, Detroit, 1991, p. 16.

26. Alan Altshuler and others, *The Future of the Automobile*, pp. 155–64.

27. The only official description of the plan is contained in the report published as the Carter administration was on its way out of office. See U.S. Department of Transportation, Office of the Secretary, *The U.S. Automobile Industry, 1980: Report to the President from the Secretary of Transportation*, January 1981.

28. Edward Lapham, Helen Kahn, and Jake Kelderman, "Carter Offers His Plan to Rescue Detroit: President Vows 'Close Knit' Partnership with Industry," *Automotive News*, July 14, 1980, p. 1.

29. David Hoffman, "Reagan Would 'Convince' Japan to Limit Car Exports," *Philadelphia Inquirer*, September 3, 1980, p. 9A.

30. The memo is quoted in William Greider, *The Education of David Stockman and Other Americans* (E. P. Dutton, 1982), pp. 146, 156–58.

31. Helen Kahn, "Thirty-Four Auto Regulations Shot Down," *Automotive News*, April 13, 1981, p. 2.

32. Helen Kahn, "Reagan Chops NHTSA Funds in Half," *Automotive News*, March 16, 1981, p. 1.

33. Gary C. Bryner, *Blue Skies, Green Politics: The Clean Air Act of 1990 and Its Implementation*, 2d ed. (Washington, D.C.: CQ Press, 1995), p. 103.

34. U.S. Congress, House of Representatives, Committee on Energy and Commerce, Subcommittee on Energy Conservation and Power, "Statement of Joan Claybrook," *Automobile Fuel Efficiency Standards*, Hearings on July 21, 1983, 98 Cong. 1 sess., p. 123.

35. Jake Kelderman, "Ford, GM Fail on '83 CAFE," *Automotive News*, July 9, 1984, p. 1; Helen Kahn, "Makers Face No Penalties for Missing CAFE Goals," *Automotive News*, July 25, 1983, p. 1; "Lower Fuel Standard Proposed by NHTSA for '85 Trucks," *Automotive News*, May 28, 1984, p. 3; and U.S. Department of Transportation, National Highway Traffic Safety Administration, "Passenger Automobile Average Fuels Economy Standards of Model Year 1986," *Federal Register* 50 (October 4, 1985), p. 40528.

36. Matt DeLorenzo and Helen Kahn, "White House Urges Repeal of CAFE Laws," *Automotive News*, March 2, 1987, p. 1.

37. U.S. Congress, House of Representatives, Committee on Energy and Commerce, Subcommittee on Energy Conservation and Power, "Statement of Robert M. Sinclair, Vice President, Chrysler Corporation," *Automobile Fuel Efficiency Standards*, pt. 2, hearings on July 31, 1984, 98 Cong. 2 sess., p. 171.

38. John F. Stacks, "The Administration Split on Auto Imports," *Fortune*, May 4, 1981, pp. 156–63; and "Voluntary Curb on Japanese Car Imports Said to Be 'Consensus' of Reagan, Advisors," *Wall Street Journal*, March 20, 1981, p. 1.

39. "GM's Chairman Calls for Automobile Import Restrictions," *Philadelphia Inquirer*, March 16, 1981, p. 3.

40. David Stockman, *The Triumph of Politics: How the Reagan Revolution Failed* (Harper and Row, 1986), p. 155.

41. Ibid., p. 157.

42. See Robert E. Scott, *Short-Sighted Solutions: Trade and Energy Policies for the U.S. Auto Industry* (New York: Garland Publishing, 1994), table 11, p. 136. Scott reviewed six different economists' efforts to estimate the VRA's impact on employment and found that they varied from a low of 4,598 jobs saved to a high of 137,900 jobs preserved.

43. Ibid., p. xviii.

44. U.S. International Trade Commission, *The Internationalization of the Automobile Industry* (GPO, 1981), pp. 29–45.

45. Congressional Budget Office, *Has Trade Protection Revitalized Domestic Industries?* (GPO, 1986), p. 88.

46. The low figure of $1.1 billion per year is accepted by William A. Niskanen, former chief economist for Ford Motor Co. and a member of President Reagan's Council of Economic Advisers at the time of the VRA. See his memoir, *Reaganomics: An Insider's Account of the Politics and the People* (New York: Oxford University Press, 1988), p. 40. As his source Niskanen cites the 1984 Federal Trade Commission study by David Tarr and Morris Morke, *Aggregate Costs to the United States of Tariffs and Quotas on Imports*. The high estimate of $5 billion is accepted by Murray Weidenbaum, who was chairman of the Council of Economic Advisers (and hence Niskanen's boss), in his book *Rendez-vous with Reality: The American Economy after Reagan* (Basic Books, 1988), p. 117. Weidenbaum cites as his source the Brookings study by Robert W. Crandall, "Import Quotas and the Automobile Industry: The Costs of Protection," *Brookings Review* 2 (Summer 1984): 8–16.

47. For a description of how Japanese bureaucrats and auto executives learned the new rules of the international auto trade regime, see James A. Dunn Jr., "Automobiles in International Trade: Regime Change and Persistence," *International Organization* 41 (Spring 1987): 225–52.

48. Calculated from American Automobile Manufacturers Association, *Motor Vehicle Facts and Figures 1996* (Washington, D.C.: 1997), pp. 17–19.

49. Ibid.

50. Bryner, *Blue Skies, Green Politics*, p. 148.

51. Quotations from the announcement text are from the White House, Office of the Press Secretary, *Historic Partnership Forged with Auto Makers Aims for Threefold Increase in Fuel Efficiency in As Soon As Ten Years*, press release.

52. On GM's unveiling of its "portfolio" of high-efficiency power plants at the 1997 North American auto show, see Bill Visnic," GM Shows Its High-Tech Cards," *Ward's Auto World* 32 (February 1997): 58–59. For Ford's response see "Ford Supercar Averages More than 60 MPG," *Ward's Auto World* 33 (April 1997): 25–26. See also Gary S. Vasilash, "On the Road to Supercar," *Production* 108 (January 1996): 40–42; and Steven Ashley, "Steel Cars Face a Weighty Decision," *Mechanical Engineering* 119 (February 1997): 56–61.

53. For a good survey of all the possibilities, see Robert Q. Riley, *Alternative Cars in the 21st Century: A New Personal Transportation Paradigm* (Warrendale, Penn.: Society of Automotive Engineers, 1994).

54. Amory B. Lovins, "Hypercars: The Next Industrial Revolution," in *Transportation and Energy: Strategies for a Sustainable Transportation System*, ed. Daniel Sperling and Susan A. Shaheen (Washington, D.C., and Berkeley, Calif.: American Council for an Energy Efficient Economy, 1995), pp. 78–79. See also Amory B. Lovins and L. Hunter Lovins, "Reinventing the Wheels," *Atlantic Monthly* (January 1995): 75–93.

55. Lovins, "Hypercars," pp. 87–89.

56. National Research Council, *Review of the Research Program of the Partnership for a New Generation of Vehicles: Third Report* (Washington, D.C.: National Academy Press, 1997).

57. Ibid.

58. Albert Gore, *Earth in the Balance* (Houghton Mifflin, 1992).

59. Daniel Sperling, *Future Drive: Electric Vehicles and Sustainable Transportation* (Washington, D.C.: Island Press, 1995), p. 143.

60. Wyn Grant, *Autos, Smog and Pollution Control: The Politics of Air Quality Management in California* (Aldershot, U.K.: Edward Elgar, 1995), p. 54.

61. Sperling called it "the single most important event in the history of transportation since Henry Ford began mass-producing cars eighty years ago." See Sperling, *Future Drive*, p. 2.

62. Reports of such a possible trade-off are cited in Grant, *Autos, Smog and Pollution Control*, p. 128; and by Michael Shnayerson, *The Car That Could: The Inside Story of GM's Revolutionary Electric Vehicle* (Random House, 1996), p. 169.

63. California Air Resources Board, *Zero-Emission Vehicle Program Memoranda of Agreement: Fact Sheet,* 1996, p. 1.

64. California Air Resources Board, *ZEV Incentives*, 1997, p. 1.

65. Shnayerson, *The Car That Could*, p. 253.

66. In 1966 there were 53,041 deaths from motor vehicle accidents in this country. There were only 43,900 in 1995, despite a 119 percent increase in the total number of vehicles, and a 234 percent rise in the total miles driven. Measured as a public health problem, the rate of motor vehicle deaths per 100,000 population declined from 27.1 to 16.7. American Automobile Manufacturers Association, *Automobile Facts and Figures 1996* (Washington, D.C.: 1997), p. 91, citing data provided by the National Safety Council.

67. Compared with a baseline vehicle before federal emissions standards were introduced, a new 1995 automobile produced 96 percent fewer grams of hydrocarbons per mile, 96 percent less carbon monoxide, and 90 percent less nitrogen oxide. Ibid., p. 88, citing data provided by the Environmental Protection Agency. The average fuel economy, for the domestic new-car fleet rose 115.2 percent between 1974 and 1996, from 13.2 miles per gallon to 28.7 miles per gallon. Ibid., p. 85, citing data from the U.S. Department of Transportation.

68. David L. Greene, Daniel Sperling, and Barry McNutt, "Transportation Energy to the Year 2020," in *A Look Ahead: Year 2020*, ed. Transportation Research Board (Washington, D.C.: National Research Council, 1998), pp. 216, 220.

69. See the two reports by the consulting firm Energy and Environmental Analysis, Inc., *Revised Projections of Fuel Economy and Technology in Highway Vehicles*; and *Analysis of the Capabilities of Domestic Auto Manufacturers to Improve Corporate Average Fuel Economy* (U.S. Department of Energy, 1983).

70. Robert W. Crandall and others, *Regulating the Automobile* (Brookings, 1986), p. 121.

71. Ibid., pp. 135, 158.

72. Robert W. Crandall and John D. Graham, "The Effect of Fuel-Economy Standards on Automobile Safety," *Journal of Law and Economics* 32 (April 1989): 94–118.

73. Pietro S. Nivola and Robert W. Crandall, *The Extra Mile: Rethinking Energy Policy for Automotive Transportation* (Brookings, 1995), p. 6.

74. Bryner, *Blue Skies*, p. 261.

75. The competition is already under way, at least in the media. See "Big Three Roll Out Green Cars in a Bow to the Environment," *Philadelphia Inquirer*, January 11, 1998, p. G1. See also H. Josef Hebert, "Researchers Claim Success on Gas-Fired Electric Car: Eighty MPG and No Batteries to Recharge," *Philadelphia Inquirer*, October 22, 1997, p. A1.

76. See John H. Cushman Jr., "Clinton Seeks Tax Credits for Fuel Savings," *New York Times*, January 31, 1998, p. A11.

77. For a readable overview of the technological possibilities, see Riley, *Alternative Cars*. For a strong argument for electric cars, see Sperling, *Future Drive*. See also James J. MacKenzie, *The Keys to the Car: Electric and Hydrogen Vehicles for the Twenty-First Century* (Washington, D.C.: World Resources Institute, 1994).

78. Sperling, *Future Drive*, p. 58.

79. Michael Schiffer compares Thomas Edison's 1901 public proclamation that he was working on a better battery for electric cars that would soon be ready for release with the Big Three's announcement of the impending arrival of better batteries for EVs. Schiffer believes that in both cases the public got the wrong message and decided to hold off buying an electric car until the batteries improved, something he feels was unfortunate then and now. See Michael Brian Schiffer, with Tamara C. Butts and Kimberly K. Grimm, *Taking Charge: The Electric Vehicle in America* (Smithsonian Institution Press, 1994), p. 181.

80. MacKenzie, *The Keys to the Car*, p. 70.

81. Riley, *Alternative Cars*, pp. 79–87.

82. See Lester R. Brown, Christopher Flavin, and Colin Norman, *Running on Empty: The Future of the Automobile in an Oil Short* World (Norton, 1979). This Worldwatch Institute book stands as a classic example of the vanguard's wishful thinking. "The seventies have seen a fundamental transformation in the global oil outlook. . . . The beginning of the end of the oil age is now in sight," the authors wrote two decades ago (p. 33).

83. In an op-ed piece the associate director of Environmental Media Services recently warned that "our luck may be running dry. We may have less oil than we think. And there may be less time left to find [more] than we hope. . . . [E]xtraction rates will start dipping as early as 2010. . . . Given our history and current extravagant habits, the question is not if the next oil price shock will come, but only when." Chris DeCardy, "Oil Is Cheap—But It's Going Fast," *Philadelphia Inquirer*, March 24, 1998, p. A11.

84. Energy Information Administration, *Petroleum 1996: Issues and Trends*, DOE/EIA-0615, 1997, p. 9.

85. Italics in original. Ibid., p. 59.

86. David E. Sanger, "Singing the Cartel Blues," *New York Times*, March 29, 1998, p. WK4.

87. In October 1997 Honda announced it had developed an engine with a dual function catalyst that produced only one-tenth of the emissions permitted by California's ultra low emission vehicle standard. One commentator said that the new engine could "drive a stake through the heart of the electric vehicle." See Kelly L. Anderson, "Honda Unveils Ultraclean Engine," *Philadelphia Inquirer*, October 21, 1997, p. A1.

Chapter Four

1. David W. Jones Jr., *Urban Transit Policy: An Economic and Political History* (Prentice-Hall, 1985), p. 81.

2. The report was subsequently revised and published. See Lyle C. Fitch, ed., *Urban Transportation and Public Policy* (San Francisco: Chandler Publishing Co., 1964).

3. "The Transportation System of Our Nation," message from the president of the United States, 87 Cong. 2 sess., April 5, 1962, H.R. Doc. 384, cited in Delbert A. Taebel and James V. Cornhels, *The Political Economy of Urban Transportation* (Port Washington, N.Y.: Kennikat Press, 1977), p. 51.

4. P.L. 88-365, 78 Stat. 302, 49 U.S.C. 1601 et seq. The key vote came in the House, where 39 Republicans joined 173 Democrats to pass the bill by a vote of 212 to 189. The House Republicans who voted for the bill represented districts in New York, New Jersey, Connecticut, Massachusetts, Pennsylvania, Ohio, California, Washington, and Nebraska. See George M. Smerk, *The Federal Role in Urban Mass Transportation* (Indiana University Press, 1991), note 13, p. 326.

5. Emphasis in original. See Jones, *Urban Transit Policy*, p. 81.

6. The matching funds issue is complex, and the requirements have changed. From 1964 to 1973 the ratio was two-thirds federal money and one-third local money for capital construction. After July 1, 1973, the balance shifted to 80 percent federal and 20 percent local, with exceptions such as 100 percent federal funding for certain planning activities. Smerk, *The Federal Role*, p.119.

7. Ibid., p. 109

8. Ibid., p. 106.

9. Ibid., p. 125.

10. Ibid., p. 112.

11. Alan Altshuler, who was secretary of transportation in Massachusetts from 1971 to 1974, pointed out that the Boston area stood to lose nearly $700 million in federal aid because freeway revolts had led to the cancellation of further interstate construction in the Boston area. Massachusetts politicians, under pressure from business and labor interests, lobbied hard for provisions enabling a state to cancel and trade-in an interstate segment for general fund money equal in value to the highway project. See Alan Altshuler with James P. Womack and John R. Pucher, *The Urban Transportation System: Politics and Policy Innovation* (MIT Press, 1979), p. 38, note 4.

12. P.L. 93-87.

13. For a detailed description of the legislative process, see Smerk, *The Federal Role*, pp. 108–217. Summaries of transit legislation can be found in American Public Transit Association, *Transit Fact Book 1994–1995*, pp. 140–46. An incisive summary of the transit lobby's strength and legislative strategy vis-à-vis the highway coalition is given in Altshuler, Womack, and Pucher, *The Urban Transportation System*, pp. 35–42.

14. P.L. 93-505.

15. Smerk, *The Federal Role*, pp. 158–61.

16. The quoted phrase is by Altshuler. See Altshuler, Womack, and Pucher, *The Urban Transportation System*, p. 38.

17. P.L. 97-424.

18. American Public Transit Association, *Transit Fact Book, 1987*, pp. 30, 57–58.

19. John Pucher, Anders Markstedt, and Ira Hirschman, "Impacts of Subsidies on the Costs of Urban Public Transit," *Journal of Transport Economics and Public Policy* 17 (May 1983): 173.

20. Charles A. Lave, "The Private Challenge to Public Transportation: An Overview," in *Urban Transit: The Private Challenge to Public Transportation*, ed. Charles A. Lave (San Francisco: Pacific Institute for Public Policy Research, 1985), p. 11.

21. For the book that marked an intellectual turning point in the analysis of transit policy, see Altshuler, Womack, and Pucher, *The Urban Transportation System*.

22. See Arthur E. Wiese, "Money for Mass Transit: Much Talk, Little Action," *Mass Transit* (December 1977): 16; and Department of Transportation, Institute of Public Administration, *Financing Transit: Alternatives for Local Government*, 1979.

23. "The Stockman Report," *Railway Age*, February 23, 1981, p. 5.

24. Arthur Wiese, "Transit Advocates Resent Biting the Budget Bullet," *Mass Transit* (May 1981): 20.

25. "Transit Funding Triumph . . . Then Tribulation," *Mass Transit* (April 1983): 14.

26. See P. H. Bly, "Managing Public Transport: Commercial Profitability and Social Service," *Transportation Research* 21A (March 1987): 109–126.

27. Edward Beimborn and Alan Horowitz, with Julie Schuetz and Gong Zejun, *Measurement of Transit Benefits,* published in 1993 for the Urban Mass Transportation Administration, University Research and Training Program, DOT-T-93-33, pp. 126–27.

28. Michael A. Sargious and Christopher Bee, "An Evaluation of Urban Transportation Systems Using Behavioral Models and Consumer Surplus," *The Logistics and Transportation Review* 16 (1980): 129–49; and J. S. Dodgson and N. Tapham, "Benefit-Cost Rules for Urban Transit Subsidies: An Integration of Allocational, Distributional and Public Finance Issues," *Journal of Transport Economics and Policy* (January 1987): 57–71.

29. George V. Hilton, *Federal Transit Subsidies: The Urban Mass Transportation Assistance Program* (Washington, D.C.: American Enterprise Institute, 1974).

30. Jones, *Urban Transit Policy,* pp. 28–95.

31. Lave, "The Private Challenge," pp. 26–27. See also C. Kenneth Orski, "Redesigning Local Transportation Service," in *Urban Transit,* pp. 272–74.

32. Robert Cervero, *Transit Service Contracting: Cream Skimming or Deficit Skimming?* (Washington, D.C.: Urban Mass Transportation Administration, 1988).

33. The authors of a study of privatization efforts around the world conclude that "rail transit offerings may not be the most appropriate mode for infrastructure privatization initiatives." See José A. Gómez-Ibáñez and John R. Meyer, *Going Private: The International Experience with Transport Privatization* (Brookings, 1993), p. 253.

34. See James A. Dunn Jr. and William B. Felix, "Privatizing Local Services as a Federal Policy Goal; The Case of New Jersey Transit" (paper presented at the annual meeting of the Southern Political Science Association, Atlanta, 1990). At the time of these events, I was the chairman of New Jersey Transit's South Jersey Transit Advisory Committee and my coauthor was an employee of the New Jersey Department of Transportation who managed federal transit grants. For a shorter and more one-sided view, see Jerome Premo, "Privatization in Practice: The Case of New Jersey Transit," in *Private Innovations in Public Transit,* ed. John C. Weicher (Washington, D.C.: American Enterprise Institute, 1988), pp. 16–20.

35. Jack R. Gilstrap, *Comments of the American Public Transit Association on Guidance on Documentation of Private Enterprise Participation in Urban Mass Transportation Programs,* March 26, 1986.

36. *Making Appropriations for the Department of Transportation and Related Agencies,* conference report accompanying H.R. 5205, 100 Cong. 2 sess., 1987, pp. 28–29.

37. Robert Guskind, "Leave the Driving to Us," *Planning* 53 (July 1987): 6–10.

38. Smerk, *The Federal Role,* pp. 265, 289.

39. The totals on federal funding and purchases of new transit equipment from 1961 to 1987 have been compiled from Jo Tucci, *1987 Urban Mass Transportation Grants Assistance Program Statistical Summaries* (Washington, D.C.: UMTA, 1988), tables B, 22 and 23; and for 1988 to 1995 from American Public Transit Association, *Transit Fact Book, 1994–1995,* tables 31 and 50.

40. Smerk, *The Federal Role*, pp. 265–72.

41. APTA, *Transit Fact Book, 1994–1995*, pp. 62, 74.

42. David Jones is a transit supporter who recognizes the uneconomic aspects of the benefits regime behind federal transit policy. See Jones, *Urban Transit Policy*. A representative critic of the benefits regime is Charles A. Lave. See Lave, "The Private Challenge."

43. Mathew J. Lawlor, "Federal Urban Mass Transportation Funding and the Case of the Second Avenue Subway," *Transportation Quarterly* 49 (Fall 1995): 52.

44. Don H. Pickrell, "A Desire Named Streetcar: Fantasy and Fact in Rail Transit Planning," *Journal of the American Planning Association* 58 (Spring 1992): 158–75.

45. Calculated from U.S. Department of Transportation, Bureau of Transportation Statistics, *National Transportation Statistics 1995*, 1995, p. 64.

46. Kevin Starr, "What the MTA Debate Is Really About," *Los Angeles Times*, September 7, 1997, p. M1.

47. For a concise overview of the politics of rail rejuvenation in Los Angeles, see Wyn Grant, *Autos, Smog and Pollution Control: The Politics of Air Quality Management in California* (Aldershot, U.K.: Edward Elgar, 1995), pp. 148–68.

48. Ted Rohrlich, "Common Sense Didn't Ride This 'Money Train,'" *Los Angeles Times*, January 15, 1998, p. A1.

49. David Willman, "Misalignments Found in New Subway Tunnels," *Los Angeles Times*, April 14, 1994, p. A1; Eric Lichtblau and Richard Simon, "MTA Official Charged with Taking Kickbacks," *Los Angeles Times*, February 2, 1994, p. A1; and Mark A. Stein, "One Year Later, Blue Line Is Having a Bumpy Ride," *Los Angeles Times*, July 14, 1991, p. B1.

50. Grant, *Autos, Smog and Pollution Control*, p. 158.

51. Ibid., pp. 154–55.

52. Ibid., p. 160.

53. Metropolitan Transportation Authority, *Annual Report 1993–1994*, p. 3.

54. "Transit Dream Derailed, Reality Prevails," *Los Angeles Times*, February 15, 1995, p. B6.

55. Eric Lichtblau, "Whistleblowers Win $1.2 Million in MTA Case," *Los Angeles Times*, May 5, 1995, p. A1.

56. "Chief of Crisis-Prone Los Angeles Transit System Is Dismissed," *New York Times* December 22, 1995, p. A25.

57. Richard Simon, "MTA Pledges Better Bus Service in Suit Accord," *Los Angeles Times*, September 26, 1996, p. A1.

58. James Bornemeier, "Key House Chairman Favors Busways over Subway for Los Angeles," *Los Angeles Times*, February 26, 1997, p. B3.

59. Jeffrey L. Rabin and Josh Meyer, "Airport Revenue Dispute May Imperil Subway Funds," *Los Angeles Times*, March 21, 1997, p. A1; Richard Simon, "MTA to Suspend Work on Three Key Rail Lines," *Los Angeles Times*, January 15, 1998, p. A1; and Tom McClintock, "Mass Transit without the Masses," *Los Angeles Times*, January 18, 1998.

60. Simon, "MTA to Suspend Work," p. A1.

61. See Peter Gordon, "Beyond Polycentricity: The Dispersed Metropolis, Los Angeles, 1970–1990," *Journal of the American Planning Association* 62 (Summer 1996): 289–95; Peter Gordon, Harry W. Richardson, and Myung-Jin Jun, "The Commuting Paradox: Evidence from the Top Twenty," *Journal of the American Planning Association* 57 (Autumn 1991): 416–20; and Peter Gordon and Harry W. Richardson, "Notes from Undergound: The Failure of Urban Mass Transit," *Public Interest* 94 (Winter 1989): 77–86.

62. Harry W. Richardson and Peter Gordon, "Counting Nonwork Trips: The Missing Link in Transportation, Land Use, and Urban Policy," *Urban Land* (September 1989): 11.

63. Gordon and Richardson, "Notes from Underground," pp. 83, 85.

64. Ibid., p. 85.

65. For a spirited call for recreating the monocentric metropolis of yore, see William B. Shore, "Recentralization: The Single Answer to More than a Dozen United States Problems and a Major Answer to Poverty," *Journal of the American Planning Association* 61 (Autumn 1995): 496–503.

66. Mathew L. Wald, "The Fight for Transit Money: It's Amtrak against Everyone on the Road," *New York Times*, October 8, 1995, p. E5.

67. Frank R. Baumgartner and Bryan D. Jones, *Agendas and Instability in American Politics* (University of Chicago Press, 1993), pp. 32–35.

68. Unpublished tables from *Consumer Expenditures Survey 1993*, cited in U.S. Department of Transportation, Bureau of Transportation Statistics, *Transportation Statistics Annual Report 1995: The Economic Performance of Transportation*, 1995, p. 37.

69. APTA, *Transit Fact Book 1994–1995*, pp. 82–85.

70. Smerk, *The Federal Role,* pp. 260–309. The Camelot and cathedrals analogies may have been triggered by the title of the last chapter, "The Once and Future Program of Federal Mass Transit Policy." I hasten to add that the analogies are mine, not Smerk's.

Chapter 5

1. Albro Martin, *Enterprise Denied: The Origins of the Decline of American Railroads, 1897–1917* (Columbia University Press, 1971).

2. Gabriel Kolko, *Railroads and Regulation, 1877–1916* (Princeton University Press, 1965).

3. Stephen Salsbury, *No Way to Run a Railroad* (McGraw-Hill, 1982).

4. Stephen B. Goddard, *Getting There: The Epic Struggle between Road and Rail in the American Century* (Basic Books, 1994), p. xi.

5. Gregory Lee Thompson, *The Passenger Train in the Motor Age: California's Rail and Bus Industries, 1910–1941* (Ohio State University Press, 1993), p. 10.

6. Ibid., p. 153.

7. Claiborne Pell, "Saving the Railroads," *Commonweal*, November 22, 1963, p. 249; see also Claiborne Pell, *Megalopolis Unbound* (Praeger, 1966).

8. Donald M. Itzkoff, *Off the Track: The Decline of the Intercity Passenger Train in the United States* (Greenwood Press, 1985), p. 99.

9. "Money Is Roadblock to Revival of Passenger Trains," *Congressional Quarterly Weekly Report*, February 6, 1970, p. 352.

10. R. Kent Weaver, *The Politics of Industrial Change: Railway Policy in North America* (Brookings, 1984), p. 93.

11. My analysis draws on Anthony Perl and James A. Dunn Jr., "Reinventing Amtrak: The Politics of Survival," *Journal of Policy Analysis and Management* 16 (Fall 1997): 598–614.

12. Itzkoff, *Off the Track*, pp. 80–85.

13. Ibid., pp. 110, 112.

14. Frank N. Wilner, *The Amtrak Story* (Omaha, Neb.: Simmons-Boardman Books, 1994), p. 99.

15. Anthony Perl, "Financing Transportation Infrastructure: The Effects of Institutional Durability in French and American Policymaking," *Governance* 4 (1991): 365–402.

16. Wilner, *The Amtrak Story*.

17. Itzkoff, *Off the Track*, p. 126.

18. *Background on Amtrak* (Washington, D.C.: Amtrak, 1979), p. 10.

19. General Accounting Office, *Intercity Passenger Rail: Financial and Operating Conditions Threaten Amtrak's Long-Term Viability* (GPO, 1995).

20. Thomas M. Downs, "A TQ Interview," *Transportation Quarterly* 48 (Autumn 1994): 355–68.

21. Congressional Research Service, Library of Congress, "Amtrak and the 104th Congress," *CRS Issue Brief*, May 15, 1995.

22. Thomas M. Downs, *Testimony before the House Appropriations Transportation Subcommittee, March 2, 1995* (Washington, D.C.: Amtrak, 1995); and *Amtrak Tomorrow: Reinventing the National Railroad Passenger Corporation: FY 1996 Legislative Report and Federal Grant Request* (Washington, D.C.: Amtrak, 1995).

23. Details on the legislative politics of the Amtrak reform bills in both houses are taken from the *Washington Letter on Transportation*, published fifty-one weeks a year by Linton, Mields, Reisler & Cottone, Inc., Washington, D.C., and from *The AASHTO Journal Weekly Transportation Report* (Washington, D.C.: American Association of State Highway and Transportation Officials).

24. Mathew L. Wald, "The Fight for Transit Money: It's Amtrak against Everyone on the Road," *New York Times*, October 8, 1995, p. E5; see also Jack R. Glistrap, "Does Weakening Peter to Strengthen Paul Really Help the Travelling Public?" *Transit News*, September 12, 1995.

25. Chris Mondics, "Congress Gets Aboard Amtrak Funds Bill," *Philadelphia Inquirer*, November, 14, 1997, p. A1.

26. Don Phillips, "Amtrak, Union Reach an Accord to Avert Strike," *Philadelphia Inquirer*, November 3, 1997, p. A2.

27. "Amtrak's Strategic Business Plan established federal funding require-ments of $4.3 billion through 2002. Enactment of the Taxpayer Relief Act of 1997 (TRA) provides Amtrak with $2.2 billion, or approximately one-half of the plan's federal requirement." Amtrak, *FY 1999 Amtrak Legislative Report and Federal Grant Request*, February 13, 1998, p. 2.

28. Jim Abrams, "Lott Says No New Funds for Amtrak," *Philadelphia Inquirer*, November 5, 1997, p. A12.

29. U.S. Congress, House of Representatives, Committee on Appropriations, Subcommittee on the Department of Transportation and Related Agencies, *Hearings on Department of Transportation and Related Agencies Appropriations for 1999*, "Testimony of Jolene M. Molitoris, Federal Railroad Administrator," 105 Cong. 2 sess., March 11, 1998, pp. 29–30.

30. U.S. General Accounting Office, *Intercity Passenger Rail: Financial Performance of Amtrak's Routes*, GAO/RCED-98-151, 1998, pp. 2–3, 18. See also U.S. General Accounting Office, *Intercity Passenger Rail: Outlook for Improving Amtrak's Financial Health*, "Statement of Phyllis F. Scheinberg before the Subcomittee on Transportation, Committee on Apppropriations, U.S. Senate on March 24, 1998," USGAO/T-RCED-98-134.

31. The critics attack Amtrak's long-term burden on the taxpayers, its overly generous labor agreements, and the fact that much of its ridership is middle class and includes business travelers who can afford unsubsidized alternatives. They also argue that because of its low market share, Amtrak does little to relieve con-gestion, fight pollution, and promote energy efficiency. One study even claims that diversion of all rail passengers in the Northeast Corridor to airlines would fill only one-quarter of the unused seat capacity of existing flights. Thus, even if Amtrak were to disappear, the transportation system could easily absorb the loss, its critics say. See Jean Love, Wendell Cox, and Stephen Moore, "Amtrak at Twenty Five: End of the Line for Taxpayer Subsidies," *Policy Analysis*, no. 266 (Washington, D.C.: The Cato Institute, 1996).

32. José A. Gomez-Ibanez and John R. Meyer, *Going Private: The International Experience with Transport Privatization* (Brookings, 1993), p. 272.

33. Joseph Vranich, *Derailed: What Went Wrong and What to Do about America's Passenger Trains* (St. Martin's Press, 1997), p. 211.

34. Ibid., p. xiii.

35. Itzkoff, *Off the Track*, p. 62.

36. Joseph R. Daughen and Peter Binzen, *The Wreck of the Penn Central* (Little, Brown, 1971), p. 136.

37. Itzkoff, *Off the Track*, p. 92.

38. Weaver, *The Politics of Industrial Change*, pp. 211–24.

39. Ibid., p. 249.

40. Mathew L. Wald, "Builder Is Chosen for Speedy Trains on Northeast Run," *New York Times*, March 16, 1996, p.1.

41. Amtrak High Speed Rail Project Office, Old Saybrook, Conn., *Quarterly Report on Amtrak's Northeast High-Speed Rail Improvement Project*, April 2, 1996, p. 2.

42. U.S. General Accounting Office, *Intercity Passenger Rail: Prospects for Amtrak's Financial Viability*, report to the Honorable Frank R. Wolf, chairman, Subcommittee on Transportation and Related Agencies, Committee on Appropriations, House of Representatives, GAO/RCED-98-211R, June 5, 1998, p. 5.

43. James A. Dunn Jr. and Anthony Perl, "Policy Networks and Industrial Revitalization: High Speed Rail Initiatives in France and Germany," *Journal of Public Policy* 14 (1994): 311–43.

44. Mitchell P. Strohl, *Europe's High Speed Trains: A Study in Geo-Economics* (Praeger, 1993), p. 83.

45. Joseph Vranich, *Supertrains: Solutions to America's Transportation Gridlock* (St. Martin's Press, 1991). The author was formerly executive director of the High Speed Rail/Maglev Association.

46. Federal Railroad Administration, U.S. Department of Transportation, *High Speed Ground Transportation for America: Overview Report* (GPO, 1996), p. 5.

47. Ibid., p. 6.

48. Ibid., p. 47.

49. William C. Vantuono, "Despite Setbacks, High Speed Rail Moves Ahead," *Railway Age* (April 1994): 57–67.

50. P.L. 103-440; 108 Stat. 4615.

51. Dick Netzer, "An Evaluation of Interjurisdictional Competition through Economic Development Incentives," in *Competition among States and Local Governments*, ed. Daphne A. Kenyon and John Kincaid (Washington, D.C.: The Urban Institute Press, 1991), pp. 219–46.

52. Ohio Railway Organization, Inc., *Implementation Plan for High Speed Rail in Ohio*, June 1992.

53. John S. Robey, "High Speed Rail in Texas: Its Rise and Fall," *Transportation Quarterly* 48 (Autumn 1994): 403–21.

54. "Tracking the (High Speed) Fox," *Mass Transit* 22 (July/August 1996): 32–43.

55. Florida Department of Transportation, "Florida DOT Receives High Speed Rail Plans," press release, November, 13, 1995; and "Florida Department of Transportation Selects Florida Overland eXpress as High Speed Rail Franchisee," press release, February 27, 1996.

56. "The Fox Proposal," *Mass Transit* 22 (July/August 1996): 32.

57. Florida Department of Transportation, "Fox and FDOT Take Next Step in High Speed Rail Process," press release, August 2, 1996.

58. Florida Department of Transportation, "Florida Department of Transportation (FDOT) Signs Agreement with Florida Overland eXpress (FOX) to Continue High Speed Rail Creation," press release, November 12, 1996.

59. The analysis in this section draws on James A. Dunn Jr. and Anthony Perl, "Building the Political Infrastructure for High Speed Rail in North America," *Transportation Quarterly* 50 (Winter 1996): 5–22.

60. On the obstacles still remaining, see National Academy of Public Administration, *State Departments of Transportation: Strategies for Change*, National

Cooperative Highway Research Program, Report 371 (Washington, D.C.: National Academy Press, 1995).

61. Dunn and Perl, "Policy Networks and Industrial Revitalization," p. 335.

62. Karen Borlaug, "The Perspective of the Freight Railroads on Rail Passenger Issues," *Transportation Research Circular*, no. 484 (March 1998): 44–47.

63. Marcia D. Lowe, *Back on Track: The Global Rail Revival* (Washington, D.C.: Worldwatch Institute, 1994).

64. Dunn and Perl, "Policy Networks and Industrial Revitalization," p. 329.

65. Vranich, *Supertrains*, pp. 264–313.

Chapter 6

1. For an explanation of these two concepts, see the chapter entitled "Transportation, Mobility, and Accessibility: An Introduction," in U.S. Department of Transportation, Bureau of Transportation Statistics, *Transportation Statistics Annual Report 1997: Mobility and Access*, BTS97-S-01, 1997, pp. 135–46.

2. Charles E. Lindblom, *Politics and Markets: The World's Political Economic Systems* (Basic Books, 1977).

3. Rationalization policy based on a trade-off of mobility for accessibility is not new in the 1990s. See K. H. Schaeffer and Eliot Sclar, *Access for All* (Penguin, 1975). But it has come back strongly in the debate over automobile-generated social problems.

4. Dwight Young, *Alternatives to Sprawl* (Cambridge, Mass.: Lincoln Institute of Land Policy, 1995), p. 4.

5. Ibid., p. 5.

6. See Real Estate Research Corporation, *The Costs of Sprawl* (Washington, D.C.: GPO, 1974).

7. Alan Altshuler, with James P. Womack and John R. Pucher, *The Urban Transportation System: Politics and Policy Innovation* (The MIT Press, 1979), p. 393. On the positive aspects of sprawl from a practical planner's point of view, see Wayne A. Lemmon, "Can Sprawl Be Good," *Planning Commissioners' Journal*, http://www.plannersweb.com/sprawl/lemm.html.

8. U.S. General Accounting Office, *Intermodal Freight Transportation: Combined Rail Truck Service Offers Public Benefits, but Challenges Remain*, 1992.

9. "Under the current mode-based institutional structure, connections between modes are at the edge of every organization's responsibility. In a true intermodal organization, these connections would be recognized as the heart of the system." National Commission on Intermodal Transportation, *Toward a National Intermodal Transportation System: Final Report,* Washington, D.C., 1994, p. 17.

10. Daniel Carlson, with Lisa Wormser and Cy Ulberg, *At Road's End: Transportation and Land Use Choices for Communities* (Washington, D.C.: Island Press, 1995), p. 156. This book was sponsored by the Surface Transportation Pol-

icy Project, and it is one of the clearest and most comprehensive statements of the new paradigm and its implementation strategies.

11. Ibid., p. 156.

12. Ibid., pp. 79, 154.

13. Ibid., p. 13.

14. Ibid., p. 81.

15. Ibid., p. 156.

16. William Fulton, "The New Urbanism Challenges Conventional Planning," *Land Lines* 8 (September 1996) at http://www.lincolninst.edu/land-line/1996/september/newurb2.html.

17. Andres Duany and Elizabeth Plater-Zyberk, *Towns and Town-Making Principles*, ed. Alex Krieger with William Lennerz (Rizzoli, 1991); see also Andres Duany and Elizabeth Plater-Zyberk, "The Second Coming of the American Small Town," *Wilson Quarterly* 16 (Winter 1992): 19–50.

18. Peter Calthorpe, *The Next American Metropolis: Ecology, Community, and the American Dream* (New York: Princeton Architectural Press, 1993), pp. 15, 17. See also Sim Vander Ryn and Peter Calthorpe, *Sustainable Communities: A New Design Synthesis for Cities, Suburbs, and Towns* (San Francisco: Sierra Club Books, 1986).

19. Calthorpe, *The Next American Metropolis*, p. 32.

20. Ibid., p. 52.

21. Fulton, "The New Urbanism."

22. In 1997 some 135 New Urbanist projects were in the design or construction phase, and they ranged from small pedestrian pockets of fifty units to the thousands of units in Disney's Celebration. See *New Urban News* 2 (September-October 1997): 10–13.

23. Michael Southworth, "Walkable Suburbs? An Evaluation of Neotraditional Communities at the Urban Edge," *Journal of the American Planning Association* 63 (Winter 1997): 43.

24. Randall Crane, "Cars and Drivers in the New Suburbs: Linking Access to Travel in Neotraditional Planning," *Journal of the American Planning Association* 62 (Winter 1996): 51–52.

25. Michael Pollan, "Town Building Is No Mickey Mouse Operation," *New York Times Magazine*, December 14, 1997, pp. 62–63.

26. Marlon Boarnet and Randall Crane, "L.A. Story: A Reality Check for Transit-Based Housing," *Journal of the American Planning Association* 63 (Spring 1997): 201.

27. The New Urbanists would argue that this is merely leveling a field unfairly tilted by the postwar biases of zoning laws, federally insured mortgages, and interstate highways.

28. See Gerrit Knaap and Arthur C. Nelson, *The Regulated Landscape: Lessons on State Land Use Planning from Oregon* (Cambridge, Mass.: Lincoln Institute of Land Policy, 1992); Alan Artibise, Anne Vernez Moudon, and Ethan Seltzer, "Cascadia: An Emerging Regional Model," in *Cities in Our Future: Growth and Form, Environmental Health and Social Equity*, ed. Robert Geddes (Washington, D.C.: Island Press, 1997), 147–76; and Young, *Alternatives to Sprawl*. For a

thorough comparison of Portland's success in controlling sprawl with Denver's relative failure, see Paul G. Lewis, *Shaping Suburbia: How Political Institutions Organize Urban Development* (University of Pittsburgh Press, 1996). For a description of how popular Portland has become with visitors from the United States and as far away as China, see Alan Ehrenhalt, "The Great Wall of Portland," *Governing* 10 (May 1997): 20–24.

29. Lewis, *Shaping Suburbia*, pp. 169, 195.

30. Ehrenhalt, "The Great Wall," p. 24.

31. Lewis, *Shaping Suburbia*, pp. 162, 204, 206.

32. Ibid., pp. 114, 191.

33. Ibid., p. 219.

34. Ehrenhalt, "The Great Wall of Portland," p. 20.

35. Lewis, *Shaping Suburbia*, pp. 259–60, note 13.

36. Ibid., p. 80.

37. For an overview of the issues and descriptive studies of ten major metropolitan areas, see H. V. Savitch and Ronald K. Vogel, eds., *Regional Politics: America in a Post City Age* (Sage, 1996).

38. Indeed, the "Charter of the New Urbanism" explicitly states: "The metropolitan region is a fundamental economic unit of the contemporary world. Governmental cooperation, public policy, physical planning, and economic strategies must reflect this new reality." The charter calls for tax revenues to be "shared more cooperatively among the municipalities and centers within regions to avoid destructive competition for tax base and to promote rational coordination of transportation, recreation, public services, housing, and community institutions." See http://www.cnu/charter.html.

39. Myron Orfield, *Metropolitics: A Regional Agenda for Community and Stability* (Brookings, 1997).

40. Orfield notes that of the twenty-five largest U.S. urban areas, the Twin Cities had the shortest average commuting time in 1990. He also observes that Minnesota's Constitution prohibits diversion of gas tax revenues. There did not seem to be any great push to change either of these facts of life in Minnesota. Orfield, *Metropolitics*, p. 68.

41. Anthony Downs, *Stuck in Traffic: Coping with Peak-Hour Traffic Congestion* (Brookings, 1992), p. 162.

42. Ibid., pp. 162–64.

43. Anthony Downs, *New Visions for Metropolitan America* (Brookings, 1994), pp. 136–41.

44. Ibid., pp. 218–27.

45. Ibid., pp. 195–97.

46. Ibid., p. 196.

47. Edward Weiner, *Urban Transportation Planning in the United States: An Historical Overview* (Praeger, 1987), p. 19. Regional planning agencies in New York, Philadelphia, Chicago, and Detroit can trace their roots to the metropolitan transportation studies sponsored by state highway departments in the 1950s. See U.S. Advisory Commission on Intergovernmental Relations, *Toward More Bal-*

anced Transportation: New Intergovernmental Proposals (GPO, 1974), pp. 55–124.

48. The background of the statute and its language, as well as an analysis of the EPA guidance document, are given in Pamela S. Reiman and Stephen C. Yohay, "Compliance with Clean Air Act Employer Trip Reduction Requirements," Employee Relations Law Journal 19 (Spring 1994): 621–38.

49. C. Kenneth Orski, "Employee Trip Reduction Programs—An Evaluation," Transportation Quarterly 47 (July 1993): 327–41.

50. Ibid., p. 340.

51. Ibid., p. 341.

52. California Air Resources Board, Evaluation of Selected Projects Funded by Motor Vehicle Registration Fees, cited in Craig N. Oren, "Getting Commuters Out of Their Cars: What Went Wrong?" Stanford Environmental Law Journal 17 (January 1998): 234.

53. Chang-Hee Christine Bae, "Air Quality and Travel Behavior," Journal of the American Planning Association 59 (Winter 1993): 71.

54. Arnold M. Howitt and Joshua P. Anderson, "Crash Course: Cars and Clean Air Are Colliding," Governing (April 1995): 52–54.

55. See, for example, William Vickery, "Some Implications of Marginal Cost Pricing for Public Utilities," American Economic Review 45 (1955): 605–20; Herbert Mohring, "The Peak Load Problem with Increasing Returns and Price Constraints," American Economic Review 60 (1970): 693–705; and T. E. Keeler and Kenneth A. Small, "Optimal Peak-Load Pricing, Investment, and Service Levels on Urban Expressways," Journal of Political Economy 85 (1977): 1–25.

56. See Anthony Perl and Jae-Dong Han, "Evaluating the Environmental Component of Automobile Pricing Schemes," World Transport Research: Proceedings of the Seventh World Conference of Transport Research, Vol. 3: Transport Policy (Tarrytown, N.Y.: Elsevier Science, 1996), pp. 265–75.

57. Charles Komanoff, "Pollution Taxes for Roadway Transportation," Pace Environmental Law Review 12 (Fall 1994): 121–60.

58. Anthony Downs notes that for road pricing to be effective in southern Califonia, peak-period charges would have to reach approximately 65 cents per mile in urban areas. A ten-mile trip to work on urban expressways could cost as much as $13 a day round trip. See Downs, Stuck in Traffic, pp. 51–52. In 1997 a New York court held that the Triborough Bridge and Tunnel Authority could not refuse to turn over its E-Z Pass electronic toll account information to police in connection with a homicide investigation. "New York Agency Must Turn over Electronic Toll Records," Computer Law Strategist 14 (July 1997): 6.

59. See Sanford F. Borins, "Electonic Road Pricing: An Idea Whose Time May Never Come," Transportation Research 22A (January 1988): pp. 37–44.

60. George James, "E-Z Pass: The Early Reviews," New York Times, December 21, 1997, p. NJ 8.

61. See Charles Lave, "The Demand Curve under Road Pricing and the Problem of Political Feasibility," Transportation Research 28A (March 1994): 83–92.

62. See the cover story by Eric Pooley, "The Great Escape: Americans Are Fleeing Suburbia for Small Towns: Do Their New Lives Equal Their Dreams?"

Time, December 8, 1997, pp. 52–65. On how this trend might affect the old distributive struggle for public resources between suburb and center city, see Thomas Hylton, "A Real Place to Call Home: Suburban Sprawl Is Self-Destructive. Instead, States Should Reinvest in Their Small Towns and Cities," *Philadelphia Inquirer*, December 5, 1997, p. A43.

Chapter 7

1. Deborah Gordon, "Sustainable Transportation: What Do We Mean and How Do We Get There?" in *Transportation and Energy: Strategies for a Sustainable Transportation System*, ed. Daniel Sperling and Susan A. Shaheen (Washington, D.C., and Berkeley, Calif.: American Council for an Energy-Efficient Economy, 1995), p. 1.

2. Ibid., pp. 4–5.

3. For a scientist's readable overview of the points of contention among scientists, see S. George Philander, *Is the Temperature Rising? The Uncertain Science of Global Warming* (Princeton University Press, 1998).

4. William H. Calvin, "The Great Climate Flip-Flop: Global Warming Could, Paradoxically, Cause a Sudden and Catastrophic Cooling," *Atlantic Monthly* 281 (January 1998): 47–64. See also Michael L. Parsons, *Global Warming: The Truth behind the Myth* (Plenum Press, 1995); E. William Colglazier, "Scientific Uncertainties, Public Policy, and Global Warming: How Sure Is Sure Enough?" *Policy Studies Journal* 19 (Spring 1991): 61–72.

5. Marvin S. Soroos, *The Endangered Atmosphere: Preserving a Global Commons* (University of South Carolina Press, 1997), p. 279.

6. David L. Greene, "Transportation and Energy: The Global Environmental Challenge," *Transportation Research* 27A (May 1993): 163–66.

7. Soroos, *Endangered Atmosphere*, p. 278.

8. Daniel Sperling, *Future Drive: Electric Vehicles and Sustainable Transportation* (Washington, D.C.: Island Press, 1995), p. 11.

9. In Detroit jargon this is expressed as: "Higher fuel economy standards could significantly degrade vehicle affordability . . . [which] would effectively eliminate the opportunity for consumers, on average, to continue to upgrade as they purchase new vehicles." See Paul McCarthy, "How Government and Industry Can Cooperate to Promote Fuel Conservation: An Industry Perspective," in *Transportation and Energy: Strategies*, p. 271.

10. Dean A. Drake, "Technology, Economics, and the ZEV Mandate: A Vehicle Manufacturer's Perspective," in *Transportation and Energy*, p. 253. Drake was a manager on General Motors' environmental and energy staff.

11. See National Research Council, Energy Engineering Board, Committee on Automobile and Light Truck Fuel Economy, *Automobile Fuel Economy: How Far Should We Go?* (Washington, D.C.: National Academy Press, 1992).

12. See Alex Trotman, "The Climate for Change: The Environment and How to Preserve It," *Vital Speeches of the Day*, vol. 63, December 1, 1996, pp. 121–23.

Compare the sweet reason of Trotman, the chairman and CEO of Ford Motor Company, with GM chairman James Roche's diatribe against the industry's critics in a 1972 speech to the Chicago Executive Club. Roche, "The Chairman of the Board of General Motors Speaks: Ralph, You're Wrong!" in *Nader: The People's Lawyer*, ed. Robert F. Buckhorn (Prentice-Hall, 1972).

13. H. Josef Herbert, "Big Three Automakers to Build Cleaner Cars for Northeast," *Philadelphia Inquirer*, February 5, 1998, p. 1. See also "Super-Clean Cars May Be Imminent," *AASHTO Journal*, December 19, 1997. See http://www.aashto.org/journal/a-j.html.

14. David L. Greene and K. G. Duleep, "Costs and Benefits of Automobile Fuel Economy Improvement: A Partial Analysis," *Transportation Research* 27A (May 1993):. 234.

15. Charles River Associates, *Policy Alternatives for Reducing Petroleum Use and Greenhouse Gas Emissions*, report prepared for the Motor Vehicle Manufacturers Association, 1991.

16. McCarthy, "An Industry Perspective," p. 275. Broad-based carbon taxes or Btu taxes on all fuels would be preferable, he says, to motor fuel taxes. More recently, Detroit has been making favorable references to the energy-saving possibilities of congestion pricing schemes.

17. Jerry L. Mashaw and David L. Harfst, *The Struggle for Auto Safety* (Harvard University Press, 1990), pp. 210–12.

18. Gasoline was cheaper in 1998 (in inflation-adjusted dollars) than at any time since the early1950s. In current dollars gasoline is cheaper than bottled water or Coca-Cola. Motorists can afford, and governments can use, the extra revenue from moderate increases in gasoline taxes.

19. It remains to be seen how effective the TEA-21 "firewall" negotiated by Representative Bud Shuster and his allies will actually be at protecting highway spending from pressure for cuts by the administration and congressional budget and appropriations committees.

20. See James A. Dunn Jr., "The Politics of Motor Fuel Taxes and Infrastructure Funds in France and the United States," *Policy Studies Journal* 21 (Summer 1973): 271–84.

21. C. Kenneth Orski, ed., "Public Transit—Searching for New Paradigms," *Innovation Briefs* 8 (September/October 1997): 1–2.

22. Ibid., p. 2.

23. H. V. Savitch and Ronald K. Vogel, "Perspectives for the Present and Lessons for the Future," in *Regional Politics: America in a Post-City Age*, ed. H. V. Savitch and Ronald K. Vogel (Sage Publications, 1996), p. 298.

24. See James A. Dunn Jr., "Coordination of Urban Transit Services: The German Model," *Transportation* 9 (Spring 1980): 33–43.

25. James A. Dunn Jr., *Miles to Go: European and American Transportation Policies* (The MIT Press, 1981), chaps. 4 and 5.

26. John Pucher, "Urban Travel Behavior as the Outcome of Public Policy: The Example of Modal Split in Western Europe and North America," *Journal of the American Planning Association* 54 (1988): 509–20; and John Pucher, "Capitalism, Socialism, and Urban Transportation: Policies and Travel Behavior in the East

and West," *Journal of the American Planning Association* 56 (1990): 278–96. See also Anthony Perl, "Financing Transport Infrastructure: The Effects of Institutional Durability in French and American Policymaking," *Governance* (October 1991): 365–402; and Anthony Perl, *Comparative Transport Finance: The Institutional Logic of Infrastructure Development in Canada, France and the United States*, Ph.D. diss., University of Toronto, 1993.

27. John Pucher and Christian Lefèvre, *The Urban Transport Crisis in Europe and North America* (Macmillan, 1996), p. 201.

28. Alex Marshall, "Eurosprawl," *Metropolis* (January/February, 1995). See http://www.metropolismag.com/archives/10195.2html.

29. Pucher and Lefèvre, *The Urban Transport Crisis*, p. 22.

30. Ibid.

31. See James A. Dunn Jr. and Anthony Perl, "Policy Networks and Industrial Revitalization: High Speed Rail Initiatives in France and Belgium," *Journal of Public Policy* 14 (1994): 311–43.

32. Gary Stix, "Maglev: Racing to Oblivion?" *Scientific American* 227 (October 1997): 109.

33. Pucher and Lefèvre, *The Urban Transport Crisis*, p. 16, table 2.4.

34. When Mayor Rudolph Giuliani's administration prohibited pedestrians from crossing on one side of ten busy intersections along 49th and 50th streets between Lexington Avenue and the Avenue of the Americas to make it easier for cars (and buses) to make a left turn, native New Yorkers were outraged. "The idea that automobiles should get priority in the city is insane," said one resident. "What they ought to do is charge everyone from New Jersey and Long Island $10 to come into the tunnels." See Alan Finder, "Footloose Pedestrians Are Just about in Lock Step: They Hate Traffic Plan," *New York Times*, January 3, 1998; see also the paper's editorial on the same day, "Wrong Turn on City Traffic?" p. A10.

35. M. A. Hughes, "Employment Decentralization and Accessibility: A Strategy for Stimulating Regional Mobility," *Journal of the American Planning Association* 57 (1991): 292.

36. Martin Wohl, "Increasing the Taxi's Role in Urban America," in *Urban Transportation: Perspectives and Prospects*, ed. Herbert S. Levinson and Robert A. Weant (Westport, Conn.: Eno Foundation, 1982), pp. 329–32.

37. Peter Suzuki, "Vernacular Cabs: Jitneys and Gypsies in Five Cities," *Transportation Research* A 19 (July 1985): 337–47.

38. For an intriguing proposal for far-reaching deregulation in urban transit, see Daniel B. Klein, Adrian Moore, and Binyam Reja, *Curb Rights: A Foundation for Free Enterprise in Urban Transit* (Brookings, 1997).

39. Ronald F. Kirby, "Targeting Money Effectively: User-Side Transportation Subsidies," *Journal of Contemporary Studies* 4 (Spring 1982): 45–52.

40. William Plowden, *The Motor Car and Politics in Britain* (Harmondsworth, U.K.: Penguin, 1971).

Index